LIGHT AND SHADOWS

WALTER BRANDMÜLLER

LIGHT AND SHADOWS

Church History amid
Faith, Fact and Legend

Translated by Michael J. Miller

IGNATIUS PRESS   SAN FRANCISCO

Original German edition:
*Licht und Schatten: Kirchengeschicte
zwischen Glaube, Fakten und Legenden*
© 2007 by Sankt Ulrich Verlag GmbH, Augsburg

Cover photograph: © James Thew/iStockphoto

Cover design by Roxanne Mei Lum

© 2009 Ignatius Press, San Francisco
ISBN 978-1-58617-273-2
Library of Congress Control Number 2008936284
Printed in the United States of America ∞

CONTENTS

ACKNOWLEDGMENT

The present volume is a collection of texts, revised and without the original scholarly footnotes, that were written for various occasions and published in various places.

My sincere thanks to Dr. Susanne Siegl-Mocavini and Dr. Barbara Dienst-Friedrich for their valuable collaboration in preparing the manuscript.

TRUST THIS CHURCH?

Occasionally the Church is compared with Noah's ark: only his sons and daughters, only those animals that Noah took with him into the ark were saved from the great flood. In a similar way, the Church is supposed to be man's only rescue from the final catastrophe.

When discussion turns to the Last Things, to man's eternal fate, then the question assumes the utmost urgency: To whom can he entrust his eternal fate and himself? What can he rely on in life and death? Now, since the Church makes the exclusive claim to be the saving ark, this claim must be so solidly established that it does not mean a leap into uncertainty when man puts his trust in this ark.

Questions about Questions

To many of our contemporaries, such trust in the Church appears to be nothing less than an unreasonable demand upon sound common sense. Aren't there countless facts (the objection goes) that demolish the credibility of the Church?

Many people have read the numerous books or seen the television programs that deal with the subject of the Qumran community and seem to offer proof that the beginnings of Jesus of Nazareth and of Christianity ought to be portrayed in a completely different way from what is recorded

9

in the Gospels and the rest of the New Testament. Many have also seen the earthenware receptacle containing human remains that was found in Jerusalem, on which the names Joseph, Mary and Jesus were inscribed. Isn't this compelling evidence that Jesus did not rise bodily from the dead and that Mary was not taken body and soul into heaven? With that, however, the foundations of the Christian faith crumble into dust and ashes! Many people today suspect that this is so.

Furthermore, the Church—as they say—through clumsy errors made by her official teaching authority on numerous occasions, has repudiated her claim to hold the truth infallibly. Let us listen to Hans Küng, who lists the "classic errors of the Church's Magisterium, most of which have been admitted". First he mentions the "excommunication of the Ecumenical Patriarch of Constantinople, Photius, and of the Greek [Byzantine] Church, which formalized the soon-to-be millennial schism with the Eastern Church". Then Küng adduces "the prohibition against charging interest [on loans] at the beginning of the modern era, whereby the Church's Magisterium changed its opinion much too late, after various compromises". Then (what else could you expect?) he also cites the trial of Galileo in 1616 or else in 1633 and other things of this sort. The most recent major error of the Magisterium, in his view, is its rejection of artificial contraception.

Others before and after him have pilloried the Church on account of the Crusades, the Inquisition and the witch trials, and anyone who is still not satisfied is referred to the financial scandal of the Vatican Bank and the murder conspiracy against Pope John Paul I, who was so likeable: Mafia in the Vatican, at the heart of the Church. From another corner the cry is that a power-hungry clique of Freemasons already replaced Paul VI with a double whom they could control and that the Lodge in general seized power in the Vatican long ago—and so on. Therefore, who can still trust such a Church?

If you are really going to ask the critical question about reliability, however, then direct it not only at the Church but also at the objections that are raised against her.

Justified Criticism?

The Qumran Theme

The most popular books about Qumran, *The Dead Sea Scrolls Deception* by Baigent and Leigh, and *Jesus und die Urchristen* [Jesus and the Early Christians] by Eisenmann, as well as other comparable publications on this topic, have been exposed by serious researchers as clumsy concoctions. The books are partly the result of scientific incompetence; to some extent they are based on deliberate, malicious falsification of the facts. It is precisely the archaeological findings at Qumran that, quite to the contrary, shed an extremely interesting light on the New Testament and even clear up riddles. And as for the ossuary with the names of Joseph, Mary and Jesus [Joshua], which actually comes from Jerusalem and dates back to the time of Jesus, the names mean nothing at all, when you consider that they were as common and therefore as insignificant as the names Miller, Fields and Smith would be today.

Similarly, with regard to Hans Küng's "errors" of the Church's Magisterium, we are dealing more with the errors of Hans Küng than with those of the Church. First of all, in page after page, he confuses Patriarch Photius with Patriarch Michael Cerullarius. Then Küng fails to mention that Photius was excommunicated because he had become Patriarch in an unlawful manner and furthermore had accused Rome of heresy and had tried to depose Pope Nicholas I by means of a manipulated synod. Depending on how one views the particular historical circumstances of this case, one could possibly speak about a wrong decision in ecclesiastical politics or an unjust excommunication, but never about an error of the Church's Magisterium.

The same is true for the prohibition against lending at interest and its gradual abolition by the Church. This prohibition against charging interest was based on the Old Testament and had been confirmed by popes and councils. Why this was so becomes clear when you consider that in antiquity and in the medieval world, charging interest was most often identical to usury. Lending at interest lost this sinful character, however, with the transformation of commercial structures in the late Middle Ages. Thus the reason for the prohibition against charging interest became moot over the course of time, and from then on the only concern was with the question of determining the just rate of interest. The general prohibition had thereby become null and void. So where in all this is there an error of the Church's Magisterium?

The condemnation of Galileo's teaching about the fixed position of the sun and the movement of the earth, which is also so often described as an error of the Church's Magisterium, proves upon closer inspection to have been justified at the time. With the scientific methods at his disposal, Galileo could not offer a proof that would convince the specialists either of his day or of ours that that is really the case, nor could he explain, before the discovery of gravity by Isaac Newton, how the earth could possibly revolve at breakneck speed around the sun and around its own axis while at the same time nothing of the sort is perceived by us, since everything on earth stands firm and secure instead of being tossed about in a tumultuous whirl. Most importantly, though, the whole legal proceeding against Copernicus and Galileo resulted in not one single magisterial statement that could have been described as a dogma and on that account would have been irrevocable. In this case, too, the critics fail to take into consideration the many events and facts in intellectual, cultural and scientific history that explain this decision. Furthermore, the most recent scientific findings vindicate the Church of 1633.

A comparably nuanced, careful and comprehensive approach should be taken to the problems connected with the touchy subjects of the Crusades, the Inquisition and the witch trials. In light of recent findings and the latest research, these subjects prove to be many-layered and much more complicated than the superficial observations of those who look at them as a source of ammunition against the Church. Moreover, anyone who has even the foggiest notion of the complexity of Financial-political activities and their worldwide interconnections and knows, furthermore, what sort of possibilities they offer for manipulation, will assume that the aforementioned Vatican financial scandal resulted from excessive gullibility or perhaps incompetence or even frivolity in financial matters on the part of the ecclesiastical authorities rather than from criminal intrigues.

As for an opinion of Yallop's book, *In God's Name*, which maintains that John Paul I was murdered, it is enough to read the first thirty pages in order to pass judgment. On these pages there is talk about the popes of the nineteenth century, and so much of it is false that it is hard to imagine that the author used even an encyclopedia—for that would have sufficed to prevent the numerous errors. If Yallop does not report correctly what everyone can easily find out, how are we supposed to be able to believe him when he cites conversations and events for which, by the very nature of the matter, there can be no witnesses except those who were supposedly involved? No doubt, nothing more should be said about the double of Paul VI and other such luxuriant outgrowths of overheated imaginations.

All these things and many others besides are alleged in order to shake confidence in the Church. As we have shown in these all-too-brief remarks, however, in all these cases that supposedly vitiate the Church, historical and theological knowledge about the subject is enough to prove that such accusations are groundless.

But What about the Moral Failings?

One can with good reason retort that the most extensive knowledge about a subject of this kind will not suffice to excuse the religious and moral failings of important members of the Church throughout the centuries and in every locality, down to the papal adulterer Alexander VI. But then the question arises, on what do we actually base the trust that we place in the Church?

The real basis for our trust can never be a splendid spiritual, moral and religious manifestation of the Church in this world. This has existed and indeed does exist always and everywhere—but one likewise finds always and everywhere the much more conspicuous opposite. Thus all romanticism about the early Church, a romanticism that imagines it sees in the first generations of Christians nothing but holiness and greatness, necessarily runs aground on the hard facts: the Christian married couple Ananias and Sapphira tried to defraud the Apostle Peter; in Paul's congregation at Corinth, there was a case of incest and rebellion against the Apostle; in Philippi, Saint Paul's committed female co-workers Euodia and Syntyche quarreled with each other so much that Paul had to give them a serious warning. Indeed, Paul himself parted with Mark and Barnabas during one of his journeys due to differences of opinion that were evidently insuperable. Finally, as early as the year 70, according to the latest research, there was an uprising in Corinth against the priests, such that the Bishop of Rome had to intervene forcefully.

Thus the Church has never had that spotlessly radiant appearance that she ought to have. So it is no wonder, either, that those who believed that they were especially devout were scandalized again and again by this and founded their own "church of the blameless". In contrast, the Church has always shown herself to be a great realist who has always and everywhere reckoned with the failure of her members. Not for nothing did the Lord Jesus himself, who searches and knows the depths of the human heart, institute the sacrament for the forgiveness of sins.

It cannot be said, either, that the shepherds and members of the Church have always and everywhere reacted correctly to the challenges of history. On the contrary, many mistakes have been made that subsequently became notorious. For example, was not it disastrous that Pope Clement V allowed himself to be intimidated by the demands of the French king Philip and abandoned the order of Knights Templar, who as a whole were certainly innocent, to a downfall that was in large part bloody? Entire episcopates—today we would say bishops' conferences—fell into heresy during the Arian crisis of the fourth and fifth centuries. In the sixteenth century the bishops of England, with the exception of Saint John Fisher, followed King Henry VIII into schism out of weakness and cowardice, and similarly the French episcopate, during the conflict over the freedom of the Church from the state, stood beside Louis XIV against the pope. For almost two centuries the French bishops promoted the heresy of Jansenism. There were not many exceptions. And how did the German bishops conduct themselves during the eleventh- and twelfth-century Investiture Controversy? In 1080 a majority of the German bishops, under the influence of Emperor Henry IV, made an attempt at a synod in Brixen to depose Pope Gregory VII and to elect an antipope. Those German bishops who found themselves confronted with the religious division of the sixteenth century no doubt failed in large measure, too.

Truly, all of this does not make for glorious pages in the ecclesiastical chronicles. In the end, therefore, we cannot place our trust in the wisdom and power of the shepherds, either. No promise was ever made to the Church that her shepherds and her faithful would be irreproachable or capable. What her Founder, the God-man Jesus Christ, did guarantee, nevertheless, is that she will continue unshakably and stand fast immovably in the truth until his return at the end of time. This means that the Church can never proclaim an error in matters of faith whenever she speaks in a form that is ultimately binding; that her sacraments always produce their characteristic effects of grace, provided that they are administered according to the Church's directions; and that her hierarchical-sacramental structure comprising the ministries of primacy, episcopacy and priesthood will always be maintained intact. Precisely thereby it is guaranteed that the graces of redemption will continue to be available to the people of all generations, until the Lord comes again.

Is There Such a Thing as Legitimate Change?

At this juncture we should address a widespread misunderstanding. Again and again there are earnest Christians who call precisely this durability of the Church into question, since the Church in the year 2000 is no longer identical, by any means, to the Church that the Apostles left behind at their death. Many think, too, that they can cite the changes that have taken place over the course of recent decades as proof that the Church does not endure, while others describe these changes as a falling away from the truth. Not uncommonly, the result is that trust in the Church is shaken. These doubts soon prove to be unfounded, however, provided that we are willing to make necessary distinctions.

Indeed, whereas changes in the binding dogmas of the faith, in the essential elements of the sacraments and in the core features of the hierarchical-sacramental ministries are unthinkable and have never occurred, changing with the times in other departments of the Church's life over the course of her history is not only possible but also necessary if the Church is to accomplish her mission faithfully under the altered circumstances and conditions of the day. Thus, for example, ecclesiastical ministries have been created and abolished, religious orders have been founded and have declined, devotions have been introduced and consigned to oblivion. Feast days and seasons for fasting were subject to regional differences and temporal modifications—and since the Eucharistic celebrations of the Apostles, numerous forms of the liturgy have developed and then become outmoded, to be followed in each case by new liturgical reforms. The last-mentioned fact in particular should be considered when people here and there bitterly debate about the "old" and the "new" Mass.

Even the aforementioned change in the Church's legislation and practice with regard to lending at interest was an objectively correct and completely consistent change— demanded and made possible by the changed circumstances of commercial life.

The same is true for the repeal of the prohibition against cremation in connection with Vatican II. Although this practice was once a protest against the belief in the resurrection of the body and therefore had to be rejected, in present-day conditions cremation has lost its anti-Christian character and thus could be permitted, where it serves a purpose.

Yet many Christians think that they can see instability in the aforementioned core area of dogma, hierarchy and sacraments. The Orthodox, for instance, accuse the Catholic Church of having made absolutely inadmissible changes by inserting the *Filioque* into the profession of faith and by proclaiming the new dogmas of the Immaculate Conception of the Blessed Virgin Mary (1854), the infallibility and the universal primacy of the pope (1870) and the bodily Assumption of Mary into heaven (1950), and they view these innovations as a falling away from the faith of the Church Fathers.

But that is precisely what these dogmas are not: here we are dealing not with a change but rather with an organic development of the faith under the guidance of the Holy Spirit. That this is so is already evident in the fact that not one of these "new" doctrines of the faith contradicts traditional teaching about revealed truth at any point. Rather, they fit harmoniously into the whole organism of the truths of the faith; indeed, they are no less than a logical conclusion from the Church's doctrinal Tradition, which thereby is deepened and clarified.

Biblical Foundation

Now, we have already mentioned that Jesus Christ guaranteed that his Church would be indestructible and abide intact in the truth. Given all the aforementioned denials and misunderstandings, this needs to be substantiated more thoroughly, based on the Sacred Scriptures of the New Testament.

Our Lord's declaration to Peter, which is recorded in chapter 16 of the Gospel of Matthew, should be seen as the decisive argument for the indestructibility of the Church: "You are Peter, and on this rock I will build my church, and the powers of death shall not prevail against it." "The gates of hell", as some translations render it, signify the power of death, which makes everything else on earth fleeting and transient. That means that Jesus promised his Church permanence: she will never pass away, as long as this world lasts.

The image of building on the rock, moreover, intends to say the same thing. An earlier hymn of praise from Qumran (IQH VI 26–28) reads: "And I rejoiced in your truth, my God / for you lay a foundation upon a rock . . . to build a strong wall / that will not be shaken / and all who enter shall not falter."

Also, in the parable of building a house on sand or else on a rock, the rock foundation is required if the house is to withstand every storm (Mt 7; Lk 6). The spiritual reason for this is the constant presence and working of Jesus Christ in his Church; he promised his Apostles: "Lo, I am with you always, to the close of the age." Paul expresses this assurance when he says in First Corinthians 11:26: "As often as you eat this bread and drink the cup, you proclaim the Lord's death until he comes." This means that the Church will continue to exist only until Christ's second coming at the end of time.

Intimately connected with the indestructibility of the Church is her infallible abiding in the truth; the truth of her teaching, after all, with God's revelation as its contents, is the indispensable requirement for her existence. This means that the Church would cease to exist if she were to depart from the foundation of this truth in even one point. And that is precisely what can never happen, because of Jesus' promises; he assured the Apostles that during the time when he was physically absent, "I will pray the Father, and he will give you another Counselor, to be with you for ever, even the Spirit of truth" (Jn 14:16). And later in the same chapter: "But the Counselor, the Holy Spirit, whom the Father will send in my name, he will teach you all things, and bring to your remembrance all that I have said to you" (Jn 14:26). Both characteristics, the indestructibility and the infallibility of the Church, are implied by the Apostle Paul in his First Letter to Timothy (3:15), when he calls the Church "the pillar and bulwark of the [divine] truth". Furthermore, the scriptural images that describe the Church as a building, a people, in short as a work of God, as the Body of Christ, point to her divine institution and thus to her permanent nature, which is impervious to the destructive forces of this world.

Now someone can of course object that such a line of argument will hardly be convincing to people outside of the Church, since for them Jesus Christ is at most an important historical personage who naturally, like any other human being, is by no means free from all error. But if we are willing to accept in faith God's revelation in Jesus Christ, indeed, to acknowledge him as God incarnate, then the persuasive force of the above-cited passages from Sacred Scripture becomes evident to us also, because we recognize that it is God's Word. And then these promises acquire their full import.

Two Thousand Years without Shipwreck

Now let us approach the problem from a completely different angle. If our findings thus far are indeed true, then Christ's promises must have stood the test. And that can easily be verified by looking back over two thousand years of Church history. Yet the fact that today we can ask this question in the first place already anticipates the answer. We could not do this at all as Catholics if the Church had meanwhile ceased to exist. The mere existence of the Church in the year 2007 is therefore already an irrefutable proof for her permanence.

The full persuasive force of this proof is manifested, however, when we survey in retrospect the historical conditions under which this permanence of the Church has had to stand the test of time until now. It becomes clear, then, that even the beginnings of the Church were encumbered by both the internal oppositions and the external persecutions resulting from her doctrinal and institutional separation from the synagogue. Likewise beset with problems was the inculturation of the early Church into the *Imperium Romanum* with its Greco-Roman culture. These historical conditions

were the underlying cause not only of the oppressive measures of the Roman state but also of the development of the
early heresies connected with the name of Marcion or the
concept of gnosis, for example.

Therefore the latter conflicts, those concerning the doctrine of the faith, were by no means ended by the official
recognition of Christianity starting with Constantine the
Great, but rather intensified, as the decades-long Arian crisis shows. This crisis was so widespread, and it managed
to shake the foundations of the Christian faith so seriously,
that at times the Arian party, in alliance with the imperial
power, acquired almost exclusive authority in the East, while
someone like Saint Athanasius was not only driven repeatedly from his episcopal see but even had to fear for his life.
In the same way, the Germanic tribes fell into Arianism
for two centuries. Arianism's victory, though, would have
meant the end of the true Christian faith.

Late antiquity was characterized also by other doctrinal
errors that cropped up again and again—we have only to
think of the Monophysite, Monothelite, and Donatist heresies, among many others. Despite this history of heretical
challenges and, of course, threats to the genuine Christian,
Catholic faith has continued constantly, aside from brief interruptions, and it finally culminated in the Great Schism
of the sixteenth century, a high point in hostilities that
has not been reached again since. Specifically in German-
speaking lands around the year 1530, almost nine-tenths of
the population had fallen away to follow Luther and the
other innovators, and the others were screaming, "Death to
the pope!" England, Scotland, Scandinavia, parts of Poland,
Hungary and significant portions of France separated from
the Church. Italy and Spain, Bavaria and the principalities
of Cologne and Münster, ruled by bishops who took their

political cues from Bavaria, essentially remained faithful, the last-mentioned two with some difficulty. In contrast, violent political campaigns to suppress the Church, for instance during the French Revolution and the atheistic dictatorships of the twentieth century, cost the Church many bloody sacrifices but endangered her continued existence far less than the forces of error at work within her.

Be that as it may: the Church has withstood the storms that have raged within and about her for two thousand years —not always splendidly, not triumphantly, but still unbroken. Although the bark of Peter has sprung leaks here and there, and has often had a broken mast and a tattered sail, it has not sunk. And if this has been so until now, it will— even by merely human reckoning—remain so, too.

We should consider, however, not only the often difficult survival of the Church in the tempests of history but also the great spiritual, intellectual, cultural and moral values that she has secured for mankind. It is indisputable and undisputed that everything that we regard today as our Western cultural heritage, from art to science and even technology, grew on the native soil of the Church. That institution which led scholarly and scientific progress during all those centuries, the university, is a legitimate daughter of the Church, to say nothing about all the branches of art: Where did the arts find a home until the cultural revolution of the sixties and seventies—which called everything into question—if not in the Church?

Above all, though, that respect for the personhood and freedom of the individual, resulting from the fact that man is created in God's image and is called to salvation in Christ —a respect that of course has long since become secularized —is hardly recognized at all today as the heritage from a past that was lived out in the spirit of the Church. Fundamentally new features of that respect—as compared to all pre- and non-Christian cultures, with the exception of Judaism—are compassion, love of neighbor and love of enemy, which the Church has heralded from the very beginning. After all, where, outside the spiritual milieu of the Church, has there ever been a movement like the *treva Dei* ["truce of God", the cessation of feudal hostilities during certain seasons of the liturgical year] in the eleventh and twelfth centuries?

We could mention here many other things that, like the moral attitudes just listed, logically disappear from social reality wherever the formative power of the Church's proclamation is no longer effective.

The Witness of the Saints

All that we have said finds its most convincing expression, its unsurpassable realization, from the beginning of Church history down to our own day, in the lives of those whom we call the saints of the Church. The number of them in every century is so great that just the accounts of their lives down to around the end of the Middle Ages fill up some seventy-two folio volumes of the *Acta sanctorum*. These were people in whose lives faith, hope, love of God and of neighbor, justice, honesty, selflessness, magnanimity, piety and devotion —in short, everything that makes a man precious—was evident in exemplary fashion. All of them attained this greatness as members of the Church. It was her teaching, her guidance, her dispensation of graces—in short, the Church herself—that brought the saints forth, as a tree brings forth its fruits. But how good must the tree be that bears such fruits! Indeed, it is the saints who present the most impressive reason for our trust in the Church.

Anyone who tries to reply that the world has not become any better despite two thousand years of the Church's influence will have to entertain the question: What would the world look like without the work of the Church? And, can the stream help it if the gravel lying in it is still hard and dry inside after two thousand years? Conversely, however, we should say that in every place where the Church's proclamation is heard, understood and put into practice, "a kingdom of truth and life, a kingdom of holiness and grace, a kingdom of justice, love and peace" has taken shape (Preface for the Solemnity of Christ the King): the kingdom of God.

II

THE PAPACY: GUARANTOR
OF UNITY AND TRUTH

On July 18, 2005, it had been 135 years since the First Vatican Council comprehensively described and proclaimed for the first time the position of the pope. Thunder and lightning filled the skies over Saint Peter's in Rome while Pius IX read aloud the constitution *Pastor aeternus*, thereby putting it into force. To some the thunderstorm signified the protest of heaven, while others took it as the raging of hell. The conciliar constitution, you see, contained the two dogmas of the universal primacy and the magisterial infallibility of the pope.

Days later, cannon fire thundered along the Rhine—the Franco-Prussian War had broken out. The council dispersed to the four winds, and its work remained a torso that waited until Vatican II for its completion.

What Does "Papal Primacy" Mean?

Let us now examine the contents of the constitution *Pastor aeternus*. It teaches that Jesus Christ himself conferred upon Saint Peter supreme pastoral authority over the entire Church and that his primacy continues in the Bishops of Rome. Concerning this supreme pastoral ministry, it then says:

We teach and declare that the Roman Church, by the dispo-
sition of the Lord, holds the sovereignty of ordinary power
over all others, and that this power of jurisdiction on the
part of the Roman Pontiff, which is truly episcopal, is immediate; and with respect to this the pastors and the faithful of whatever rite and dignity, both as separate individuals and all together, are bound by the duty of hierarchical
subordination and true obedience, not only in things which
pertain to faith and morals, but also in those which pertain
to the discipline and government of the Church [which is]
spread over the whole world, so that the Church of Christ,
protected not only by the Roman Pontiff, but by the unity
of communion as well as of the profession of the same faith,
is one flock under the one highest shepherd. This is the
doctrine of Catholic truth from which no one can deviate
and keep his faith and salvation.

Now, this means, first, that the pope is the supreme leg-
islator, who can enact binding laws for the entire Church
as well as for individual parts thereof. By virtue of the same
authority, he can repeal or modify the laws of his predecessors or even those of general councils, insofar as they do not
involve divine right or the truth of the faith. To him belongs
also the authentic interpretation of ecclesiastical laws. The
same applies for the convocation, direction and conclusion
of general councils and the final confirmation thereof. The
limits to papal authority are, as we said, divine right, natural
law and the truths of the faith.

Together with the supreme legislative authority goes the
supreme administrative power. Accordingly, the pope alone
can erect or suppress dioceses, and so forth. He creates cardinals, appoints or approves bishops and in principle can fill
all ecclesiastical offices. The regulation of the liturgy, beatifications and canonizations, the granting of indulgences,

and the approval of religious communities and their rules are the pope's prerogative, too. Furthermore, to him belongs the supreme management of all Church property and also the right to organize collections for the administration of the universal Church. The pope exercises these rights to this extent only in the Latin rite Church, however; the Eastern Catholic Churches have their own canon law—which of course was also enacted by the pope—that provides for many other regulations suited to the tradition of the Eastern Churches.

The exercise of the ministry of the supreme pastor then requires also a supreme right of supervision over the whole Church, which the pope exercises through nuncios, legates and other officials.

Finally, the pope is the authority of the last resort for all members of the Church who think that their rights have been impaired. The organs employed by the pope in carrying out this task are the individual congregations and offices of the Roman Curia.

Very important also is the supreme judicial authority of the pope. He has to see to it that ecclesiastical laws are observed, and he is the final appellate authority for all decisions of subordinate ecclesiastical jurisdictions. The pope exercises this function through the tribunals of the Sacra Romana Rota and of the Signatura Apostolica.

It is important, furthermore, that the pope represents the Church and her interests vis-à-vis the secular powers.

To the Holy See belong from time immemorial the rights of a legal person as understood in civil law—independently of the fact that the pope, since the Lateran Agreement of 1929, has also been the sovereign of the Vatican City State, which ensures that the pope is no one's subject and therefore can lead the universal Church in complete freedom. All of these rights are derived from the spiritual, plenipotentiary authority that is proper to the successor of Peter.

This delineation of the universal primacy of papal jurisdiction definitively rejects interpretations—for instance, those of Orthodoxy, but also of episcopalism and Gallicanism in the West—which are willing to concede to the Bishop of Rome only a primacy of honor but not the supreme pastoral authority. The idea of the pope serving as a sort of "general secretary of the united Christian denominations" thus proves to be absolutely impossible.

Whereas the jurisdictional primacy just described constitutes the real essence of the papal ministry, the supreme teaching authority (which is included in the former), that is, the infallible magisterium of the pope, is by far better known and also more controversial.

Vatican I teaches about this in chapter 4 of *Pastor aeternus*, and this passage is the actual formulaic definition:

> The Roman Pontiff, when he speaks *ex cathedra*, that is, when [in] carrying out the duty of the pastor and teacher of all Christians in accord with his supreme apostolic authority he explains a doctrine of faith or morals to be held by the universal Church, through the divine assistance promised him in blessed Peter, operates with that infallibility with which the divine Redeemer wished that his Church be instructed in defining doctrine on faith and morals; and so such definitions of the Roman Pontiff from himself, but not from the consensus of the Church, are unalterable.

An attentive reading of this text makes it clear that a series of objections that are usually raised against this doctrine of the faith are without basis. For example, not by the furthest stretch of the imagination can anyone say that this passage declares that the pope cannot sin, cannot make mistakes, is right about everything that he says, and so forth. Instead, the council restricts the pope's real freedom from error in two ways: with respect to the content of infallible teaching, it is limited to doctrinal matters of faith and morals; formally, infallible teaching is limited to statements that the pope makes *ex cathedra*. And the council defines *ex cathedra*: the pope must explicitly invoke his supreme apostolic authority and direct what he says to the entire Church. Only when these criteria are satisfied can one speak about an infallible decision and therefore about a decision that is per se unalterable. Furthermore the decision is attributed to the divine assistance that is promised to Saint Peter. Therefore, an *ex cathedra* statement does not depend on a creative dogmatic act on the part of the pope but rather on the divine guarantee that the Gospel of Jesus Christ will always be preserved from falsification. So says the First Vatican Council.

Vatican II reaffirms these teachings in their entirety and merely supplements them by emphasizing the pope's position as the head of the college of bishops. The successor of Peter is therefore the supreme pastor of the Church and the authentic interpreter of divine revelation. Through his worldwide primacy of jurisdiction and his magisterial infallibility, he is enabled to guarantee both the unity of the Church of Jesus Christ throughout the world and also the integrity of her deposit of faith.

Church without a Papacy

Just how important—indeed, how necessary—this Petrine ministry is for the very existence of the Church becomes evident in an especially impressive way when we look at those areas of Christendom in which the mission and authority of the papacy are not recognized. Thus, for example, since their separation from Rome, the Orthodox have not succeeded in holding another general council and instead have drifted away from each other into national Churches. And in the territories affected by the Reformation, the departures from the Gospel of Christ and the fragmentation in doctrine and fellowship are so obvious that nothing more needs to be said on the subject. Already in the seventeenth century, the distinguished Protestant jurist Samuel Pufendorf remarked:

> And although Luther had been the first to bell the cat, yet the others are unwilling to follow his opinion at each and every turn and want to have something to say, too. Hence disputes arose among them, too, and because there was no one who could have decided them *pro auctoritate*, but each one insisted stubbornly on his opinion, soon there were internal divisions, and everyone forgot the common enemy and got into each other's hair. And so the Papists have this advantage over the Protestants, that the former all acknowledge the pope as the supreme head of their Churches and are united in faith at least externally and by lip service. In contrast, the Protestants have no visible spiritual head and are wretchedly divided amongst themselves. For—to say nothing about the smaller sects of the Arminians, Socinians, Anabaptists, and the like—the main body has been divided into two almost equal camps, of Lutherans and of Reformed Christians, many of whom are almost as bitterly opposed to one another as they are to the Papists. Moreover, among them there is no general constitution for the good of religion, but instead each state governs itself in these matters as it sees fit.

The decisive question now is not whether the primacy and the infallibility of the Bishop of Rome serve a purpose and are necessary or advantageous for the Church. The one and only important consideration is whether or not primacy and infallibility are rooted in the apostolic tradition, that is, whether they were intended as such by Christ and instituted as part of the Church. Indeed, this is precisely what has been disputed again and again over the course of the centuries.

Criticism of the Papacy

While preparations were still being made for the council that convened in 1869–1870, Ignaz von Döllinger, a famous Church historian from Munich, had written that "the papacy, as it has developed, appears [today] as a disfiguring, malignant, suffocating growth on the organism of the Church, which hampers and undermines the better vital forces within her." With his extravagant polemics against the council, Döllinger was largely responsible for the Old Catholic schism.

Not a hundred years before that, in 1786, the archbishops of Mainz, Trier, Cologne and Salzburg had gathered under the protection of Emperor Joseph II [of Austria-Hungary] at the so-called Congress of Ems in order to protest against the Roman claim. In doing so, they relied on several canonists who owed much to the Enlightenment; according to them, the pope is indeed the Church's *centrum unitatis* and possesses a right of supervision over the bishops. On the other hand, the real power in the Church, in their view, belongs to the council, and the pope merely has to carry out its decisions. Decisions that he makes between councils would require the approval of the universal Church. In formulating their demands, the archbishops went so far as to require the consent of the local bishop in order to make papal bulls, doctrinal statements, and so forth, binding in the individual dioceses. They also claimed for the bishops unrestricted power to bind and loose.

Although some of their demands, which have not been listed here exhaustively, were not entirely without justification, and formulating them did not ipso facto make the archbishops heretics and schismatics, their program nevertheless fostered an internal dynamic that tended toward the dissolution of Church unity and a fragmentation into national Churches. In particular, the intention of making the validity of papal decisions, whether doctrinal, administrative or judicial, dependent upon the consent of the individual bishop struck at the heart of the papal ministry. Meanwhile, together with the princely glory of the protesting archbishops and the *ancien régime*, the demands made at Ems were swept away by the deluge of the French Revolution and Napoleonic rule, as the Imperial Church ended in secularization.

Their ideas, however, continue to simmer under a lid even today. The same is true of the Synod of Pistoia in the same year, which was likewise nourished by the intellectual heritage of the Enlightenment. That synod wanted to demote the pope to a sort of executive officer who received his authority from the universal Church. The powers of the bishops—indeed, of parish priests—were extended so far that the pope would have become de facto superfluous.

If we go even farther back in history, we encounter in the person of Martin Luther the most radical No to the papacy that has ever been uttered. His oft-repeated remark is well known: "*Pestis eram vivus, moriens ero mors tua, papa!*" ("I was a plague to you, O pope, when I was alive—when I die, I will be your death!"). He entitled one of his late works "On the Papacy in Rome, Founded by the Devil", and in it he says that they should "take the pope, the cardinals, and all the servants of his idolatry, and tear the tongues of those blasphemers out from the back of their throats and nail them to the gallows." He challenges his followers to fetter the pope, and so forth, outside Ostia and drown them in the sea, and in another passage, Luther calls on the German princes to exterminate the whole crew of the Roman Sodom and to wash their hands in their blood.

Compared with such outbursts, the aspirations of conciliarism in the preceding fifteenth century appear downright innocuous. Certainly those with such aspirations aimed to restrict papal powers of jurisdiction, legislation and administration in favor of a council or the bishops. Certainly quite a few people also maintained the supremacy of a general council over the pope, and some circles of council fathers at Constance and Basel thought that they could depose popes. Yet at the Council of Constance, with regard to John XXIII and Benedict XIII, it is quite certain that the bishops had not been dealing with legitimate popes, and so the claim of the fathers of Constance was inconsequential. And when the council fathers at Basel in 1439 thought that they had deposed the legitimate pope, Eugene IV, the failure of their attempted revolution was foreseeable.

There was criticism of the papacy in the High Middle Ages, too—expressed by both saints and heretics: the person of the pope and the exercise of his ministry were the object of these critiques. There was talk about pride, avarice and abuse of power, but there was no question about the Petrine ministry and its plenipotentiary authority.

All this notwithstanding, this papacy has existed for two thousand years, and despite all challenges from within and persecution from without, it has developed over those two millennia into the precise form in which the last two councils have presented it to our view.

This Roman papacy has not only survived the vicissitudes of its two-thousand-year history but has emerged again and again from dangers, periods of decline, and upheavals renewed and strengthened; this fact is a historically unprecedented phenomenon. More than 150 years ago, the English historian Macaulay marveled at it:

> The proudest royal houses are but of yesterday, when compared with the long line of the Supreme Pontiffs. . . . The republic of Venice came next in antiquity. But the republic of Venice was modern when compared with the Papacy; and the republic of Venice is gone, and the Papacy remains. The Papacy remains, not in decay, not a mere antique, but full of life and youthful vigour [while all the other kingdoms that were of the same age have long since disintegrated into dust]. . . . It is impossible to deny that the polity of the Church of Rome is the very master-piece of human (!) wisdom.

In his last comment, the learned historian is mistaken. The reason he mentions for this permanence and indestructibility of the papacy is not truly sufficient. It must be due to something more: the papacy is very deeply rooted in the authentic Tradition of the Church and thus in divine revelation.

Deep Roots

Let us attempt now this historical demonstration as well. Going back in time from Vatican I, we note that the previous council, namely the Council of Trent, did not even treat this theme explicitly; nevertheless, through its structures and its proceedings, it showed clear signs of papal influence. The Fifth Lateran Council, which had reached its conclusion a half century before that, had already brought about the definitive victory over conciliarism, after the Council of Florence in 1439 had taught the following, in connection with the union with the Eastern Church:

> We likewise define that the holy Apostolic See, and the Roman Pontiff, hold the primacy throughout the entire world; and that the Roman Pontiff himself is the successor of blessed Peter, the chief of the Apostles, and the true Vicar of Christ, and that he is the head of the entire Church, and the father and teacher of all Christians; and that full power was given to him in blessed Peter by our Lord Jesus Christ, to feed, rule, and govern the universal Church.

These sentences are taken from the bull *Laetentur coeli*, which was signed also by the Orthodox delegation together with the emperor of Byzantium so as to effect the Union of Florence.

With a pointed allusion to the supreme teaching office of the pope, the earlier Second Council of Lyons (1274), which was likewise attended by an Orthodox delegation, had already taught as follows:

> [The] holy Roman Church holds the highest and complete primacy and spiritual power over the universal Catholic Church which she truly and humbly recognizes herself to have received with fullness of power [*plenitudo potestatis*] from the Lord Himself, in Blessed Peter, . . . whose successor is the Roman Pontiff. And just as she is bound above all to defend the truth of faith, so too, if any questions should arise regarding the faith, they must be decided by her judgment.

At the same time, it is emphasized that the Roman Church is the supreme judicial authority and that all other Churches are subject to her.

Finally, we should mention the profession of faith that was formulated by Pope Hormisdas on August 11, 515, and was supposed to be signed by the clerics who were returning to the Church from the Acacian schism. This formula, which was signed in 519 by the emperor and the Patriarch of

Constantinople together with more than two hundred bishops from the East and which was again confirmed at the Fourth Council of Constantinople, declares that Catholic truth has always been preserved intact by the Apostolic See and that full and true adherence to the Christian religion is to be found in communion with it. One cannot ignore the saying of Our Lord Jesus Christ: "You are Peter, and on this rock I will build my church." Thus Rome was recognized as the final norm for the truth of the faith and for ecclesial communion.

This conviction, however, was by no means new. Pope Leo the Great had already given the classical expression to this papal-Petrine understanding of his own ministry in the middle of the fifth century, while he was striving to gain acceptance for the doctrinal teachings of the Council of Chalcedon.

Now, all of this is not disputed in the least. The disputed point is that this primacy has its roots in the original apostolic faith and goes back to the will of Jesus Christ in instituting the Church. Legitimate development—or pathological growth? That is the question. Let us examine therefore the oldest testimonies for the office of the successor to Peter; only the most important ones, of course, can be presented here.

As our first witness, let us hear Bishop Irenaeus of Lyons, who suffered martyrdom around the year 202. To his pen we owe priceless testimonies to the Church's faith in the second century, which he records in his work *Adversus haereses* (Against Heresies). In this book, he comes to speak about Rome as well. He writes:

For with this Church, because of her more powerful pre-eminence, all Churches must agree, that is, the faithful who

come from every part [of the world]; and it is in her that
the tradition that was handed from the Apostles has always
been maintained by the faithful who come from every part.

Now, over and over again the attempt is made to weaken
the force of this otherwise clear testimony for a primacy
of leadership and the normative character of the Church
of Rome. Some say, for instance, that Irenaeus meant that
we must seek the true apostolic tradition in the Churches
founded by the Apostles. That means Rome, of course, but
also Ephesus, Corinth or Antioch. One must look to that
sort of Church! But that is precisely what Irenaeus is *not*
saying! He says, rather, that *this* Roman Church is the one
that should be considered as the stronghold of the true Tradition. By no means is Rome mentioned here as the first example of an apostolic Church that happened to occur to the
bishop of Lyons, or because two Apostles, Peter and Paul,
worked there at the same time. Ephesus, too, could cite two
Apostles—Paul and John—as its authorities, even though
a *potentior principalitas*, a more powerful preeminence, had
never been attributed to it; after all, this is about Peter! And
about the whole Church, for immediately in the next sentence, Irenaeus says that the Apostles then conferred upon
the successor of Peter, Pope Linus, *"episcopatum administran-
dae ecclesiae"*, the office of overseeing the Church—but not
just this Roman Church, but the Church in general. Then
there is the opinion that Irenaeus had in view only a preeminent ranking of Rome over the Churches of the West,
but this cannot be proved, either.

This passage from *Adversus haereses*, therefore, presents
to us, from the second half of the second century, a testimony to the preeminent rank of the Roman Church—and
that means of her bishop—over the universal Church. The
same conclusion follows from the dispute between Bishop

Polycrates of Ephesus and Bishop Victor of Rome about the correct date for Easter in the years 189 through 199. Whereas the Churches in the province of Asia followed the Jewish calendar to determine the date, the other Churches celebrated Easter on the Sunday after the first full moon in spring, as we still do today.

From the reports about this very intense dispute handed down to us in the Church history of Eusebius (fourth century), it is clear, first of all, that Victor of Rome knew that he was authorized to call the Churches in Asia to order in this matter. He insisted that Bishop Polycrates convoke a synod; the latter did so, and the other bishops obeyed. In debating the matter itself, they vehemently opposed the Roman demand, whereupon Victor excommunicated the Christian communities of Asia, which in turn evoked the protests of many, including of the aforementioned Irenaeus of Lyons. However much many observers now criticized Victor's imprudence and harshness and tried to persuade him to be more conciliatory, they still did not doubt Victor's authority to proceed as he had done. Nor did he revoke his decision in any way. Finally, the Roman practice, approved by the Council of Nicaea in 325, was generally accepted.

If we go back now to the beginning of the second century, we come upon Bishop Ignatius of Antioch, who suffered martyrdom in Rome around the year 109. Letters from him to several Christian communities have been preserved, among them one to the community in Rome. This letter is different in several respects from the other letters. Whereas the others all contain emphatic admonitions and warnings against heresies, there is not a trace of such things in the letter to the Romans. Instead, we find high praises.

In particular, however, the introductory passage is interesting in this context. Not only does Ignatius commend the community in Rome as an example of Christian unity and an invincible bulwark against heresies, but he also says that it has the law of Christ—obviously in a qualified way that distinguishes it from the other Churches. It is especially significant, however, when he says that the Roman Church presides. The fact that this conviction—expressed by the bishop of Antioch, a renowned Church located in the East —was in no way a novelty but rather was based on authentic Tradition, is demonstrated by the First Letter of Clement, which was composed more than ten years before the letters of Ignatius.

Clement of Rome—and Rome is the issue here—demanded in this letter not only the submission of the agitators in the Church of Corinth to the presbyters whom they had driven away. He demands of them nothing less than their exile from Corinth. This demand for obedience is reinforced with sanctions, and furthermore, his awareness of his authority can be seen in the following sentence: "You will certainly give us the keenest pleasure if you prove obedient to what we have written through the Holy Spirit." The fact that the writer of the letter is exercising authority not only in word but also in deed is clear from what he says about his representatives who conveyed the letter, Claudius Ephebus, Valerius Biton and Fortunatus: "Send them back to us at an early convenience, full of peace and joy, that they may without delay bring tidings of peace and concord—the object of our most ardent desires—and that we in turn may without delay rejoice in your tranquillity." Thus, in friendly and modest terms, immediate compliance and a report thereon are demanded, whereby the sender of the letter does not doubt for a moment that this will take place.

In order to appreciate the full import of this letter, we must also note that Corinth was likewise an apostolic foundation —indeed, it was a thoroughly Pauline community and even older than the one in Rome. Moreover, there is no indication that the Corinthians had requested Roman intervention or rejected it when it was forthcoming. It is remarkable, too, that the Roman letter writer sees no need whatsoever to justify his intervention in Corinth. And, a hundred years after its composition, this letter was still read aloud during the Divine Liturgy of the community in Corinth, just like the Sacred Scriptures, as Bishop Dionysius assures Pope Soter in writing. Irenaeus, too, is acquainted with the letter—he calls it *"potentissimas litteras"*, an extremely powerful letter.

When we go back to the First Letter of Clement, we stand at the threshold of the apostolic era, properly speaking. John was still living in Ephesus, which was half as distant from Corinth as Rome was, and yet Rome intervened and he did not. But it is, after all, the Gospel of John that contains that twenty-first chapter in which we read about the commission given by Jesus to Peter: "Feed my lambs."

In response to the aforementioned historical evidence for a preeminence of the Roman Church, of the Bishop of Rome, in governing the whole Church, the objection is immediately raised that this was in no way intended to be a primacy of jurisdiction, as has been claimed since Vatican I and II. Therefore, such a primacy cannot be traced back to Jesus Christ, either, but is merely the result of a human historical development. And so—the argument goes—under suitable conditions, for instance for the sake of ecumenism, it can and also must be limited again to its original dimensions or abolished entirely.

Organic Development

What actually comes to light is an unfolding of the Petrine ministry that runs parallel to the development of the Church as a whole, from the community of disciples in Jerusalem down to the worldwide Church of the twenty-first century. In the process, the original knowledge about the "religious and spiritual significance of the Roman Church" was distilled into the insight that Rome must be considered "a place of privileged tradition", which is why Rome was increasingly recognized and acknowledged as the "center of the *communio*", from which "leadership of the universal Church" was exercised to an ever-greater extent. This was the case, however, at least since the time of Leo the Great, if not earlier (K. Schatz).

Catalysts for this process were the concrete problems of ecclesial communion—problems that arose with increasing frequency and urgency—and the need to fend off heresies, to maintain the unity of *communio* and to ensure independence from worldly powers. In this perspective, it is remarkable that over the course of all those centuries no other episcopal see ever raised the same claim that Rome did.

How are we to evaluate this now theologically? If we start with the foundation of the Church by Jesus Christ and with his promises to the Church—that he will be with her always until the end of the world, that he will send her the Holy Spirit to be her counselor, that the powers of hell will not prevail against her—then it is simply unthinkable that this Church could ever have changed so much over the course of history as to lose her identity, that is, that there could ever be such erroneous developments in her dogma or in her sacramental-hierarchical structure that they could lead to the loss of her identity. The developmental processes within this most intrinsic and essential area of the Church can therefore be nothing other than a genuine unfolding of what Christ had placed within her from the very beginning —comparable to the unfolding of an organism according to its genetic code.

Now, if several general councils, which after all are organs of the infallible Magisterium of the Church, have taught this primacy of the Bishop of Rome by means of increasingly precise formulas, then the primacy of the pope belongs to the inalienable deposit of faith of the Church of Jesus Christ.

The Protest Persists

Regardless of this, what remains is—as Hans Urs von Balthasar puts it—the "anti-Roman attitude", which can be observed again and again down through the centuries. "In fact, what else remains common to the churches separated from Rome and dispersed in all directions but the rejection of the center's rightly or wrongly assumed claims of God-given authority, claims that keep the No of the dissidents alive and embittered?" This No from outside is accompanied today to an unusual extent by protest against the pope from inside the Church, and it seems as though an antiecumenism were forming, which indeed has as its common basis not a Yes to the Catholic faith but rather the repudiation of the pope. And so the Rock of Peter proves again and again to be a "stumbling stone", "a rock that will make [men] fall" and a "sign that is spoken against" [i.e., a "sign of contradiction"]. Now, this really demonstrates that the disciple is not above his teacher and must share his teacher's fate. Yet this is precisely what proves the authenticity of his discipleship. The papacy—and every individual pope—therefore participates in the *scandalum incarnationis* [scandal of the Incarnation]: "Is not this the carpenter's son?" (Mt 13:55). Just as Jesus' opponents were not willing or able to recognize the divine mystery of his Person, so too the many opponents of the Roman papacy, both outside and inside the Church, are incapable of seeing in it anything more than human power structures or, at best, a historical development thereof.

Of course, one should immediately concede that there is a whole series of psychological reasons excusing those who find the papal claim intolerable; yet their protest is based most often on the manner in which the Roman authority is exercised. Again and again over the course of history this authority has been exercised harshly, inflexibly, or even in the service of political, financial or egotistical interests; many times it has been abused. And have there not been popes who by their way of life, which contradicted God's commandments, repudiated their claim to be Christ's representative on earth? No doubt about it. But there is no doubt, either, about the fact that God makes use of weak human beings in order to accomplish his work of salvation. Peter himself had proved his fragility before he was nevertheless made the Rock, the Keeper of the Keys and the Chief Shepherd of Christ's Church. Thus the anti-Roman attitude is ultimately unmasked as merely a special case of the protest against the God who appeared as man among us and against his revelation.

But this, too, no doubt, is part of God's plan of salvation. We might still ask: What good is this vexing phenomenon supposed to accomplish?

Once again, von Balthasar has a profound insight when he points out how relentlessly God himself demanded unconditional obedience from the patriarchs, Moses and the prophets—and above all from the Servant of God par excellence, Jesus, and how Jesus himself deals subsequently with Peter "as if the heedless disobedience of Adam and Eve could be balanced only by a similarly heedless demand of obedience". Man, who was unwilling to obey his Creator, because he himself wanted to be like God, must now obey a man, if he wants to have—by grace—a share in the divine nature.

Therefore, the Petrine ministry, the Roman primacy, participates in the "mystery of the Church", the "mystery of redemption". The papacy, too, is revealed only in faith. A believer's view of the papacy, far from being a superficial devotion to the person of the pope, results in that reverence, that obedience—indeed, that love—with which a Catholic greets the Vicar of Christ.

Not the least important motivation for this love and obedience is the historical experience that the storms of two millennia could not shake the Rock of Peter upon which the Lord built his Church. Thus it is true for the future also: "*Non praevalebunt*"—they, the powers of hell, shall not be able to prevail against her.

III

THE CATHOLIC CHURCH AND
THE UNIFICATION OF EUROPE

Is European union a vision of the future or a lost heritage? Putting the alternative this way brings the historical dimension into play. In this chapter, we will try to shed some light on it and gain from it insights into the future.

Starting from this point of departure, we immediately come across the unique historical phenomenon of the Roman Empire, which for many long centuries was the principal factor in the cultural and political unity of a much larger geographical region than modern-day Europe. The empire's center was the Mediterranean Sea, which was divided by the Italian peninsula into an eastern and a western half. In the middle of the peninsula stood the city of Rome. From there the empire expanded in all directions, until it reached as far as Mesopotamia in the east and Egypt in the south, and extended to the Atlantic in the west and to the north as far as the *moles Hadriani*, the present Scottish border.

Early Christianity saw, in the very existence of the Roman Empire, Divine Providence at work, ordaining the birth of Jesus Christ at a time when the world was ruled by a single government in Rome, so that the spread of the Gospel would not be hindered by borders between countries and kingdoms. So does Origen remark in *Contra Celsum* 2, 30. With the fall of the Roman Empire during the mass migration of peoples, this unity broke apart. After that, the Islamic invasion at the beginning of the seventh century tore the eastern part and the southern rim of the former empire away from its central regions. At the same time, the center of political action shifted toward the north, where a new focal point arose in the kingdom of the Franks.

The momentous consequences of the resulting separation between the Greek East and the Latin West have yet to be completely overcome. After the decline and fall of the empire, what could now replace it and restore order?

Institutions of the Unification

Out of the rubble of the *Imperium Romanum* arose, in a process that lasted a good two hundred years, medieval Christendom. Its most important structural element—which we will discuss soon—was the axis between Rome and Aachen, between the Roman Church and the Frankish kingdom. For a millennium the harmonious but periodically controversial cooperation between the two poles of *sacerdotium* and *imperium*—papacy and imperial power—determined the fate of Christendom. However, until the discovery of the New World, Christendom was essentially identical to Europe, to a Europe whose boundaries moved east and north with the advances of Christian missionary work around the year 1000.

This historically unique phenomenon of Christendom was, as we have indicated, comparable to an ellipse whose two foci, the papacy and the empire, had a tense relationship to each other and yet held the whole thing together.

The Papacy

Of these two unifying institutions, we will look first at the papacy, not only because of its priority in time but also, as we will demonstrate, for other objective reasons. As the Gospel of Matthew says (16:16–19), Jesus Christ founded his Church on Peter, the Rock. This should be regarded as the foundational charter of the papacy, which subsequently has withstood not only the oppressive measures taken by the Caesars but also the attempts of the Christian emperors to domesticate it politically. It also survived the downfall of the Roman Empire.

Furthermore, the Roman successors to Peter were the only authority whose mission extended beyond the boundaries of the newly formed ethnic kingdoms and who claimed universal validity.

In the wake of this development of various ethnic kingdoms, ecclesiastical life was formally characterized by "national churches" and therefore by a rather loose connection to the Roman papacy; after that phase and from the seventh century on, Rome once again assumed a prominent position in early medieval Christendom—this time no longer as the imperial capital but rather as the burial place of the Apostles Peter and Paul, as the see of the successors of Peter. At the Synod of Whitby in the year 664, the Anglo-Saxon Church, which until then had lived in relative independence, adopted the Roman forms of ecclesiastical life in her liturgy and discipline. It was precisely from the Anglo-Saxon world that the custom of making a pilgrimage to the tombs of the Roman Apostles began, also at a very early date.

As far as political conditions allowed, the Roman popes for their part exercised their ministerial powers to an increasing extent over all of Christendom. Even the Christian East did not doubt that in the final instance Rome issued the judgment in ecclesiastical matters, whether they concerned the faith or canon law.

Consequently, all of the ethnic kingdoms, which were no

longer held together by the *imperium* and from which modern Europe would evolve, had a common center, a common point of reference: the pope in Rome. No more did one find in Rome, as in antiquity, a center of political power; that was long gone, despite the ecclesiastical state that developed in the eighth and ninth centuries. Instead, people recognized in Rome a stronghold of faith and law. An eloquent expression of this view of Rome is the letters of Saint Boniface (d. 754), which he wrote to the popes of his day, requesting and receiving from them guidance and instruction for his missionary work among the Germanic tribes.

Out of this exchange between the periphery and the center arose medieval canon law. Whereas conciliar canons had regulated ecclesiastical life until the end of the fourth century, now papal decisions in individual cases became increasingly important: the so-called decretals. A disputed case was referred to Rome and decided there. Thus medieval canon law came about. Its greatest hour—indeed, that of European law in general—arrived around the year 1144, when the monk Gratian from Bologna—nothing more than his name is known about him—compiled the entire legal tradition of the Western Church from the documents in which it lay scattered about, systematically ordered it, harmonized contradictory decretals and published the results under the title *Concordantia discordantium canonum*. Generally known by the name *Decretum Gratiani*, this private scholarly work was de facto the first statute book of the Western Church and became the cornerstone of the *Corpus iuris canonici* that built upon it and remained in force until Pentecost 1918 [when the 1917 Code took effect].

What came about thereby was nothing less than pan-European law; it immediately pertained only to ecclesiastical life yet had a profound influence on civil life, if you consider how intensively the ecclesiastical and secular realms permeated each other for centuries. Canon law was a unifying factor of the first order for Europe during its formative period. Very closely connected with it was the ecclesiastical judicial system, the official channels of which led from the local tribunal via that of the Metropolitan to the Sacra Romana Rota or the Signatura Apostolica, the latter two being the papal tribunals that decided a final appeal. Because the two last-mentioned tribunals made their judgments independently of and uninfluenced by local and territorial authorities, a maximum of legal reliability was guaranteed by the papal courts. Even though the late-medieval papal Curia had a bad reputation (it was said that you could obtain anything there for money), nevertheless the papal courts of justice enjoyed the highest esteem, and their judgments were respected from Reykjavik to Catania.

In a certain sense the much-reviled papal fiscal system, as it developed during the so-called Avignon papacy (essentially the fourteenth century), had a unifying effect as well. This was a refined system for regulating the contributions sent to the Apostolic Treasury from individual dioceses, abbeys and even smaller churches. Raising these revenues was the responsibility of the institute of papal collectors, who worked as local representatives or were sent specially from Rome. If nothing else, the flow of information between the center and the periphery was fostered in this manner. Not infrequently, such collectors served also as papal diplomats.

With that, however, we have already mentioned an additional factor in European unification, namely, papal diplomacy. Papal diplomacy was already developing during the late Middle Ages from the system of legates: as needed, the popes sent to the periphery high-ranking representatives vested with more-or-less comprehensive powers so as to exercise through them their papal ministry as supreme pastor and to regulate disputed ecclesiastical affairs, to carry out reforms and to vanquish heresies. Especially in the late Middle Ages we encounter such legates acting also as mediators who were sent to make peace between hostile kings or princes.

A forum for unification par excellence, however, were the general or ecumenical councils convoked by the popes and presided over by them or else by their legates. We are speaking here about a gathering of the bishops of the whole Church for the purpose of exercising collectively their teaching or pastoral ministry; the decrees of such a council are —still today—binding for the entire Church. The circumstance that in medieval Christendom the ecclesiastical and secular realms interpenetrated one another led also to the custom that kings and princes were present or represented at councils and exerted considerable influence, although without the right to vote. Naturally, high-ranking clerical and university professors were present, too, in varying but large numbers.

It is not difficult to appreciate what it meant for council participants from every country to meet in great numbers daily in a restricted space for a long period of time, indeed, even for years. This was the intellectual, cultural, religious and also political elite of Europe, and their common participation in the council offered them a rare forum for the exchange of ideas, knowledge and experiences. The periphery gathered in the focus of ecclesiastical and also of political events. A particularly impressive example of this is the Council of Constance (1414–1418), which has to rank as the largest gathering of the leading class of Europe in the Middle Ages and has been surpassed in this respect only by the Second Vatican Council.

The aforementioned centripetal dynamic that is inherent in councils was matched on the other hand by a movement running in the other direction, from the center to the periphery. Whatever doctrinal decrees and laws were formulated and decided at a council and confirmed by the pope were addressed in fact to the entire Church and were supposed to be put into action in the individual dioceses, and so forth.

In this way—although of course not always and everywhere in the same manner, because of various sorts of resistance—ecclesiastical life and in many respects civil life as well throughout Europe were to a great extent uniformly regulated. An eminent example of this is the Council of Trent, which lasted, with long interruptions, from 1546 until 1564. With its doctrinal decrees, to say nothing about its canons for reform, it inspired that unique phenomenon in cultural history, the "Catholic Baroque" period, which transformed all departments of life in those regions of Europe that remained Catholic and, despite all the geographical differences, left on them all a uniform, magnificent stamp that is still visible today.

The Emperor and the Empire

The second focus of the "Christendom-Europe ellipse" is the *imperium*, the empire. However much the medieval emperors regarded themselves as the successors to the Roman Caesars, there was an essential difference between the latter's *imperium* and that of their successors, namely with regard to their credentials. The Roman Empire of Augustus, into which Jesus Christ was born, had a long and glorious history behind it, and it had just reached the apogee of its expanding power. Christ and Christianity were born into this empire; they found it there already.

The situation was quite different when it was a matter of restoring the *imperium* after the downfall of the Caesars' empire. When the Frankish majordomo Pippin set about wresting the kingship from the Merovingian dynasty after having seized power—since the one who holds the power should rightly be called the king—he saw that he was in need of credentials. The idea that the legitimacy of the kingly throne depended on the descent of the occupant from a royal bloodline was deeply rooted in the Frankish people; the king was thought to be sacred because of his lineage. But this is precisely what Pippin lacked, for he was not of royal lineage—although he, like his father Charles Martel and his grandfather Pippin before him, wielded the real power in the Frankish kingdom. If he was now going to strive for the kingship, he needed a legitimation that significantly surpassed that of a hallowed lineage. And this legitimation could come only from the supreme sacral authority: from the successor of Peter in Rome. Now, when Pope Stephen II anointed Pippin as king in 754 in the Church of Saint Denis and bestowed on him together with his sons Charles and Carloman the title of *patricius Romanorum* [patrician of the Romans], and finally when Leo III crowned Charlemagne as emperor on Christmas Day in the year 800, the *renovatio imperii* occurred, and this restored empire was henceforth the *Sacrum Romanum Imperium*. Yet the Church, the papacy, had stood by the cradle of this Holy Roman Empire. As late as the fifteenth century, when Pope Clement VII crowned Charles V emperor in Bologna in 1530, the emperors received their crown from the hands of the pope. Although the power of these emperors was soon increasingly restricted by the up-and-coming "national" kingdoms, the sacral dignity of their empire nevertheless made them an important unifying factor for a Europe that was drifting apart more and more.

One last time, the unifying force of the empire appeared impressively in the person of Emperor Sigismund from the house of Luxemburg (crowned 1433, d. 1437), who at the time had not yet been crowned but was still called by that title everywhere. Ever since the election of an antipope to rival Urban VI (September 20, 1378), a papal schism had existed, which had been so aggravated by the unsuccessful attempt at unification at the Council of Pisa (1409) that now three pretenders claimed to be the pope. Because of this papal schism the world of European states was torn apart also, at first into two and then into three blocs, each of which supported "its pope". In this situation, which was both ecclesiastically and politically perverse, it was the "emperor" who, after all attempts at restoring unity had failed, managed, by discharging the duties of his office as *advocatus ecclesiae*, to assemble the hostile parties at the Council of Constance (1414–1418), which then in fact was able to restore the lost unity through the unanimous election of Pope Martin V (1417–1431).

It is impressive to see how the mutual cooperation of the two foci, emperor and pope, stabilized the unity of Europe. In the measure in which the empire subsequently lost its sacred character, its significance within Europe decreased as well. What remained was a ranking, a matter of protocol. At the same time, however, the disintegration of Europe proceeded apace.

University

When historians speak about the pillars that supported medieval society, they like to list, in addition to the Church and the empire, the university—resulting in the triad *sacerdotium, imperium, studium*. By way of analogy to the myth of the *translatio imperii*—the transfer of the empire from Constantine to the pope and from the pope to the [Holy Roman] emperor—scholars in the Middle Ages spoke also about a *translatio studii*, in this case from Athens via Rome to Paris.

This may not correspond to the facts so much as it testifies to an awareness of larger continuities—and these, too, are a reality. Be that as it may, there is no doubt that the papacy was a godparent at the baptism of *studium*, the university, just as it had stood by the cradle of the *imperium*. Yet the metaphor does not correspond exactly to the reality: the university is not a godchild; it is the legitimate daughter of the Church. The consolidation of schools that had provided for the education of clerics, notaries and judges, and physicians resulted at the end of the twelfth century in the institution of the *studia generalia*, first in Paris and Bologna. Although this process was not chronologically or geographically uniform, it was the pope who bestowed canonical form upon this loose association and the *universitas magistrorum et scholarium* [university of teachers and students] that developed around it. Only in a second phase did secular princes grant privileges to these centers of learning.

Another important factor was the decision to ensure the livelihood of the professors and students, to a great extent through the assignment of income-producing Church lands. Once again it was the popes to whom the universities submitted their *rotuli*, collective applications for the conferral of ecclesiastical benefices upon the professors. The preferential treatment of university professors in the assignment of benefices by the popes was an important topic at late medieval councils. The students, too, provided that they had received the tonsure and thus had been accepted into the clerical state, became the beneficiaries of such subsistence allowances, on an appropriately more modest scale, of course: the medieval *Bafög*, whereby they were exempt for the duration of their studies from the duties connected with their stipends.

Thus after the year 1200 a wide-meshed network of institutions of higher education spread over all of Europe: the universities of Bologna, Paris, Oxford, Cambridge, Salamanca and Coimbra came into being, and Padua and Montpellier as well before the close of the thirteenth century. One exception was the founding of the University of Naples in 1220 by Frederick II, which took place without papal assistance. The fourteenth century then witnessed a boom in university foundations: the first one in imperial territory was the foundation by Charles IV in Prague in 1348. Around the year 1300 there were thirteen universities in all of Europe; toward the end of the century, twenty-eight, and around 1500 there were sixty-eight of them.

But what does this "*studium* pillar" have to do with European unification? Well, these institutions of higher education had essentially identical structures, and the examinations as well as the subjects taught were the same—Christian revelation and the ancient Greco-Roman tradition. Furthermore, the academic degrees were valid everywhere. Finally, every master or doctor had the *licentia ubique docendi*, the general authorization to teach. This, however, was awarded by delegated papal authority.

Thanks to this and also to the Latin language, which was in everyday use at the universities (and far beyond them), there was great mobility among the masters and students, who traveled from one university to another so as to follow the most famous teachers or to find the best conditions for teaching. In this way a "pan-European" class of *literati* arose, who had been molded by the same subjects, experiences and training and soon populated not only the lower schools but also the chanceries of bishops and princes and the courts of justice and gained increasing influence, if not power.

This cultural-sociological development reached its high

point in the age of the Renaissance and humanism. The guild of humanists, which was decisive for intellectual life throughout Europe and looked to Erasmus of Rotterdam as its universally revered head, felt so duty-bound by its common ideal of education that the initial attempts to overcome the [Protestant] schism that broke out in the sixteenth century started within its ranks. The university should be highly esteemed as a unifying factor in Europe, particularly in the Middle Ages, when intellectual life in its entirety developed upon a common spiritual foundation.

Expressions and Practices of European Community

The Calendar

Spend a week in Jerusalem, and you experience something that a European is completely unaccustomed to: three different calendars, like interfering radio waves, define the rhythm of a city's life. On Friday the Muslims observe their holy day, on the next day the Jews keep their Sabbath, and finally the Christians celebrate their Sunday, with the respective consequences for their work schedules, and so forth. Ever since Emperor Constantine declared Sunday the work-free day reserved for divine worship, this became throughout the empire and afterward through the newly developing "Europe" a prominent structural element defining everyday life. Much the same thing is true of the Church's great feast days and her seasons for feasting and fasting, particularly since the time of Pope Leo the Great.

Since deeds of purchase and sale, last wills and testaments, contracts and peace treaties, and even private letters were now dated according to the liturgical calendar of the Church, even profane events were—conspicuously—brought into relation with salvation history. Moreover, since the sixth century (Dionysius Exiguus, d. c. 550), years were reckoned with reference to the birth of Christ as *anni Domini*, *anni salutis*, *anni Incarnationis Domini*, and so forth [years of Our Lord, years of salvation, years of the Lord's Incarnation]. The fact that the beginning of the year was variously observed on December 25 (the birth of Christ), on March 25 (the Annunciation) and on other days, until the date of January 1 finally prevailed, to all appearances causes contemporary historians more difficulties when they are dating old documents than it did to the people who lived in the Middle Ages. The essential thing is that the rhythm of daily life in medieval Europe was determined by the Church calendar, and thus the general consciousness of transcendent realities found its expression in this way of reckoning time and organizing the year.

Interestingly enough, the European disintegration process of the modern era also found a calendar-related expression. When Pope Gregory XIII reformed the calendar and abolished the Julian calendar that had been valid until then, so as to introduce the Gregorian calendar, which was named after him, both the Protestant and the Orthodox countries refused to comply with this reform, even though it was a marked improvement.

The most decisive break with the Christian tradition occurred two hundred years later, on July 14, 1790, with the revolutionary calendar that was introduced in France, which no longer counted years of salvation but rather years of "liberty". Even the biblically based seven-day week was abolished, and Sunday along with it. After all houses of God had been closed, this was supposed to wipe out the last remnant of religion. On December 31, 1805, this aberration in the calendar vanished again by a decree of Emperor Napoleon.

In contrast, the Fascist way of reckoning years, introduced by Mussolini in 1922—beside the "normal" number of the year, one would write the number of the year in the Fascist era—was not a real change; it, too, vanished with the end of Mussolini's regime.

Language

Language has much more significance as a unifying factor than the common Church and civil calendar. Whereas the many peoples of the Roman Empire had found a *common* language in Koiné, the Greek spoken in late antiquity— "common" is precisely what κοινή means—the lingua franca of developing Europe was Latin. It was certainly not at the level of Ciceronian Latin, and often in everyday use it was more like the "English" that is spoken in the British Commonwealth; nevertheless, the common Latin language represented an outstanding opportunity for communication. Once again it was the Church that made Latin at home north of the Alps, not only through her schools, but above all through the use of the Latin language in her liturgy, government and administration of justice.

Furthermore, it was not only scholarship that used the language of Rome in instruction and literary production. The merchant from Norway, too, ordered his bolts of cloth in Florence in Latin, and the traveler asked for directions or inquired about lodgings in that language.

Latin was of particular importance, however, for intellectual life. It made possible "pan-European" communication among the universities of the different countries, to an extent unknown even today. The mobility of professors and students was therefore extremely great until the early modern period. The German elite of the fifteenth and early sixteenth centuries used to study effortlessly in Bologna,

Padua, Pavia and Siena, without having to learn a foreign language first. And professors could easily exercise their right to teach *ubique terrarum*; everywhere the common language of instruction, the language of academic disputations and examinations, was Latin.

This made it possible to have an extremely intensive exchange of scientific knowledge: problem-free scholarly discussion, which contributed to the formation of a "pan-European" academic elite. In the age of humanism, this elite became that guild of scholars and literati who looked to the great Erasmus as their head and esteemed model. In these circles, Latin experienced throughout Europe a renaissance at the highest level.

Consequently it was possible, well into the nineteenth century, to compose in Latin not only writings in the field of the humanities but also scientific works. Copernicus, with his *De revolutionibus orbium caelestium* [On the revolution of the heavenly bodies], is a world-renowned example of this; and for the nineteenth and even the twentieth centuries, we mention also the series entitled Monumenta Germaniae historica, critical editions of historical documents with Latin introductions and notes.

Pilgrimages

The notion that medieval man was so tied to the soil that he hardly ever left his village, his monastery or his city and had acquired almost no knowledge of what lay beyond his own narrow horizon is based on an error.

Aside from the fact that commercial life flourished even in the Middle Ages, it is above all the custom of going on pilgrimage that illustrates what a high degree of mobility was taken for granted in that society, a mobility that received its impetus from a pious love of the Church. From the very beginning it drew believers not only to the places where Jesus had lived but also to the tombs of the Apostles and saints, in whose intercession with God they trusted.

Besides the Holy Land, the chief places of pilgrimage were the tombs of the Apostles Peter and Paul in Rome, the tomb of Saint James in Santiago de Compostela and finally the shrines of the Archangel Michael on Monte Gargano in Apulia, Italy, and on Mont-Saint-Michel in Normandy. The tomb of Saint Thomas Becket in Canterbury was also the destination of European pilgrimages. With his *Canterbury Tales*, Geoffrey Chaucer constructed a literary monument to it.

But what significance did this have? No more and no less than the fact that thousands of Christian believers, both men and women, made their way to these holy places along the roads of Europe. In doing so, they left their homes, crossed boundaries, became acquainted with foreign lands and peoples and returned home with an abundance of impressions that they could not have imagined at their departure—to say nothing about the real religious benefits of the pilgrimage. If we are to give credence to contemporary sources, again and again there were crowds of pilgrims along these roads that are reminiscent of modern-day traffic jams. Not only were there travel or pilgrimage guidebooks (printed ones in the late Middle Ages) for pilgrims who had decided to set out on their journey, but along the way the pilgrim found a logistically well-planned system of hostels that provided lodgings and even hospitals for travelers who fell ill. It is not difficult to imagine what sort of company sat there by the fireside in the evening—pious and impious folk thrown together from every land and nation—and what a jumble of languages—interspersed with Latin words—could be heard.

Along those pilgrim paths and at those shrines, Christendom met itself, Europe encountered itself, and European consciousness could develop under the banner of sanctity. Even such remotely situated destinations as Santiago, at the *finis terrae* [end of the earth], or Canterbury, across the Channel, were connected by pilgrimages with the center of the continent. The pilgrimage was—and is becoming again in our day—an important factor for the spiritual unification of Europe.

The Spiritual Foundations of Europe

Only a thumbnail sketch could be given of those institutions and customs that defined the life of the European continent for more than a millennium; we ought to have included many additional details. Although the ideals were often put into practice in a fragmentary manner, there is no other way to describe that life than as magnificent. It has been said occasionally that everything great in the history of Europe arose upon the foundations associated with Jerusalem, Athens and Rome.

In this remark Jerusalem stands for the knowledge that man and the world are ultimately related to the Creator God, to whom they owe their existence and from whom they await their definitive fulfillment.

Man's understanding of himself and of his fellow man as the image and likeness of God, as part of creation and at the same time as a steward who helps to shape it, as God's partner, as a person endowed with freedom and called to responsibility in God's sight, along with the knowledge that man is presently still on the way to his destination, his eternal perfection: all this necessarily left an enduring impression on the European's outlook on life, his relation to his fellow man and to the world.

No doubt, individuals were aware of all this to varying degrees, depending on their capacity for understanding. It is quite certain also that, despite this noble heritage, the powers of evil were not simply banished from the life of the individual or of society. Yet this very knowledge about sin and guilt, about the necessity and possibility of repentance and forgiveness, was the undisputed common property of this Christian society. Without this background, it seems impossible to explain the mighty accomplishments in science and art, in European culture as a whole. Rather, we can tell from the results what a creative cultural force it was for the inhabitants of a continent to share the same ideals in life and the same moral norms for a millennium.

Whereas Jerusalem stands for the predominant relation of old Europe to the transcendent, Athens stands for the primacy of the intellect that defined European culture. It was not the Sophists, who spoke about the utilization of knowledge, but rather Socrates, Plato and Aristotle who became the philosophical foster fathers of the European continent. Disinterested striving for knowledge about the ultimate foundations of being—*theoria* [contemplation], which is fascinated by the truth, the goodness and the beauty of all that is—characterized the intellectual efforts of the Middle Ages as well as the search for the norm for right living that is grounded in existence itself.

In the lofty school of Athens, great minds of the early Church—think of the "three great Cappadocian Fathers", Basil, Gregory of Nazianzen and Gregory of Nyssa—sought and found the intellectual tools for their profound treatises, in which they attempted, not to decode the mysteries of the Christian faith, especially the belief in one God in three Persons, but rather to provide intellectual insights into them. The harmonious synthesis of Greek philosophy and

Christian revelation that is associated with the names of Augustine, Albert the Great and Thomas Aquinas found in the works of those theologians an expression that has hardly ever been surpassed since. The Scholasticism of the High Middle Ages, which was reaching its apogee at the same time as the rise of the universities, taught Europe the intellectual discipline and conceptual precision that became the prerequisite for the whole scientific development in the history of our continent. Without Scholastic distinctions and "hairsplitting", there would be no splitting of the atom in the modern era.

Finally the aphorism mentions Rome, and immediately we associate the name of this city with the concepts of authority and law. Certainly, the ideas of power and war come to mind as well. But power and war do not characterize Rome's history-making heritage; what does characterize it, rather, are the other two: authority and law. Whereas philosophy has its home in Athens, Rome brought forth jurisprudence. The *ius Romanum* became the foundation of all jurisprudence, even in our day, and thus became also the basis of legislation and legal systems [*Rechtskultur*, including the courts and the legal profession]. Although there has often been a gulf between the reality and the ideal, nevertheless there is no disputing the fact that law has always been able to rein in authority. Principles such as the one declaring that contracts must be honored—*pacta sunt servanda*—have set standards for the social life of peoples to this day. Faith in the rule of law in the common life of individuals and peoples is indisputably part of the Roman heritage.

To have combined Old and New Testament revelation and Greco-Roman culture with the Germanic-Celtic element into a history-making synthesis, in which the Christian revelation revealed its formative power, was the epochal accomplishment that resulted from the collaboration of the papacy (or the Church) with the restored empire in a magnificent effort of both spiritual and political forces at the turn of the ninth century and basically continued its development until the French Revolution. This event indicates a caesura that not only distinguishes "classical" Europe from today's Europe but also marks a historical break between the two.

The Denial of the Roots

The last two centuries of European history are in fact characterized by a break, on a wide range of fronts, with the spiritual and intellectual tradition of more than one and a half millennia. It is enough to quote Goethe's assessment of Europe's past, upon which the Church had in fact left her mark: "The whole history of the Church is a mishmash of error and violence" ("Tame Xenia" IX). Even more radical is his refusal: "Give thanks to the Sleeping One up there for saving us? I should honor thee? What for?" ("Prometheus"). And the frighteningly prophetic passage: "Here I sit and make man in my own image, a race that will be my equal . . . and will pay thee no heed, as I don't!" (ibid.). What is expressed here is the fundamentally transformed Enlightenment outlook on life, out of which nineteenth-century Europe was formed, scarcely tempered by the interlude of Romanticism.

Whereas the Hegelian Right produced the totalitarian state, from Hegel's leftist followers came, with completely logical consistency, the *homo Sovieticus* of Lenin and Stalin and of the entire former East Bloc. There is not much to distinguish it from the racially pure *homo Nordicus*, and the *homo oeconomicus* of the capitalist world is not much better, just different. They, these prototypes of the new European, shaped their world, their state, their culture after their own image. The catastrophes of the twentieth century, from the insatiable mechanized battles of the First World War to the death camps of the Third Reich and the Gulag Archipelago, are the results of this break that Europe made with its heritage from Jerusalem, Athens and Rome. To the extent in which the Christian view of man and the world vanished under the influence of the rationalistic philosophy of the Enlightenment, the path led to the fang-and-claw society of social Darwinism, the ultimate expression of which is the abortion, euthanasia and cloning society of our day. At the beginning of this dire trend—as we said—was the denial of the foundations for the cultural development of a Christian millennium.

Now, however, we must speak about Europe's responsibility for the rest—the incomparably greater rest—of the world.

Europe's former greatness was also relevant to the fact that its spiritual, intellectual and cultural heritage was accepted in all those parts of the world, such as North and South America and Australia, that came under European influence. This is not the place for a critical evaluation of Europe's interventions in countries overseas and of the methods that it employed. The phenomenon of colonialism eludes a simple value judgment because of its complexity. Just one question, though: Without the Spanish Conquest, would the Aztecs and Mayas not have continued for a long time to worship the stars and to offer multitudes of human sacrifices, as they were still doing at a time when European Renaissance culture was at its zenith?

Apart from the Far East and Africa, Europe put its cultural stamp on the world. With this exportation of European culture, which increased steadily from the time of the geographical discoveries, the "Old World" took on also a burdensome—indeed, an oppressive—responsibility. Whereas in the mid-eighteenth century, more-or-less atheistic rationalism was among the European "exports" to Latin America, in the nineteenth century it was ideologies that had originated in European minds. The conceptual baggage of the Hegelian Left, down to Marx and Engels, of positivism, popular materialism and nationalism (which was particularly virulent) produced their effects both in Latin America and also, especially, in Asia. If you ask where the great revolutionary leaders of the Third World in the nineteenth and twentieth centuries had their intellectual formation, their academic training, you invariably encounter the important universities of the Old World. That is where those philosophical ideas developed which, when translated into sociopolitical reality, have led to the most brutal totalitarian regimes. Chou En-lai and Deng Xiaoping may be mentioned here in lieu of many others.

Allow us to ask for once, by way of exception, what might have happened instead if the aforementioned leaders, while in Europe, had become acquainted with and accepted the fundamentals of the doctrine of natural law, of a Christian anthropology, of a personalist metaphysics based on the *philosophia perennis* [perennial, i.e., Aristotelian, philosophy]!

The fact is, though, that the European intelligentsia had separated themselves from their roots in antiquity and Christianity long before that and were giving stones instead of bread to the students at the universities. Modern Europe, alienated from its origins, bears its full share of guilt for the intellectual and consequently the political catastrophes that have occurred, not only in its own house but also in the rest of the world.

The Catholic Contribution to the Future of Europe

We are talking about the importance of the Church as a factor, if not the main factor, in the unification of Europe. As we have seen, much evidence can be adduced for her contributions in the past.

It is considerably more difficult to answer the question as to whether the Church could have an analogous role for the future as well. In comparison with the past, the conditions for such a role have changed fundamentally. The break is marked by the triumphant march of the Enlightenment and the French Revolution. Concomitantly, the self-evident character of the Christian faith that supported the intellectual and political life of Europe for a millennium was shattered. Henceforth the Christian faith had to compete with "modern" philosophies and ideologies, with indifferentism and agnosticism. The number of believers and their social and political importance determined from now on the extent of the Church's influence on European society. Incidentally, this state of affairs, which still obtains today, should also be taken into account when "the Church" is blamed for flawed developments, crimes and omissions—for instance, in connection with totalitarian regimes. The Church has only as much influence and power as society concedes to her. The negative events in Europe's Christian past are not the results of putting Christian maxims into practice but rather of turning away from them.

This already demonstrates the limits to ecclesiastical action on behalf of European unification. It should be pointed out also that [German] Christians today, in contrast to the late nineteenth century and the Weimar period, no longer have a political arm available of the sort that used to be found in the Christian political parties of the past.

Then, too, there is the "intra-Christian" fact of the schism in the sixteenth century, which is associated with the names of Luther, Zwingli, Calvin and Henry VIII of England. What can be heard of the Gospel since then, with regard to quite a few topics, is a very dissonant concert. This is true precisely of those doctrines and moral norms that immediately concern the life of society. Suffice it to mention the subjects of marriage, family, abortion, homosexuality, in vitro fertilization and euthanasia: in reference to these, the Catholic Church stands practically alone on the grounds of genuine Christian Tradition. In these areas—and no doubt there will be still others—she will not be able to rely on any outside support in bringing the authentic Christian standpoint to bear on a secularized society. On the contrary, she sees herself confronted by a growing ideological opposition that launches attacks on her from the camps of liberalism, individualism and relativism. An essential feature of all these ideologies is that they recognize no suprasubjective, that is, objectively valid truth or moral norms that oblige all human beings equally inasmuch as they are human beings. The Catholic Church, however, claims to declare such truth and such norms—citing as her authorities the order that is inherent in creation itself and divine revelation (the Bible)— and thus elicits opposition. Under these conditions, then, what chance, if any, does she still have of helping to shape the Europe of the future? The only thing that she has left is the power of argumentation. And the crucial argument, aside from any other, is a question—indeed, a utopian question: What sort of society could develop in the new Europe, what culture would be created, if today's Europe, at least in its intellectual circles initially, decided to found the culture of this coalescing continent upon the Magna Carta of the Catholic understanding of man and the world?

That would mean nothing less than this: natural law, as classically understood, the Decalogue of the Old Testament and the Sermon on the Mount from the New Testament would provide the standard against which norms for private as well as for societal life would have to prove their worth. It is unquestionable that such a society would be more humane by far than one in which the power of those who are stronger can pave the way for the boundless egotism of the individual—a society in which the weak have no chance and in which money, power and pleasure are considered the highest goals in life.

If, on the other hand, the inviolability of the human person, the responsibility of the individual for the whole, reverence for the Creator and for creatures, the dignity of marriage and family were acknowledged as having a "constitutional status", so to speak, then—although even that would certainly not produce a paradise on earth—nevertheless, despite the fragmentary nature of all earthly accomplishments, a much more human-friendly society could arise on this basis than the one in which we live today. Would it be a utopia like the one described in Kant's "Eternal Peace"? As we can see from the Marxist utopia of the classless society, however, utopias unleash their own forces—in that case worldwide destructive forces. Why shouldn't the utopia of a Christian Europe demonstrate its own formative, constructive dynamic? By now Europe can look back on a century of catastrophes. These resulted from the ultimate logical consequences of National Socialist [Nazi] and Marxist ideologies, the misanthropic errors of which were then so drastically demonstrated. At the moment, after their downfall, it seems that the ideology of liberalism is aspiring to power. Of course, we are not speaking here about that liberalism that has inscribed on its banners the freedom of the citizen from patronizing treatment by the state. We mean the liberalism that rejects any subordination of the individual to universally valid truth and norms. This kind of liberalism, which vindicates the individual's right to follow his own individualized moral code, "his own truth", seems in fact to be at work in society today. The forms in which it expresses itself are too well known to require description here. No doubt, however, these social expressions are such that, if this ideology ever prevails to the same extent as National Socialism and Marxism, it would necessarily lead to the perhaps noiseless but all the more destructive catastrophe of the twenty-first century. Aldous Huxley's *Brave New World* could be a vision of the future. In this situation the question arises whether today's Europe might not be able after all to muster the curiosity and daring to risk the "Catholic experiment".

When the influential Scottish statesman and historian Thomas Babington Macaulay reviewed Leopold von Ranke's study *The Ecclesiastical and Political History of the Popes of Rome* in the *Edinburgh Review* in 1840, he wrote:

> There is not, and there never was on this earth, a work of human policy so well deserving of examination as the Roman Catholic Church. . . . No other institution is left standing which carries the mind back to the times when the smoke of sacrifice rose from the Pantheon, and when camelopards and tigers bounded in the Flavian amphitheatre. The proudest royal houses are but of yesterday, when compared with the line of the Supreme Pontiffs. . . . The Papacy remains, not in decay, not a mere antique, but full of life and youthful vigour. The Catholic Church . . . may still exist in undiminished vigour when some traveller from New Zealand shall, in the midst of a vast solitude, take his stand on a broken arch of London Bridge to sketch the ruins of St. Paul's.

There is no reason why Macaulay's vision should not become a reality. What would Europe have to lose, therefore, if it placed its trust in an enterprise that has withstood two thousand years without going bankrupt? But—that is, as we said, a utopia.

IV

NEW AWAKENINGS IN THE
CHURCH, PAST AND PRESENT

Anyone who illuminates time and the world with the spotlight of his momentary concerns and—necessarily—leaves yesterday and the day before in the dark, along with the rest of the surrounding area, should not think that he is a realist. Applied to our present ecclesiastical situation in German-speaking lands, this means that fixing our sights on universally known phenomena of crisis and decline causes us to overlook the whole picture. This is true geographically: the Church encircles the whole world, not just German-speaking lands, and it is also true with respect to time. The Church did not begin her existence today.

There is another false view of reality, namely the view through the lenses of evolutionism. History, development —of the Church as well—is not simply a constant development toward ever higher and more perfect forms. In human life—and therefore also in the life of the Church—there are peaks and valleys, ups and downs, decline and flourishing. If we look at reality, ecclesiastical reality, from these perspectives, we arrive at a truly realistic observation resulting in powerful impulses for present-day action.

In the Dark Ages

What Saint Boniface experienced when he first arrived in Germany must have been a real shock. Accustomed to the highly cultivated intellectual, cultural and religious milieu of his English homeland, he found himself in barbarian conditions again: episcopal sees in the hands of money-hungry men who indulged in usury and fornication; priests, deacons with four or even more concubines who nevertheless became priests or even bishops. Given to drink and the pleasures of the hunt and indolent about their ministerial duties, they were a scandal without equal. Boniface learned from one priest that he didn't even know the correct baptismal formula. He baptized *"in nomine patria et filia et spiritus sancti"*. If that was the sort of shepherds he encountered, what must the average Christians have been like?

What a catastrophic scenario emerges from the letters of Saint Boniface! Yet scarcely fifty years after his martyrdom, the observer of the Church in Charlemagne's empire met with a completely different picture: dioceses and monasteries had come into being, in which schools had been founded, like at the cathedrals; catechesis and liturgy were cultivated; and Roman sacred music, Gregorian chant, was propagated through choir schools. The arts and sciences flourished, and the testimonies to them in the museums still cause us to marvel.

Synods were held so as to bring order to the everyday life of the Church, and even the laws that Charlemagne enacted, the so-called capitularies, read in some passages like sermons. An intensive Christianization of the people had begun to bear its first fruits. With good reason, historical scholars speak about a "Carolingian renaissance". It then reached its apogee under Charlemagne's son and successor, Louis "the Pious".

The principal agents in this religious and cultural movement in central and western Europe were outstanding bishops and, above all, monks. Now, for the first time, with the help of Abbot Benedict of Aniane, Benedictine monasticism spread and made decisive contributions to the Christianization of the Germanic tribes. After many declines and collapses, the region then experienced the so-called Ottonian renaissance of the tenth century and the Gregorian reform of the eleventh and twelfth centuries; and finally, thanks to the influence of the mendicant orders in the thirteenth century, certain signs of weakening were followed again and again by such new awakenings. These were spiritual awakenings in the truest sense of the word, when for instance at the University of Paris, seventy professors and students requested the Dominican habit in one day, or a century earlier, the young knight Bernard of Clairvaux with more than twenty friends and relatives sought admission at the gate of the monastery of Cîteaux. The Middle Ages—far from being a monolithic block—were extremely animated times, noted for a whole series of new spiritual and religious movements.

From Luther and Calvin to the Council of Trent

If we skip over a couple hundred years, however, we arrive in central, northern, eastern and western Europe around the middle of the sixteenth century. Since the protest movement of Martin Luther, Calvin and Zwingli, the storm of schism had swept over these lands, leaving in its wake a landscape of religious ruins. Already at the Diet of Worms in the year 1521 the papal delegate Aleander reported: "There is a threat of a popular uprising, or rather, all of Germany is in an uproar. Ninety percent of the people are shouting "Luther!" and the other ten percent at least have "Death to the Roman court" as their slogan.

In the following years, countless consecrated religious left their cloisters, hundreds of priests married, and the most powerful princes—with the exception of Bavaria—became followers of Luther and stamped out all Catholic life. The collapse, which finally involved all of northern, central and eastern Germany together with the southwest, was almost total. Immorality and religious confusion were widespread —did the people still have any idea whether they believed the Catholic or the Lutheran faith?—and profound uncertainty and discouragement prevailed even among the clergy who had remained Catholic. This was the ecclesiastical situation in Europe in 1546 when the Council of Trent convened.

Once again, half a century later, a new awakening occurred, which was so unexpected and far-reaching, so powerful and impressive, that the renowned Church historian Hubert Jedin has described it as "the miracle of Trent". The miracle was the unprecedented phenomenon of the Catholic Baroque. Much more than referring to an artistic style, the term designates a whole cultural period in which the Catholic faith permeated all areas of culture, art, science, religion and everyday life with a new, powerful vitality and inspired the people of that period to achieve great things in all those fields, masterpieces that are still unsurpassed today. Furthermore, what the Catholic Church had lost through the Reformation, she now regained among the peoples of Asia and the Americas, where the Catholic remnant of Europe was pursuing a daring missionary outreach. A century of saints had dawned. So great was the attractive force of the Church that emerged from the Council of Trent renewed and strengthened that many Protestants—princes, scholars, theologians and townspeople—went over to the Catholic Church. A collection of very brief biographies of prominent converts alone, from the beginning of the Reformation to the end of the eighteenth century, fills thirteen volumes!

After the Great Revolution

As a third example of an ecclesiastical new awakening, we should mention the one that France experienced after the Revolution of 1789. The persecution of the Church that had gradually increased in ferocity since the outbreak of the Revolution reached its high point in late August of 1792, when all the priests loyal to Rome who could be seized were deported. In the so-called September massacre in Paris alone, three hundred priests, among them three bishops, were martyred. In 1793, priests who had not yet left France were threatened with the death penalty, to be carried out within twenty-four hours; a "violent wave of dechristianization" deluged the land from the summer of 1793 until the summer of 1794. In those twelve months alone, there were records of 22,938 executions or murders.

Most Church buildings were closed and plundered, or even torn down; Sunday was abolished; the Revolution's own cult of the goddess Reason was supposed to replace divine worship. Only a few thousand priests persevered in the underground, risking their lives in order to administer the sacraments to the remaining faithful. In all, approximately five thousand Catholics, among them more than one thousand priests, may have died as martyrs in the proper sense. Thanks to the heroic fidelity of many priests and laypeople, who had stood fast during the Reign of Terror, the motto proved true again: *"Succisa virescit"*—from the stump of the felled tree spring fresh green shoots!

What happened now, once the revolutionary regimes had been replaced, was astonishing. Whereas the concordat that Napoleon signed with Pius VII made it possible to rebuild ecclesiastical structures—dioceses and parishes —despite considerable shortages, writers like Joseph de Maistre and François-René de Chateaubriand opposed the "enlightened", rationalist spirit of the age in their widely circulated works and managed to demonstrate impressively the truth and the beauty of the Catholic faith.

The Holy Year in 1803 jump-started, so to speak, a comprehensive new missionary effort to reevangelize France, which at first, however, had a more profound effect only in intellectual circles. In the following decades, though— during the pontificates of Gregory XVI and Pius IX—an amazing number of religious communities came into being. As of 1814, 1,253 new communities not only had been founded but had also received ecclesiastical approval. That means that thousands of young women and men were willing, in extremely difficult circumstances, to place themselves at God's service for the benefit of mankind.

Thus France became a center for far-reaching missionary activity as well, especially in Asia. The missionary impulse, however, is the unerring barometer for the spiritual vitality of the Church. The splendid example set by France influenced the rest of Europe, and everywhere, in a society roiled by the aftermath of the Enlightenment, by the socialism of Marx and Engels, by the vulgar materialism of thinkers like Büchner and by godless liberalism, a religious revival took place that must be ranked as equal to the one during the post-Tridentine period. Even though books such as *The Life of Jesus* by Ernest Renan, reprinted many times, were able to destroy the faith of many people, the great number of newly founded or revived religious communities, with their apostolic, charitable and missionary works, proved their power to attract enthusiastic Catholic young people in almost every country in Europe and America, who now placed themselves at the service of the Church.

Forces and Factors

Now, however, the question arises as to the motivating forces of those new awakenings. Two factors are especially evident: the renewed certainty about the faith and close ties with Rome.

Now, as far as the Middle Ages are concerned—that is, during the reform of Saint Boniface, and the Carolingian renaissance—the certainty of the faith was taken for granted; even the pagan Germans and Celts did not find it difficult to recognize the reality of God and of the supernatural. They experienced the powerful superiority of the Christian God —for instance, Chlodwig through victory in battle, and the Saxons when they witnessed how Boniface felled the sacred oak trees.

The renewed certainty of faith that inspired the Catholic contemporaries of the Council of Trent had a completely different quality. After decades of being exposed to the attacks of Luther, Calvin, Zwingli and their followers, the Catholics had grown profoundly uncertain about their faith convictions. Was the new faith that was proclaimed with such enthusiasm, force and success perhaps really the true faith after all? Wasn't the Reformers' criticism of the papacy, the Church and the sacraments justified? Hadn't Rome in fact distanced itself from the Gospel? And finally, didn't the new Gospel truly correspond to a new demand of the age?

It was precisely this uncertainty about the faith that had

led to the confusion of minds and had thus made a decisive response to the Reformers' challenge impossible at first. But now the Council of Trent had spoken, had drawn the line between error and Catholic truth and had set the latter back on the lampstand. The whole world knew now what true Catholic and apostolic faith was. Uncertainty and lack of clarity no longer sapped the Church's strength; instead, new joy in the faith gave her wings, and the "miracle of Trent" occurred.

The situation was similar with the new awakening after the French Revolution. In this period, too, the Catholic faith had been challenged and threatened. This time the attack was carried out in the name of reason. Believers were branded obscurantists; wits like Voltaire regarded the faith as "fanaticism"; and there was no more room in an enlightened, modern world for those who resisted the bright, clear light of reason. "*Écrasez l'infâme*" ["Crush the infamous thing"] and "*Die Pfaffen an die Laterne*" ["Hang the priests from the lampposts"] were the battle cries of the enlightened battalions.

It is easy to gauge the effect that these slogans, announced with the passion of unbounded moral superiority, must have had on the faithful! Haven't we in fact been left behind while progress has hurried onward? After all, who wouldn't want to be enlightened, too, or to be regarded as enlightened? Intimidation gained ground while the voice of faith fell silent. Did anyone still have arguments in favor of it?

However, when the terror of reason receded and the guillotine was stilled, it dawned on the survivors that that goddess of Reason was no friend of mankind. Those Catholics who had proved faithful in the midst of the fiercest persecution, who had also been obliged to confront the Enlightenment challenge to their faith and to find convincing arguments to substantiate it, could now face the world with new-found confidence, and the message of faith received a new hearing.

Only three of these new awakenings could be presented here, but there is another element common to all of them: deliberate, close ties with Rome, with the papacy. Even the seventh-century Anglo-Saxon Church that produced Boniface, the Apostle to the Germans, had distinguished itself by its special reverence for Peter, the Prince of the Apostles. The second Christianization of the British Isles had been initiated from Rome by Pope Gregory the Great, and as it progressed, pilgrims soon began traveling to Rome to visit the Apostle's tomb.

The Roman liturgy, Roman canon law, and the Tradition taught at Rome left their imprint on the life of the English Church—and Boniface, standing in the mainstream of this Tradition, laid the foundation for a similar development in Germany. He himself had been in Rome three times and kept in very close contact with the popes throughout his life. His correspondence testifies to this.

Charlemagne acted no differently; he made sure that the popes were aware of his power, and yet he made the Roman liturgy, Roman canon law and Roman culture the basis for the organization of France. Thereby Charlemagne completed the work of Saint Boniface, who had constantly striven to lead the Frankish national Church, only loosely connected with Rome, out of her narrow provincialism and to establish for her ever-closer ties with the Roman papacy. The resulting breadth and catholicity made possible that extremely productive synthesis of Germanic culture and Roman tradition (both classical and Christian) that led to the remarkable flowering about which we have spoken.

It is true also of the second example that we have cited,

the "miracle of Trent", that close ties to Rome, to the popes, were an essential factor in this new awakening after the Reformation. Historians know that, in view of the dramatic situation of Catholicism in the Holy Roman Empire, a congregation of cardinals, the Congregatio Germanica, was instituted by Pius V to attend specifically to matters in Germany and to devise measures for the renewal of Catholic life there.

Above all, however, it was the nuncios, whether those in Cologne and Vienna or those who were expressly dispatched to individual territories with particular orders, who tirelessly strove to carry out the reform decrees of the Council of Trent. In Dillingen on the Danube, in Fulda and in Braunsberg, pontifical major seminaries financed by Rome were founded, and in Rome itself the Collegium Germanico-Hungaricum, from which a great number of zealous, well-educated and pious priests were sent to Germany from the sixteenth through the nineteenth centuries and who then assumed key positions in their homeland and thus advanced the reform.

The situation was different in postrevolutionary France. There, a remarkable reversal took place during the course of the revolutionary persecution. The "Gallican Church" had always boasted of her exceptional and extensive independence from Rome. Now, in her hour of need, a Catholic underground movement formed with the following motto: "Obey men, but God first. Profess one faith—the faith of Rome alone. Submit to the pope and likewise to the bishop. Acknowledge in them alone the Church and her pastors."

Then in 1804, when Pius VII, as a victim of compulsion and subterfuge, traveled to Paris for Napoleon's coronation, he encountered a wave of enthusiastic Catholics—an indication of the "ultramontane" movement, as it is often dis-

paragingly called, which ultimately encompassed the whole
Catholic world and made the individual believer conscious
of his personal connection with the supreme pastor of the
Church.

It was precisely this consciousness that enabled Catholics to withstand all the persecutions to which they were
subjected in the nineteenth century and later—think, for
instance, of Bismarck's *Kulturkampf*, during the course of
which more bishops and priests were in prison than in
Hitler's concentration camps.

Conclusions

From these experiences that the Church has had during the
two thousand years of her life, we can now draw conclusions
for our present day. First of all, there has to be a "Coper-
nican revolution" in our perspective: neither the earth nor
man is the center of the universe. The reality that rules over
everything is God. The first petitions in the Our Father are
extremely relevant: Thy name—Thy kingdom—Thy will!
Enough of this self-idolatry by man! That is the program for
a genuine spiritual uprising from the depths of the faith!

This spiritual uprising must then encompass theology and
liturgy as well as our prayer life and everyday moral decisions
—and then the petitions from the Our Father will begin to
be fulfilled.

The next important step is to stop seeing Rome and the
pope as bothersome monitors set over the Church's everyday
life and fettering the development of the local churches but
rather as the center of the worldwide Church, from which
impulses, encouragement and instruction go out for the benefit of all. The two million who attended World Youth Day

in Rome during the Jubilee Year had understood that. They returned home full of enthusiasm for Christ.

And in conclusion, we should finally stop being like the frightened rabbit that stares at the snake before it is swallowed by it. This defeatist attitude, this whining self-pity that has gained so much ground in German [and, generally, in Western] Catholic circles, is an insult to God. What is needed is a new, forceful consciousness of being Catholic. There is nothing that could be truer than the Catholic faith —and wherever the Catholic faith, Catholic truth and Catholic moral principles are put into action, the world, despite all human shortcomings, is put in order.

V

"CHILDREN'S STORIES"
OR CHILDHOOD HISTORY?

On the Historical Truth of the Events
at Bethlehem: A Critical Examination

As the Christmas season approaches each year, if not sooner, the urgent question arises whether the reports about the birth and childhood of Jesus in the Gospels according to Matthew and Luke are stories or history.

In this chapter, we will attempt to answer this question. Our first concern will be with the sources of our information, the Gospels.

Against a Scientific Dogma

The scholarly consensus, which for decades was taken for granted, that all four Gospels were written after the destruction of Jerusalem—Mark was usually dated around 70, and the other synoptics between A.D. 70 and 90, with John even later—has been rather shaky for some time now. As early as 1976 the Englishman J. A. T. Robinson, in his *Redating the New Testament* (which has gone through four editions and been translated into German and other European languages) has categorically supported an early dating of the New Testament writings as a whole and argued for the composition of the four Gospels before the destruction of Jerusalem. Indeed, in the English-speaking world, Robinson has met with wide agreement, whereas in German circles there has been less discussion of the thesis—one exception being the exegetes of the Evangelical theological faculty in Tübingen, for example, Martin Hengel. From his school of thought comes an important study that proves with sound reasoning that Luke, who accompanied Paul on his missionary journeys, was also the author of the Acts of the Apostles. Hengel himself has shown that Luke was personally in Palestine, where he could gather authentic information.

Much earlier, around the turn of the twentieth century, the renowned Protestant theologian Adolf von Harnack (d. 1930) had argued that the Acts of the Apostles were written before A.D. 62—the year in which James died. And Robinson agrees with this dating. Remarkably, in the Acts of the Apostles themselves, there is no mention at all of the Roman-Judean war that was being waged from 66 on, nor of the destruction of Jerusalem in 70 or the deaths of the Apostles Peter and Paul (64 or 67). Now, if we reflect that the Acts of the Apostles describe themselves as the continuation of the Gospel according to Luke, then this Gospel could not have been written after its continuation, and therefore not after 62. But we are looking then at a time in which large numbers of the contemporaries of the events that are reported were still alive and could provide eyewitness and hearsay reports. Luke could hear such reports especially in Nazareth, where branches of the Davidic line had settled after the exile (as also in the land of Batanaea) and were still residing there in A.D. 250, as Julius Africanus testifies around the year 250. From Epiphanius of Salamis (d. 403) we know that they called themselves "descendants of David"—Nazarenes. Accordingly, Nazareth was the village of the family of David.

Matthew, who did not have to travel to Palestine first, had

an even greater advantage in availing himself of these sources of information. Furthermore, the fact that the Gospels not only are based on eyewitness and hearsay reports but also were written for contemporaries made it impossible to include fictional accounts, which could have been exposed at any time as untrue by contemporaries who were still living. Therefore, there is no serious reason to mistrust what is reported by the Gospels.

After so-called external source criticism (the study of a document's provenance and tradition), the next step is to examine the contents and to ask the question whether the persons and events in the Gospels harmonize with facts that are known with certainty. We will conduct this examination by means of several examples.

The Census of Caesar Augustus

The first is the census of Quirinius. According to the commentary on Luke by Jacob Kremer in the German edition of the Bible published by Echter Verlag in 1988, there is "no extrabiblical evidence" for the general decree by Augustus that the whole world was to be enrolled. In the considerably more complete commentary by Josef Ernst in the Regensburg edition of the New Testament, and in particular in the writings of Gerhard Kroll (*Auf den Spuren Jesu* [In Jesus' footsteps], 10th ed., 1988), there is quite a different version of the facts. These commentaries provide convincing proofs for the historical accuracy of the Lucan account. Kroll shows by means of the available sources from profane history, such as inscriptions, papyrus finds, ancient historiography, and so forth, that Augustus in fact decreed a universal census of the Roman Empire. Kroll refers, for example, to the so-called *Monumentum Ancyranum*. This, an extensive inscription in the temple of Rome and Augustus in Ankara, contains a text that Augustus himself left behind toward the end of his life. The inscription was rediscovered in 1555. In it Augustus says that he ordered a census three times during his reign. The Roman jurist Tertullian (d. 220), who claims to have used the archives of the Roman state, writes in his polemical work, *Adversus Marcionem*, which was composed in Rome: "It is certain that during the reign of Augustus the census was carried out in Judea by Sentius Saturninus."

This news is startling. Wasn't Quirinius the one who carried out the census? Now, Luke is indeed the only one to report that Quirinius was governor during Herod's lifetime (d. 4 B.C.); nevertheless, none of this rules out the accuracy of the Lucan account. It can also be harmonized with Tertullian's information, for a series of references leads to the highly probable conclusion that Quirinius, during the years in question, held the superior position of an *Orienti praepositus* [commander over the East], to whom the governor of Syria was also subordinate. Consequently, Luke mentioned Quirinius as the one actually responsible for the census and omitted the name of the governor who carried it out.

Now, some scholars object that the census of Quirinius that we have known about until now took place not in Herod's time, around 4 B.C., but rather in the year A.D. 6. Is Luke's report wrong? Only if we accept the reference by Flavius Josephus to the census in the year A.D. 6 without further examination. But more than seventy years ago, the Protestant exegete Theodor Zahn had already written: "There has been no greater obstacle to a correct judgment on the census than blind faith in the reliability of Josephus and an uncritical use of his statements about Quirinius." Moreover, the exegete Joseph Blinzler thought that "caution is required in evaluating his statements" and that "his human and literary unreliability should always be taken into account." Can Josephus' silence about the census reported by Luke then be taken as evidence against the reliability of the evangelist? Interestingly enough, Josephus says only that after Archelaus was deposed, Quirinius was sent to Judea in order to carry out a census. Luke, on the other hand, speaks about his census as the first. This does not make for a contradiction. On the contrary. No one disputes the fact that the census was carried out in the provinces every fourteen years. So if we count fourteen years back from A.D. 6, we come to the year 8 B.C. At that time Herod was living, and Quirinius resided in the East as Caesar's legate. Therefore, during the years from 8 to 4 B.C.—since the census process took several years to complete—the census took place and Jesus was born. Consequently, Luke's report is astonishingly precise for an ancient historian.

How Can This Be?

But the Annunciation scene, the virginal conception of Jesus —doesn't all that have too many mythical features for us to be able to take it at face value? Isn't Jesus' divine Sonship being depicted here in a literary fashion through miraculous filigrees? Here, too, we can observe details in the Gospel of Luke that agree with well-known facts and conditions from the history of New Testament times. We will explain this by means of a further, particularly interesting, example, namely, Mary's question to the angel: "How can this be, for I know not man?" [Douay-Rheims]. In many circles this question, and the whole account of the Annunciation in the first place, is described as a literary fiction, as a Greek legend that is ultimately supposed to lead to the myth of theogamy [a god taking a human wife]. Moreover, such a question, on the lips of a Jewish girl who was still betrothed and waiting to be taken into her husband's home, would be completely unthinkable.

But dismissing the question is not that simple, especially after the so-called Temple Scroll, dating back to the time before Christ's birth, was found in Qumran. The scroll contains instructions for building the temple and organizing worship. Very general religious provisions of the Law follow at the conclusion of the scroll. Among them is the following passage, meant as a clarification of the instructions about vows in the Book of Numbers 30:4–9 [the words in italics are added to the biblical text]:

> Or when a woman vows a vow to Me [i.e., the Lord] and binds herself by a pledge *to practice continence*, while within her father's house, in her youth [i.e., before marriage], and her father hears of her vow and of her pledge *to practice continence* by which she has bound herself, and says nothing to her, then all her vows shall stand, and her every pledge *to practice continence* by which she has bound herself shall stand. But if her father expresses disapproval to her on the day that he hears of it, no vow of hers, no pledge by which she has bound herself, shall stand; and I [i.e., the Lord] will forgive her, because her father opposed her.

Then, after a lacuna in the text, it says, with regard to a married woman: "Any vow [that she takes] *to practice continence*, her husband may establish, or her husband may make void on the day that he hears it, and I will forgive her."

That means, first, that among the Essenes and in the surrounding area it was by no means unheard of that single or even married persons took a vow of continence. Against this background, Mary's question to the angel can be explained as effortlessly as Joseph's reaction to his discovery of

Mary's pregnancy, as reported in Matthew's Gospel. Therefore, there is no inherent improbability whatsoever in this account.

Born in Bethlehem

Another example of the historical reliability of the so-called infancy narratives is the report that Jesus was born in Bethlehem. On this subject, Othmar Keel and Max Küchler, in their very erudite study *Orte und Landschaften der Bibel* [Places and regions of the Bible] (Zürich and Göttingen, 1982, p. 620), speak only about legendary material: "Did Jesus have a literary birth in Bethlehem because according to Micah 5:2 [in Hebrew, 5:1] he had to be born there? This question is justified, after all, because no trustworthy historical information can be derived from the legends about the visit of the magi, the scene at Herod's court or the slaughter of the children in Bethlehem." And further on: "If Jesus was in fact born in Bethlehem, which strictly speaking cannot be proved historically on the basis of the source materials, then the Old Testament prophecy and the New Testament account would have had a lucky theological conjunction in no way inferior to the complicated astronomical conjunctions that are postulated to explain the star of Bethlehem by natural causes" (p. 621). That, of course, is unvarnished ridicule—having no other foundation than the assumption, taken for granted, that Luke and Matthew were ancient Oriental tellers of tales. Now, that cannot be proved either—rather, the contrary is true, as we have already shown in several examples.

Then there are the early testimonies concerning the Grotto of the Nativity in Bethlehem. It is quite likely that the tradition came not only from members of the Davidic family in Bethlehem but also from Mary herself, who for a long time lived in Jerusalem, only eight kilometers away. The mere fact that Emperor Hadrian found it necessary to replace the most popular Christian shrines with pagan temples so as to eradicate all thought of Christian salvation history —he even had a grove in honor of Adonis planted over the Grotto of the Nativity—shows that the memory of Jesus' birth was very much alive at the beginning of the second century. Emperor Constantine was able to rely therefore on confirmed tradition when he ordered the construction of a church over the grotto; the Church of the Nativity is still standing there today.

Recently conducted archaeological investigations of the Grotto of the Nativity and the surrounding area demonstrate that it was located in the middle of ancient Bethlehem, which is an additional sign of the place's authenticity, which was vouched for also by Justin Martyr, who was born around A.D. 100 in Nablus [ancient Shechem]. Therefore, there is no discrepancy worth mentioning between the Gospel accounts and other confirmed historical information. Why shouldn't we believe Matthew and Luke?

Son of the Virgin?

The answer most often given to the question we have just posed is: The Gospels relate something utterly unbelievable —the virginal conception of Jesus by Mary. Now, even the historian who is a most ardent believer must admit that he in fact cannot adduce any proof of this. On account of the absolute intimacy of such an event, it is downright impossible to do so. It is possible and necessary, though, to ask whether what Luke and Matthew maintain is ruled out or else supported by any confirmed facts or data. We should also ask whether the usual [rationalistic] explanations of these texts are valid.

Let us begin with the last-mentioned question. It is often said that chapter 1 of Luke is modeled on legends from Greek mythology, possibly on Egyptian ideas also. Such an assumption is belied by the very language and the overall arc of the infancy narratives. Moreover, the depiction in the Gospels has a different structure from the one in the comparable Greek and Egyptian myths. In the Greek myths, the god approaches the woman in question in the form of a bull, a swan or even golden dust, that is to say, in a material form. In the Egyptian myth, the god takes on the form of the reigning king and joins with the virginal queen. From several reports, we know that occasionally temple priests rather dubiously assumed the role of the god in question after assuring a woman that the god wanted to have relations with her in the form of a man. According to the Greek mentality, therefore, the conception results from a material union of the god with the woman, whereby the god can assume a wide variety of forms.

In contrast, Matthew's account simply says: "When his mother Mary had been betrothed to Joseph, before they came together she was found to be with child of the Holy Spirit." And Luke records the words of the angel: "The Holy Spirit will come upon you, and the power of the Most High will overshadow you; therefore the child to be born will be called holy, the Son of God." And he has Mary say: "Behold, I am the handmaid of the Lord; let it be to me according to your word." The structure of the Gospel accounts therefore is different from that of the myth.

Besides, the words for "Holy Spirit" are neuter in Greek and feminine in Hebrew, so any such notion of mythical mating is ruled out. Furthermore, it is possible, based on the sources, to demonstrate that Jesus is Mary's son but not Joseph's. Apart from the fact that the two mutually independent sources Luke and Matthew report this, another very revealing statement in Mark 6:2 weighs heavily in favor of this hypothesis. Upon entering the synagogue in Nazareth, where people must have known his family situation better than anywhere else, his opponents describe Jesus as the son of Mary: "And on the Sabbath he began to teach in the synagogue; and many who heard him were astonished, saying, 'Where did this man get all this? What is the wisdom given to him? What mighty works are wrought by his hands! Is not this the carpenter, the son of Mary?" The question "Isn't he the son of Mary?" though, probably means in plain language: Isn't he the illegitimate son of Mary? The passage is especially significant when we reflect that neither Luke nor Matthew was available during the composition of the Gospel of Mark.

In Matthew, again, the genealogy of Jesus indicates the same state of affairs. It uses the standard formula, "Abraham was the father of Isaac, and Isaac the father of Jacob . . ." until the conclusion: "and Jacob [was] the father of Joseph the husband of Mary, of whom Jesus was born, who is called Christ." Moreover, the fact that very early on, a legend circulated that Jesus was the son of a Roman legionary named Panthera shows that people ruled out the paternity of Joseph. Although we cannot discuss every single relevant argument in detail here, we can declare in summary that there is no proof from reliable sources that Luke and Matthew are not telling the truth when they speak about the virginal conception and birth of Jesus.

The Slaughter of the Innocents
and the Star of the Wise Men

Before we get to this fundamental question, however, we ought to discuss other problematic questions concerning Jesus' infancy narrative: for example, the star of Bethlehem and the visit of the magi, or even Herod's slaughter of the innocent children. Whether the slaughter of the children actually occurred is usually disputed. Weightier than the reasons against its historicity, however, are the reasons in favor of the historical facticity of that bloody deed. The first is provided by the so-called Assumption of Moses, a written work that was probably composed in Essenian circles and dates back to around the year A.D. 70. It says the following about Herod: "Then came an insolent king who was not of the priestly lineage, an audacious and godless man. He killed the old and the young, and a horrible fear of him fell over the land. He raged in their midst with murderous commands, just as it happened in Egypt." Now, what does this have to do with the slaughter of the innocents? After all, Herod had three of his own sons killed! But the remark about murderous commands in Egypt cannot refer to that. It means, rather, the command to kill the newborn boys of the Israelites. Therefore, we can hardly go wrong if we regard this as an extrabiblical reference of the slaughter of the innocents.

The fact that Flavius Josephus reports nothing about it is, in the first place, an *argumentum e silentio* [argument from silence, which is especially weak]; in the second place, his silence about a local episode should not surprise us, when we recall the great number of much more terrible bloody deeds that Herod perpetrated. Within the same year, 7 B.C. (the

year in which Jesus was born), Herod had two of his own
sons murdered along with three hundred soldiers, and then
on another occasion, six thousand Pharisees—the soldiers,
because they were his sons' sympathizers, and the Pharisees
because they refused to take the oath of loyalty to Caesar.
That being the case, who would bother to mention a dozen
infants in Bethlehem?

After that, we should discuss the question about the star of
Bethlehem, which is regarded by many exegetes as a literary
figure of speech without any basis whatsoever in historical
reality. But it is not that simple. As early as 1604, Johannes
Kepler calculated three conjunctions of the planets Jupiter
and Saturn during the year 7 B.C., specifically around June
22 at 23 degrees in the constellation Pisces, in August at 21
degrees in Pisces, and in December at 17 degrees in Pisces.
For these planets to cross paths three times within a year
happens once every 258 years (The last time was in 1940–
1941), whereas a threefold conjunction [of any two planets]
in one and the same constellation occurs only once every
794 years.

The extreme infrequency of such an astronomical phenomenon naturally aroused great attention and led to the question whether this might not perhaps explain the star of Bethlehem. In 1925 the Orientalist Paul Schnabel decoded a
two-thousand-year-old cuneiform tablet, incidentally providing a new basis for such reflections—for this clay tablet
came from the observatory of Sippar on the Euphrates River
and contains all of the more significant astronomical data for
the year 7 B.C. The main theme is the threefold conjunction
of Jupiter and Saturn in the constellation Pisces that occurred
in that year. Other observations at Sippar that can be dated
to almost that same time made it then possible to calculate
very precisely the aforesaid movement of the planets.

Now, how did the Babylonian astronomers who had observed this phenomenon hit upon the idea of looking for a newborn king of the Jews in Jerusalem? Ancient lore about the significance of a conjunction of the planets Jupiter and Saturn in the constellation Pisces can help explain this. Jupiter was generally regarded in the ancient world as the star of the worldly ruler; it was the royal star. Claudius Ptolemaeus, the most eminent astronomer in antiquity, says that Jupiter is most powerful when it is staying in its astrological house, that is, in the constellation Pisces. Interestingly enough, the Old Syrian translation of Matthew translates the "star", which is left unnamed by the evangelist, with the usual name for Jupiter. Greek astrology called Saturn the star of the Jews. Now, H. C. Rawlinson has published cuneiform writings that show that the Babylonian magi were particularly fond of speculating about the land *amurru*, that is, the West. Repeatedly there are statements of this sort: "When such-and-such happens, then a great king will arise in the West, and then justice, peace and joy will prevail in every land and give all peoples cause for rejoicing." Given these circumstances, it is quite possible to explain the fact that the Babylonian magi, upon observing the early ascent of Jupiter on March 16 in the year 7 B.C. and its first conjunction, were impressed by this extremely rare and quite splendid heavenly spectacle and came to the conclusion that the birth of a mighty king was occurring in Judea.

Then, too, there is the passage from Matthew, which reads: "When they had heard the king, they went their way: and lo, the star which they had seen [at its rising]went before them, till it came to rest over the place where the child was." In astronomical terminology, "to come to rest" or "to stand" meant (and still means today) the moment when a planet apparently stands still as it travels to and fro against the background of the fixed stars. This expression, which corresponds to visible appearances, was customary before astronomers knew that the earth and the planet that was thought to be standing still were actually traveling directly toward or away from each other at that moment. Even the expression "And lo", which sounds like lofty rhetoric to our ears, is a formula from the technical vocabulary of astronomers. Given these facts, which we owe to the research of Corrado Ferrari d'Occhieppo, we can read Matthew in good conscience as a historical source and accept the visit of the magi in Bethlehem at face value.

Believe the Unbelievable?

All this leads up to the question: Since the Gospels plainly report with historical accuracy in a whole series of verifiable cases, shouldn't we lend them credence also when they report "unbelievable" things, too—for instance, the virginal conception and birth of Jesus Christ? At any rate, Morgenstern's [satirical] axiom, "What must not be, cannot be", is of course not a principle that we should apply here. Especially since it would have been contrary to all normal human behavior if Mary, the central figure in all these events, had not spoken about everything that she had "kept in her heart", after Easter at the very latest. We can start from the premise that she too spoke about these events.

Therefore, everything comes down to the question of whether I am willing, precisely in matters involving God's salvific action, to accept events that go beyond the scope of usual human experience, or whether I am determined to declare this horizon of human experience to be the yardstick for what is possible for God. That, however, is no longer a historical question but rather a philosophical-existential pre-judgment.

No doubt many will still insist: I cannot accept the idea that angels sang the Gloria over the plains of Bethlehem. I am utterly incapable of accepting the angel's visit in Nazareth, as it is recounted in Luke, and so forth. But this objection is too shortsighted. In these two and other analogous cases, we are dealing with occurrences that belong to a category of reality that is normally not accessible to a human being. That is why he has no adequate concepts for them ready at hand. Therefore, when something of that sort happens to him, he finds that he is incapable of expressing precisely what he has experienced, seen and heard. Then, when he does try to do so, the things most likely to help him are the images and figures of speech from sacred tradition, from myth. But even these are vessels that overflow with the ineffable reality.

Therefore, when we read such texts, we must clearly realize the fact that the experienced reality was much greater, much more exalted and mysterious than even a biblical account can communicate. If one then reads the Christmas story and the infancy narrative with this previous understanding, then one will learn to marvel—and adore.

VI

THE INQUISITION: HISTORICAL REALITY AND LEGEND

For us, the Inquisition is a phenomenon that certainly deserves criticism, yet even such a historical phenomenon can be fathomed only when we look at it within the framework of its historical context and do not try to measure yesterday by today's standards. An essential step is to realize the unity of the medieval world, in which exclusion from the Church simultaneously meant exclusion from all human society. This meant, in turn, that if someone attacked a dogma, he was attacking at the same time the foundations of the societal order and hence was considered a danger to the public. Only against this background can we understand also that the state (and not the Church) took the initiative in the Inquisition and that broad sectors of the population —including Luther and Calvin, by the way—considered it lawful.

Presuppositions

An initial question arises in connection with the moment when the Inquisition began—namely, only after centuries of proceeding in a relatively mild manner. How could the practice of coercion become a method of fighting heresy? The historical answer requires an analysis of the situation in Christian antiquity.

In late antiquity, Church and empire were two clearly distinct, noninterchangeable entities, however close a mutual relationship they may have formed in the post-Constantinian period. Even when the Roman Empire had become Christian, it remained an autonomous political structure that owed neither its origin nor its continuation to Christianity. Not until the Middle Ages was the coronation of the emperor or the king introduced as a Christian liturgical rite. The emperors of late antiquity, unlike the emperors of the Middle Ages, derived their power and dignity neither from the pope nor from the Church. So thought Augustine at the turn of the fifth century, when in *The City of God* he expressed his opinion about the relation between Christianity and the *Imperium Romanum*; so thought Pope Gelasius at the end of the fifth century when he wrote: "There are two powers that rule this world: the hallowed authority of the bishops and royal power."

Although the two powers may have been in harmony with one another, their autonomy was maintained, since they rested upon different foundations. Thus, even long after the days of Constantine, it was still possible for pagans, Jews and Christians to live together in the one Roman Empire as citizens with equal rights. Similarly, the heretic who had been excluded from communion with the Church could still find a basis for his civic and social life in the empire, provided that he complied with its laws.

This changed fundamentally when the old empire collapsed under the onslaught of the barbarians. Migrating hordes streamed into the center of the ancient world, initiating an extremely complex and differentiated process of assimilation, the final result of which was a synthesis of antiquity and Teutonic culture, with the Gospel of Christ as the formative principle. This new Western culture, which in the empire of Charlemagne made its first impressive appearance as a force encompassing the West, was essentially a Christian, ecclesiastical culture. Indeed, it was the Church that had preserved the treasures of ancient learning in the stormy times preceding the break with antiquity and had handed them on to the new peoples from the north and the east. Charlemagne's most important counselors were men of the Church, and his laws—the famous capitularies —often read like conciliar canons or the admonitions of a preacher. This interpenetration of empire and Church found its most striking expression in the Carolingian imperial synods, where great men of the spiritual and temporal realms consulted and reached decisions about spiritual and temporal matters. This novelty became especially evident, however, on Christmas Day of the year 800, when Pope Leo III placed the imperial crown upon the head of Charles, king of the Franks, and thus brought about the much-discussed *renovatio imperii*, the renewal of the empire. The new empire was founded, therefore, upon spiritual authority and dignity.

The world was no longer divided into two separate realms —empire and Church; from now on, royal power and spiritual authority were ordered to each other, like the foci of an ellipse. One single human society had come into being, which was called the Church and, as of the ninth century, *Christianitas* (that is, Christendom). *Imperium* and *sacerdotium* [empire and priesthood] now appeared as the joint, coordinated structural principles of this one Christendom. This term remained in use—unaffected at first by the rise of the nation-states—well into the late Middle Ages.

The essential foundation of this Christendom, however (which is demanded by the very term), was unity of faith, sacraments and government. Now, if an individual or a whole group of Christians placed itself outside of this unity by denying a truth of the faith, they simultaneously relinquished the basis of their civil life, for exclusion from the Church meant exclusion from human, civil society. The excommunication of Emperor Henry IV and his walk to Canossa provide a good example of this state of affairs.

Moreover, if a heretic attacked a teaching, a dogma of the Church, he was at the same time undermining the foundations of the societal order, which, after all, was based upon the Christian faith. He thereby became a criminal and a danger to the public. It is interesting to observe, nevertheless, that this did not become the subject of conscious reflection when scholarly theologians became heretics as a result of their heterodox teachings but later, when whole groups of believers began to fall away from Church teaching—at first secretly, but then publicly. The change in procedure against heresy—from an ecclesiastical, theological synodal process to the persecution and killing of the heretic by the "secular arm"—was caused by the change in heresy itself, which ceased to be a private, theological-religious matter and became a social, political phenomenon.

For the inhabitants of those cities that had been struck with heresy, the discovery that, unbeknownst to them, men were living in their midst who long before had fallen away from the faith of the Church and now adhered to their own religious doctrines, was like the discovery that within the city walls a house had proved to be infected with the plague. It was like the unmasking of a group of conspirators poised to attack. What led to the persecution of heretics—more than religious intolerance or hatred—was the fear and dismay of a society that instinctively felt that its spiritual foundations were threatened. For "the heretics of the Middle Ages were the anarchists of our time" (E. Michael).

The remarks of the Church historian Döllinger in 1861

about the principal heresies of that period—of the Cathars, Albigensians, and Waldensians—corroborate this judgment:

> Those gnostic sects, the Cathari and the Albigensians, which actually occasioned the harsh and inflexible legislation of the Middle Ages against heresy and had to be battled in bloody wars, were attacking marriage, family and property. Had they triumphed, a general upheaval, a decline back into barbarism and pagan licentiousness would have been the consequence. Anyone acquainted with history knows that there was no place in the European world of that time for the Waldensians either, who in principle rejected oaths and civil criminal law.

There can be no doubt about it: the Cathars in their day were revolutionaries, anarchists, nihilists and criminals, who as such endangered the continuance of the societal order. Christians and Cathars, indeed, differed greatly in their relation to the world. Someone who sees the world as a task set before him will seek to accomplish it together with others. In contrast, someone who regards the world with distrust as the creation of the Evil One, and even condemns it, will logically view the power of the emperor which shapes that world with profound suspicion as the continuation and extension of the devil's worldly creative power.

On the other hand, the historical record seems to show that in distancing themselves spiritually from the world, the Cathars did not revolt against the secular order but rather despised it and practiced passive resistance. Nevertheless, this had a destructive effect on the state. The foundations of human life in common were endangered by their refusal to take an oath in a feudal society that was based on the oath of fealty; by their contempt for marriage; and by their practice of *endura*, that is, of almost forcing the sick to commit quasi suicide by refusing food after they had received the [so-called sacrament of] *consolamentum*.

That is also why the civil and not the ecclesiastical authorities were the first to take action against the heretics. It was not the local ordinary but rather King Robert the Pious of France who had at least twelve learned heretical canons regular burned at the stake in 1022 in Orleans. Members of the nobility in the city of Milan were the ones who dragged their heretical peers from the Monteforte castle to the stake around 1028, and the heretics of Goslar were sentenced to the gallows by Emperor Henry III "with the consent of all", as we read in the chronicle of Hermann von Reichenau. Guibert de Nogent reports in his chronicle, *De vita sua*, similar proceedings against the heretics of Soissons in the year 1115. While a council in Beauvais was deliberating about their fate, the people—"fearing the leniency of the clergy" —stormed the prison and burned the heretics outside the city gates.

The Decrees of Verona concerning Heretics

Both the development of Catharism and the Waldensian sect and their offshoots and also the fact that the Church and the secular government were equally affected by mass heresy led to an initial joint reaction of the emperor and the pope.

This is clearly evident from the Assembly of Verona in 1184 with its two decrees concerning heretics issued by the Emperor [Frederick Barbarossa] and the Pope [Lucius III], respectively. Whereas the text of the imperial decree was destroyed, that of the papal decree has been preserved. First, it declares excommunicated all those who dare to preach without an ecclesiastical mission, those who teach a different doctrine than the Church about the sacraments of the Church, and those who provide the heretics with any kind of support. Furthermore, anyone who is suspected of heresy and is unwilling to clear himself by an oath incurs excommunication. Someone who refused to take an oath thereby revealed that he was a Cathar.

A cleric found guilty of heresy was to be deposed, deprived of his living and handed over to the civil judge for punishment if he did not immediately abjure his error, publicly recant and make reparation. The same was true for a layman found guilty of heresy. Clerics who relapsed were to be handed over to the civil courts without a further hearing.

History notes that the most significant result of this meeting of Lucius III with Barbarossa was the introduction of the episcopal Inquisition. According to the pope's words, this too, like the previous ordinances, can be traced back to the advice and recommendation of the emperor and of his princes.

Now, the ordinance of Lucius III had wording that was quite similar [to that of the papal decree of Verona]. Every archbishop or bishop shall either personally or through appropriate agents visit once or twice a year those parishes in which heretics are reported to be living and oblige three or more honorable men under oath to denounce all those who are known to be heretics. Then the latter are to be summoned. Now, if they cannot clear themselves of the charge according to local custom (oath, *septima manus* ["seventh hand", a former canonical requirement that seven witnesses testify under oath to the reliability of someone who swears an oath], or ordeal), or if they fall back into error after having had the opportunity to clear themselves, they shall be punished according to the bishop's judgment. Refusal of the oath is considered proof of heresy, since the teaching of the Cathars forbade oaths. Those who hold secular authority must give assurance under oath that they will render the Church effective support in the work of battling heretics and carry out both the imperial and the papal ordinances; otherwise, they are to be punished with permanent loss of office and excommunication, and their land will be placed under interdict.

Although this law of the pope could also be deemed an imperial law, Barbarossa also issued his own constitution, in which he imposed an imperial ban on heretics. As a symbol for this, he removed his glove and threw it to the ground.

Death Penalty for Heretics

Although they not infrequently feuded otherwise, from now on imperial and ecclesiastical authorities worked together harmoniously to crush heresy as though between two millstones.

By 1213 Frederick II had promised his assistance to Innocent III, who had been reigning since 1198. Subsequently, the more firmly he established his understanding of himself as a ruler and his view of government, the more definite became also his attitude toward the powers that threatened them: heresy and the papacy. For Frederick II, securing of the empire included defending the faith, since he agreed completely with the notion of his time that a heretic rebels against the imperial power when he separates himself from the Church. As early as his coronation in 1220, when the young emperor made the ecclesiastical ordinance of the Fourth Lateran Council against heretics a secular law as well, he had justified the punishments against the Cathars by saying that it is far more serious to offend the Divine Majesty than the earthly one. Now banishment and excommunication awaited every heretic in the imperial realm. Particularly important in this regard is a letter written by the emperor in March 1224 to the imperial vicar of Lombardy, the Archbishop of Magdeburg. For in it Frederick, after referring to the terrible spread of heresy in Lombardy, threatens the heretics for the first time with the death penalty, to wit, burning at the stake. As one might imagine, such a draconian measure as burning at the stake could not be carried out without further ado. When the podesta of Rimini actually tried to burn heretics in 1226, there was an uprising. Brescia did not dare to incorporate the terrible statute into its own laws until 1230 at the behest of its bishop, a Dominican. But the emperor did not let that stop his persecution of heretics. In 1231 burning heretics at the stake was commanded for Sicily as well, and in the following year it was raised to the status of imperial law.

For the rest of his life, the emperor remained true to this policy against the Cathars, even though he became involved in a fatal enmity with the papacy and was himself repeatedly excommunicated and was even condemned at the Council of Lyons in 1245 as a heretic and a perjurer and was therefore deposed.

Ecclesiastical circles, in contrast, had not immediately agreed to the policy of killing heretics. As an example of this, we can cite Saint Bernard of Clairvaux. When a pogrom started in Cologne in 1144, during which heretics were dragged by an uncontrollable mob to the stake and burned, against the will of the clergy, Bernard also refused to approve of the people's actions. He wrote: "We applaud their zeal but do not recommend their action, because faith should be a matter of persuasion, not of force."

Bernard's opinion about the problem of heretics in general can be gathered from sermons on the Song of Songs. Although the text of this Old Testament book does not touch on the theme of heresy at all, the custom was to interpret verse 2:15—"Catch us the foxes, the little foxes, that spoil the vineyards, for our vineyards are in blossom"— in an allegorical way as a reference to heretics and to combine this passage with another passage from the Book of Judges (15:4–5) about Israel's war against the Philistines: "So Samson went and caught three hundred foxes, and took torches; and he turned them tail to tail, and put a torch between each pair of tails. And when he had set fire to the torches, he let the foxes go into the standing grain of the Philistines and burned up the shocks and the standing grain, as well as [the vineyards and] the olive orchards."

Upon learning that Bernard had begun in 1135 to preach on this text, the prior of the Premonstratensian monastery of Steinfeld-in-der-Eifel sent him news about the heretical intrigues in Cologne, because he assumed that Bernard would treat this topic. Bernard did in fact broach the subject, so that his remarks about it are our most reliable and most exhaustive source for our knowledge of those events in Cologne. Here, too (Sermon 64), we find his opinion:

> If we continue the allegory, taking vines to represent Christian congregations, and foxes heresies, or rather heretics themselves, the interpretation is simple: heretics are to be caught rather than driven away. They are to be caught, I repeat, not by force of arms but by arguments by which their errors may be refuted. They themselves, if it can be done, are to be reconciled with the Catholic Church and brought back to the true faith. This is His will, that all men should be saved and brought to the knowledge of the truth.

Despite these clear words, however, Bernard also recognizes that there is a limit to nonviolent efforts to overcome heresy by persuading its adherents. For when error not only is stubbornly affirmed but also seeks to win over others as followers, then force is called for in order to combat it. "It is better for them to be restrained by the sword of someone who bears not the sword in vain [i.e., the secular prince] than to be allowed to lead others into heresy." Nevertheless, the Abbot of Clairvaux does not specify whether the threat with "the sword of the prince" can go as far as execution.

Scholars in the flourishing discipline of canon law were the first to develop further this reflection on the justification of the death penalty for heresy. Although objections and reservations were raised again and again along the lines of the teaching and practice of the early Church Fathers, by the Fourth Lateran Council (1215) things had reached the point where the jurist Johannes Teutonicus considered himself capable of endorsing the death penalty for heretics, if there was no hope of reform.

These more severe proceedings against heretics may have been influenced by the harshness and strictness of the Old Testament, which prescribed the death penalty for idolaters and blasphemers. The decisive factor, however, was the acceptance of Roman law. Christian emperors such as Gratian and Theodosius had enacted laws that punished heretics with exclusion from divine worship, confiscation of property, loss of the freedom to make bequests, and banishment. At the beginning of the fifth century, even the death penalty was imposed on Donatists and Manichaeans. These laws then appeared in summary form in the *Corpus juris civilis* [Code of civil law] of Emperor Justinian. Heresy was considered a *crimen laesae majestatis* [crime against the sovereign power].

In [Christian] antiquity, granted, these laws had not been applied on account of the extensive passive resistance of the Church; but now with the renaissance of Roman law in the High Middle Ages, twelfth-century canonists and jurists rediscovered these old laws concerning heretics—at precisely the time when battling heresy had become a very important matter of current interest. The status of the discussion at the end of the twelfth century was characterized by Pope Innocent III when he placed heresy alongside *lèse majesté*— for the moment without drawing the logical conclusion of the death penalty for heretics. He wrote on March 25, 1199:

> According to civil law, those who commit crimes against the sovereign power are punished with death and their goods confiscated. . . . How much more justly should those who betray the faith and offend Jesus, the Son of God, be excluded from the Christian communion and be deprived of their goods, for it is infinitely more serious to offend the Divine Majesty than human majesty?

The Inquisition

Evidently Pope Gregory IX (1227–1241), a learned canonist, had observed that the decrees of Verona concerning heretics were not being applied consistently by many bishops in order to battle heresy. After all, the bishops came from the ruling classes of their native lands and were bound and obliged in many ways to noble society. Ties of kinship and various sorts of affinities [e.g., marital, feudal] may have prevented many a bishop from intervening when needed.

Now Gregory IX enlisted the newly founded mendicant orders—the Dominicans and the Franciscans—in the service of battling heretics. Beginning in November 1231, the pope on more than one occasion entrusted the Inquisition to the Dominicans, and subsequently Frederick II sent to the Dominican friaries of several German cities a new law concerning heretics that was even more severe than previous legislation: the houses of heretics are to be destroyed, one heretic can be convicted by another, and their children and heirs lose all positions and dignities, unless the children inform against their parents.

It was no longer a matter of granting a hearing to denounced heretics so as to convert or pass final judgment on them: an Inquisition was being undertaken in which heretics were to be sought out. This Dominican Inquisition was intended by Gregory IX not as a curtailment of episcopal jurisdiction but rather as a supplement to it. Meanwhile, the Inquisition was carried out in different ways in the individual countries. The individual inquisitor was appointed on behalf of the pope by his religious superiors. He was to have the following qualifications: he had to be at least forty years old and a Master of Theology, and should be distinguished by his good morals, insight, respectability, experience and education, both theological and canonical.

Now, the duty of the inquisitor was to track down heretics and bring them back to the true faith. If this was unsuccessful, then an investigation, judgment and punishment followed. In these proceedings, the individual inquisitor was strictly bound to follow the applicable rules. If he overstepped them, he himself was called to account and punished.

On the other hand, however, the inquisitor possessed special powers. Thus he could carry out his orders by threatening or imposing ecclesiastical punishments, and no other preacher was allowed to ascend the pulpit in a locality while the inquisitor was preaching as part of his duties.

The Method of the Inquisition

Since the purpose of the Inquisition consisted of rooting out heresy by bringing heretics back to the Church, the inquisitor began his work with a sermon to which he invited the populace. In it the teachings of the Church contrary to the heresy were presented. On the occasion of this sermon, which we can picture as a sort of popular mission, the inquisitor also announced a *tempus gratiae*, a grace period of anywhere from fifteen to forty days. During this time, heretics could report to the inquisitor, give proof of their conversion and accept an ecclesiastical penance. These penances for heretics consisted, for example, of wearing for a specified time a cross sewn onto the clothing, appearing at Mass with scourge in hand, attending the inquisitor's sermons, fasting, pilgrimages and so on. Any heretic who did not report during this period was accused, most often by denunciation. The fact that the accusers' names remained secret was understandable, on the one hand, as a protective measure for them; on the other hand, though, it opened the door to the basest instincts of revenge, hatred and envy. This was to be feared even more when known criminals—that is, perjurers, excommunicated persons, accomplices and even members of the same family—were admitted as witnesses. Only deadly enmity—which would necessarily be known to the public—disqualified an individual from testifying. There was no more effective way of striking or even destroying an unpopular competitor, or anyone else with whom another party had an account to settle, than to accuse him of heresy. A more-or-less well-founded suspicion of heresy—*levis* or *magna suspicio*—could be remedied on the suspect's part by gainsaying the heresy and accepting the resulting ecclesiastical penances. But in the case of an urgent suspicion—*suspicio violenta*—contrary evidence could not be presented. Then denial under oath—*abjuratio*—was required, absolution was given and penance was imposed, which in this case consisted of displaying a cross made of yellow fabric on the clothing. Refusing the *abjuratio* resulted automatically in being handed over to the secular authorities for the execution of the death penalty.

In the case where a heretic who had already converted once was found guilty a second time of heresy, no remedy remained but the stake. Two or three respectable men who were friends of the condemned man were then ordered to communicate to him the sentence of the tribunal and to admonish him to receive the sacraments remorsefully. Once that was done, the secular authority was invited to a meeting at an appointed time in a place located outside of the church, where the inquisitor then gave a sermon in the presence of the populace and the condemned man. If the latter was a cleric, he was then deposed and laicized—*degradatio*—according to the rite in the Pontifical, and then handed over to the secular authority responsible for carrying out the punishment, which then concluded the execution of the heretic.

The role of executioner was carried out by the secular authorities. The inquisitor's petition, upon handing the heretic over to them, that they spare his life was a cruel formality and a genuine mockery: if someone had dared to take this formula seriously, he himself would have incurred excommunication and the charge of heresy.

In descriptions of inquisitorial practice, the opinion is often expressed that many heresies, many sects actually did not exist at all, but were "misheard" by the inquisitor in a sort of prosecutorial eisegesis: according to this view, many simple believers were turned into heretics through hearings made up of questions that went beyond their intellectual capacity and entangled them in difficulties, confusion and errors when they tried helplessly to answer.

For this reason, one scholar has spoken of "heresy produced entirely by artificial means or else semiartificially"

(Lambert). Yet even that historian thinks that the inquisitors did not treat the suspects in a distinctly unfair manner. A serious danger was posed, nevertheless, by the misunderstandings and unwitting distortions that resulted either from all-too-sophisticated interrogation methods or from the all-too-inflexible pursuit of a preconceived notion of a heresy that had been obtained from a manual or a treatise.

A certain tendency to intellectualize, which ran through the whole Inquisition, not infrequently misled the inquisitors to suppose that their suspects were much more refined and intellectually learned than they really were. They measured the accused with their own yardstick and often entirely overestimated them. An oft-cited example of a typical hearing was reported by Bernard Guy in his book on the cunning and wiles of the Waldensians:

> The inquisitor asks the suspect about the articles of faith. The latter answers hastily, "I stand fast in the faith." The inquisitor questions him about transubstantiation. He answers, "Should I not believe that, then?" The inquisitor replies, "I am not asking you whether you should believe it, but whether you actually do," and he receives the answer: "I believe everything that you and other good teachers command me to believe." The inquisitor takes this for an evasion and continues: "Those good teachers whom you are willing to believe, are the leaders of your sect. If I think the way they do, then you believe both me and them; but if I do not, then you don't." And so the wrangling between them continues until the crafty Waldensian finally breaks down at the delicate question about taking an oath.

Actually, problems are plainly evident here of which the inquisitors probably were hardly aware and which the investigations of source criticism first brought to light. According to Herbert Grundmann, the transcripts of the hearings that he studied all follow an outline of questions that was based on the bull *Ad nostrum* by Clement V (1311), which was aimed at the heretical Beghards and Beguines. The suspects in question, therefore, were interrogated with the intention of determining whether they believed in the erroneous doctrines mentioned in the bull, so as to dissuade them.

They were not questioned about their other beliefs or about what they believed in general; instead, they were asked whether they believed the heresies mentioned in *Ad nostrum*. That is an important distinction! For this method results in statements that are just as schematic as the line of questioning that elicited them. Besides, anyone who has ever prepared the minutes of a meeting or a transcript knows how little or how much that can reflect the reality of a session.

· Of course, Grundmann also observes, in the case of a hearing in Eichstatt (1381), that the inquisitor noticed that his schema was not doing justice to his delinquent and asked him an additional question, as though to give him a chance to come closer to Church teaching. The latter availed himself of the opportunity and was acquitted after the imposition of a penance. So things could go that way, too—and how a hearing proceeded and the outcome probably depended in many instances less on the theological and canonical erudition of the inquisitor than on his ability to sympathize.

In order to make it easier for the inquisitors to conduct their proceedings, numerous manuals were soon composed; most of the authors were able to write from personal experience. Two of the manuals became especially well known: the *Directorium inquisitorum* of Nicolaus Eymericus, compiled in 1376, and the *Practica inquisitionis haereticae pravitatis* by Bernardus Guidonis, written around the year 1300. Despite these usually very detailed instructions, it nevertheless depended on the personality of the inquisitor on duty whether the inquisition turned into a fanatically manipulated regimen of intimidation or a pastoral tool for eliminating and overcoming erroneous doctrines.

Among the inquisitors, there were very learned, highly respected personages known to be of high intellectual and moral caliber—for instance, the Dominican Colda von Coldiz in Bohemia. This should not be overlooked in evaluating the Inquisition phenomenon as a whole. There were likewise tyrannical types who were a public menace. Among them, Robert le Petit has attained a sorry infamy. Robert was born of Cathar parents and was the first inquisitor in northern France. Soon it was whispered—and by no means without reason—that he was forcing innocent people to make confessions so as to be able to consign them to the flames. Gregory IX put an end to such criminal activity by deposing him, and thereupon Robert was incarcerated by his order.

Much more nuanced but therefore more difficult to judge is the case of Konrad von Marburg. He is famous not only as an inquisitor but also as the father confessor of Saint Elizabeth of Thüringen, and he successfully worked for her canonization. It is scarcely imaginable that this extraordinary woman would have entrusted the spiritual direction of her soul to a man of dubious character. Some have accused Konrad of cynicism, while describing him at the same time as a "man of personal integrity who commanded respect" (Patschovsky). Appointed inquisitor in the year 1227—thus Elizabeth observed his work for four years—he nevertheless spread fear wherever he went. Other inquisitors were appointed along with Konrad; some researchers think that this was the start of the papal Inquisition in general.

The major defects in the Inquisition trial were the impossibility of preparing a defense and the inherent tendency in the procedure to obtain confessions even by means of coercion. Against this background we can understand ordinances such as the one issued by the Synod of Narbonne in 1243, which decreed that "no one may be condemned without proofs that are clear as daylight or his own admission. It is better to leave a crime unpunished than to condemn an innocent person."

Yet this admonishment was by no means necessary everywhere. Many inquisitors in carrying out their duties were filled with genuine zeal for souls. The inquisitor of Padua —continually plagued by gout and rheum—visited forty-six localities in one year (1298), preaching and conducting hearings at each place. During the twelve years of his activity, only five heretics were condemned to death. There are similar statistics for tribunals elsewhere. The inquisitor Bernard Guy, famous as a result of the publication of his official records, handed down 930 judgments, of which 42 were death sentences. Three hundred seven sentenced the guilty parties to confinement, and the rest to pilgrimages and other works of penance. One hundred thirty-nine cases ended in acquittal.

In Carcassonne, the heartland of Catharism, 278 judgments were handed down by the inquisitor from 1249 to 1258, almost all of them calling for *servitium in terra sancta*—a pilgrimage to the Holy Land. For the diocese of Turin, during the entire fourteenth century, we know of 22 death sentences, 41 penitential crosses [i.e., cloth badges] and around 150 who were sentenced to other punishments.

Conscientious conduct in office was the rule. Nevertheless, down to the end of the Middle Ages, there were momentous cases in which the Inquisition was made the tool of political interests. Among these were, for example, the destruction of the Order of Knights Templar after 1312, the execution of Saint Joan of Arc in 1431 and the annihilation of the farmers of Steding by the Archbishop of Bremen in 1234 in a battle over dominion in the land.

Historical Evaluation

Attempting to give a historical evaluation of the Inquisition is admittedly difficult. Here, too, as with all historical judgments, one must keep prejudices, feelings, passions and the like from coming into play. The historian is neither prosecutor nor defense attorney nor judge.

As in any science, the historian must be concerned about *cognitio e causis*, about gaining the most comprehensive understanding possible of a historical phenomenon based on its causes, circumstances and effects. In this effort, one must apply the standards of the past era in question, and standards and categories from our time may be brought into play only with great care. So the first question should be: How did contemporaries see the Inquisition?

There was protest and resistance—for example, against Konrad von Marburg—and now and then someone turned to the pope in order to defend himself against the abuse of office by inquisitors (for instance, in Carcassonne in 1286). In other cases—for example, in fifteenth-century Bohemia—it was a matter of maintaining the legal jurisdiction of the city government and of the local hierarchy over against the special tribunal of the Inquisition. But opposition as such to the persecution and punishment—indeed to the execution—of heretics cannot be found in the primary sources.

The annals of the city of Worms, which sharply criticized Konrad von Marburg's conduct, plainly acknowledge that death by fire is a just punishment for heretics, and the renowned Berthold of Regensburg exclaimed, "Fie, impious heretic! Better that you should be burned at the stake before you make even one other person a heretic." In this connection we should again recall that it was in fact the populace itself that practiced this sort of lynch-mob justice ever since the first appearance of heretics—at that time still against the Church's opposition.

It can be assumed, therefore, that the death penalty for heretics was regarded as appropriate. As late as the sixteenth century, Martin Luther and Melanchthon in unambiguous terms called upon the princes to pursue the Anabaptists and other visionaries with the sword. Calvin carried out executions on account of heresy, and so did Elizabeth I of England—in great numbers—and also her predecessor, Mary I, a Catholic, after the Parliament had reinstated the old laws against heretics.

We can understand the matter-of-fact way in which the punishment of death by fire was demanded for a heretic if we situate it within the overall context of medieval criminal law praxis. The *Sachsenspiegel* [Saxony Mirror, a list of guidelines], compiled before 1250 by Eike von Repgow, states: "He who steals grain by night is liable to the gallows; if he steals by day, it may cost him his head." Or in another passage: "If he who mints coins offers a counterfeit penny with which to buy something, it may cost him his head." And further on, it says: "The Christian who does not believe or deals in magic and poison and is convicted of it, should be burned at the stake."

Against the background of this legal praxis, as experienced in everyday life, it is also understandable how Thomas Aquinas theoretically justifies the death penalty for heresy. In the *Summa theologiae* (II-II, q. 11, a. 3), he asks *"utrum haeretici sint tolerandi"*—whether heretics should be tolerated. Although—he answers—heretics do not deserve to be tolerated, one must nevertheless wait until after a first and a second warning to see whether they return to the faith of the Church. Those, however, who stubbornly persist in their error after the second summons should be not only excommunicated but also handed over to the secular princes so as to be "exterminated". Thomas continues his argument in the body of the article, saying that two things are noted with regard to heretics:

On the heretics' part a sin is committed by which they deserve not only to be excluded from the Church by excommunication but also to be wiped out from the face of the earth by death. For it is much more serious to undermine the faith, by which the soul lives, than to counterfeit money, which serves to maintain bodily life. For this reason, if counterfeiters and other criminals are legitimately handed over to death by the princes, then heretics certainly can be executed, if they are convicted.

However, on the Church's part, Thomas continues, mercy is called for, for the purpose of moving the wayward soul to conversion. That is also why the Church does not pass judgment immediately but only after the first and second admonition, as the Apostle says. But then, if the heretic still remains obstinate, the Church gives up hope of his conversion and—out of concern for the salvation of others—excludes him from her fellowship through excommunication and furthermore hands him over to the secular jurisdiction for execution.

A further thought is significant in understanding the medieval death penalty for heretics, namely, evidence of an inner connection between heresy and the *crimen laesae majestatis*. The sixth-century *Codex Justiniani* already states that it is much more serious to offend the Eternal Majesty than

the earthly one. Even the early jurists drew the logical consequences from this by carrying over into the Inquisition
trial the order of proceedings as well as the manner and degree of punishment from the trial for *lèse majesté* [e.g., for
treason]. Then in the Constitutions of Melfi (1231), Frederick II legally equated heresy and crimes against the emperor.

Understand First . . .

If we go even further, however, in assuming the intellectual
perspective of the Middle Ages, we encounter one of the
fundamental features of medieval thought that is especially
important for our topic: medieval thought was theocentric.

What this means becomes clear most readily through a
contrast with modern thought, which we can describe in relation to God as anthropocentric, and with respect to man's
social ties as individualistic. Today the self has such a high,
almost absolute, value, even for believing Christians, that everything else is measured against it. To allude to Kierkegaard,
what is true is what I recognize as being true; "my own private truth" is true. This existentially justified epistemolog-
ical relativism grants to everyone his own truth—to it are
sacrificed the objective truth of the faith and the moral norm.
God then appears actually as a means to an end, that is, a
human being's fulfillment and happiness.

One can hardly imagine a starker contrast to this intellectual attitude of modernity that has just been crudely outlined
than the theocentric view of the Middle Ages. The Middle
Ages were fascinated by the grandiose idea of the universal
orderly arrangement of everything that exists, whose source,
midpoint and summit is God, and they saw in divine revelation an absolute value. To attack this truth revealed by Christ

and entrusted to the Church was tantamount, in the Middle Ages, to a blasphemous attempt on God's infinite majesty. In addition, there was concern about the community, about the *bonum commune* [common good]. Since Christendom as a whole regarded the Church's faith as the foundations of its existence, attacking this faith of the Church simultaneously meant shaking the foundations of the societal order in general. Heresy endangered Christendom more than a contagious plague. Yet not only earthly well-being was endangered by erroneous faith; above all, eternal salvation was at stake. And so the heretic had to be stopped from doing spiritual damage to society for the sake of the *bonum commune spirituale*. Indeed, this had to be done even for the heretic's own sake, so that he himself might avoid damnation by converting and believing. Therefore, the Inquisition aimed at the conversion of heretics.

This idea developed into a grotesque parody, however, when the backsliding heretic—converted again and reconciled with God—was hauled off to the stake so as to free him from the danger of falling once more into sin. If he died now, in the true faith, he was saved for all eternity. To think this way was anything but hypocritical cynicism for a medieval inquisitor; after all, Jesus himself said: "What will it profit a man, if he gains the whole world and suffers the loss of his own soul?" [Douay-Rheims].

Medieval thinking was worlds apart from the atrocity of modern totalitarian regimes. When the Inquisition sentenced a man to death, it executed what is fleeting in order to save what is lasting. The modern tyrant, in contrast, is someone who "does not believe in the indestructible component of man and hence, unlike the Inquisition, thinks that it is extinguishing and annihilating him completely, forever" (Ernst Jünger, "Strahlungen" I, February 2, 1942).

Another very central element of the medieval sense of life should be considered: the fact that medieval man was oriented toward the next world. He was far more aware than we are today that earthly life is only a transitional stage on the way to eternal fulfillment in the presence of God. This knowledge enabled people to bear the often oppressive rigors and deprivations of everyday life. Earthly life was relativized in comparison with eternal life yet not despised. That danger existed, rather, in the heretical movements, to which the Inquisition sought to put a stop. The *endura* of the Cathars—the quasi-compulsory suicide by starvation as a substitute for the martyrs' baptism by blood and as a liberation from the sensory world—demonstrably claimed more victims than all the sentences handed down by the Inquisition.

Of course the people of the Middle Ages overlooked the fact that God also willed man's freedom and endowed him with noble dignity as his image and likeness. Through their extreme logical consistency, which indeed showed great faith yet was blind in one eye, they called forth the other extreme of modern anthropocentrism. God alone will judge guilt or innocence: it is up to us to combine what is true from these two extreme positions, so that future generations will not be able to accuse us, who blame the Middle Ages for sacrificing man to the truth, of deserting the truth for man's sake—and of betraying man also in the process.

The Lutheran legal historian Adalbert Erler writes in his article on the Inquisition in the *Handwörterbuch zur Deutschen Rechtsgeschichte* [Pocket dictionary of German legal history]:

> When it is observed from the present-day pluralistic, religiously indifferent perspective that considers itself humane, the Inquisition can naturally appear only as a product of the "Dark" Ages—unless the observer uses the available histor-

ical material to arrive at the cautionary insight that man in every era, even if he has good will, is exposed to the danger of horrific aberrations.

Our [twentieth] century, which brought forth Auschwitz and the Gulag Archipelago and in one year kills more unborn children in Germany than perished in centuries of death sentences under the Inquisition, should take care not to be indignant about the Inquisition of the Middle Ages.

VII

THE CRUSADES

The nine hundredth anniversary of the day on which Jerusalem was conquered by the knights of the First Crusade under the leadership of Count Godfrey of Bouillon—it happened on July 15, 1099—occasioned a new debate over the meaning or absurdity, the justification or injustice, of the Crusades.

Terminology

In this regard, a few clarifications seem to be appropriate. "Crusade" is normally understood to mean a military undertaking authorized by the pope in order to win back the Holy Places or to defend the population or the Christian kingdoms or even the rights of the Church. In particular, however, by "the Crusades" we mean those attempts in the eleventh through fourteenth centuries to free the Holy Land from Muslim rule, that is, from the capture of Jerusalem on July 15, 1099, until the conquest of Acre (Akko) by the Muslims in the year 1291. Usually, historians count seven Crusades, of which the first was the most famous and the fourth caused the most damage, since in the course of it Constantinople was seized and destroyed in 1204 and the so-called Latin Empire was established.

No doubt the Crusade movement originated in the pilgrimages to the Holy Land that had been customary since the second century. A new situation came about, however, with the conquest of the Holy Land by Islam in the seventh through ninth centuries. Although the Christian pilgrimages continued, they became increasingly difficult and above all more dangerous, especially after the caliph El Hakim had the Basilica of the Holy Sepulchre destroyed in 1008. As of the year 1014, during the reign of the Fatimids, approximately thirty thousand Christian churches had speedily met the same fate. Against this background, the idea of an armed pilgrimage immediately developed and spread. Furthermore, the practical necessity of protecting the pilgrims was combined with various ideological features of the feudal age. From this perspective, the Holy Land appeared to many people as hereditary property of the Lord, whose vassals now felt obliged to win back this inheritance for him—that is to say, for his vicar.

The chivalrous ideal of caring for the poor and the weak, namely the Christians who were threatened by Islam, and solidarity with one's Christian brethren were additional motives for the Crusade. The hierarchy made use of the latter motive as a reason to set limits on several attempts by the Western Crusaders to take over Constantinople. In keeping with the great Western religious movements in the late eleventh century, the ideal of the *vita apostolica* was often mentioned—imitating the example of the Apostles in following Christ—and the Crusades offered a special opportunity for realizing this ideal. The individual Crusader had to incur large expenses; he had to leave all that he had, including his family, and could not be sure whether he would ever return. "We have left everything and followed you." Evidence for this decision to leave all behind is provided, for example, by the Crusaders' last wills and testaments, which have come down to us in great numbers. There was also the overwhelming desire to see Jerusalem, the center of salvation history and the archetype of its eternal fulfillment. For this very reason, the religious motivation for participating in the Crusades must be underscored.

There is no doubt that the religious orientation of the Crusades by no means excluded other motives of a secular and material sort. Sons of noblemen who had no hereditary rights saw the Crusades as an opportunity not only to obtain salvation for their souls but also to acquire land of their own. The pope, on the other hand—we are speaking about Urban II—cherished the hope of promoting the idea of *libertas ecclesiae*—the Church's freedom—and the reunion of the Byzantine Church with the Latin Church through the liberation of the Eastern Churches from oppression by the Muslims. In particular, the Italian Crusaders regarded the Crusade as a continuation of their defense campaign against the Muslim pirates, who for decades had darkened their fatherland with fear.

Results

The first historical result of the Crusade movement was the establishment of four feudal states by the Crusaders: the kingdom of Jerusalem, the princedom of Antioch and the earldoms of Edessa and Tripolis. Their declaration and expansion was made possible thanks to the military presence of the chivalric orders that had come about precisely in this connection. These were the Knights Templar, the Hospitaller Order of Saint John the Baptist, the German Order of Knights and other smaller groups. Simultaneously, a Latin hierarchy was introduced as well, the establishment of which understandably encumbered the relations between the Latin Church and the Greek Church. There were also important results of the Crusade movement in the cultural sphere. The states of the *oltramare* [realm beyond the sea] developed their own literature, art and architecture. Above all, though, the West gained a comprehensive knowledge of Arabic philosophy and of the natural sciences, especially mathematics, medicine and pharmacology. Moreover, friendly commercial relations developed between the Islamic world and the Christian-Western world. It should be noted likewise that after 1110, the large Muslim populations of the Crusader states were able to live in peace and freedom according to their own religious laws and customs. For example, pilgrimages to Mecca were never impeded by the Crusaders. So it happened that when King Baldwin III of Jerusalem died in 1163, the Muslims spontaneously made a great public display of mourning for him.

Accusations

In public discussion about the Crusades, certain charges are usually leveled against the Western Church or the papacy. These concern on the one hand persecution of the Jews by the Crusaders, the so-called pogroms that took place in Worms, Mainz and Cologne, in Speyer and Halle before the First Crusade. Subsequently, the pogroms were limited to France and England. The ideological background for this was the crudely oversimplified application of the idea of blood feud to the relationship between Christians and Jews, whereby the latter were regarded as the murderers of Jesus.

The Church authorities usually opposed this wrath of the people but were successful in only a few cases. Saint Bernard of Clairvaux, for example, managed to prevent pogroms during the course of the Second Crusade. There was clear evidence, however, of a certain discrepancy between the official proclamation of the Church and the misunderstandings of a populace that had become fanatical—a phenomenon not restricted to the psychosocial situation of that time.

In particular, the conquest of Jerusalem on July 15, 1099, is portrayed as a bloodthirsty orgy on an unprecedented scale, perpetrated under the Sign of the Cross. If the fall of Jerusalem is portrayed in light of modern research, however—that is, on the basis of a critical examination of the contemporary Latin, Hebrew and Muslim accounts—then this event loses its exceptional character. Such an approach shows, for instance, that the intention of the medieval chronicler was something other than the simple description of the historical facts. A closer analysis of the texts demonstrates that what occurred in the year 1099 was understood by way of analogy with certain Old Testament passages, for example with Joshua 6 [verses 17, 20–21], in which the conquest of Jericho is described as follows:

> [T]he city and all that is within it shall be devoted to the Lord for destruction. . . . [T]he wall fell down flat, so that the people went up into the city, every man straight before him, and they took the city. Then they utterly destroyed all in the city, both men and women, young and old, oxen, sheep, and asses, with the edge of the sword.

Or Revelation 14:20: "[A]nd the wine press was trodden outside the city, and blood flowed from the wine press, as high as a horse's bridle, for one thousand six hundred stadia." In this manner, the medieval chroniclers attempted to express the victory of God's people over their opponents. So much for the literary form of some sources. The number of victims is therefore grotesquely exaggerated in the narrative sources. This is shown, for example, by contemporary registers that were found in the old synagogue in Cairo, which list numerous Jews, citizens of Jerusalem who had emigrated to Egypt after the city was seized. We must also understand that, in contrast to the narrative sources that speak about one hundred thousand inhabitants of Jerusalem, the real number of inhabitants in Jerusalem never exceeded ten thousand. Then, too, it had decreased significantly even before the Crusades, as a result of numerous wars with various Muslim enemies. Furthermore, many inhabitants had fled to the surrounding areas outside the city at the news that the Crusaders were arriving, while the Christians were driven out of the city, since it was feared that they would make common cause with the attackers.

Therefore, contrary to the narrative sources, it is necessary to limit significantly the extent of the bloodbath on July 15, 1099. In the extent to which atrocities occurred, the conquest of Jerusalem was no different from other comparable cases.

The Capture of Constantinople

Vehement accusations—especially on the part of the Orthodox—are made concerning the seizure and destruction of the city of Constantinople in 1204 during the Fourth Crusade. This fact is always stressed when discussion turns to the relations between Rome and Constantinople. In this case, too, the historical truth is much less simple than people usually think.

In order to procure funds for the sea voyage, the army of Crusaders under the command of the counts of Champagne, Blois and Flanders had gone deep into debt with the seigniories [in Italian: *signorie*, feudal lords] of Venice. In return, the seigniories demanded the reconquest of Zadar, a city on the Adriatic that had seceded from Venice in 1186. Despite the protests of Innocent III and against the will of one party of the Crusaders, the Christian city of Zadar was in fact seized. The pope reacted with severe rebukes and ecclesiastical penalties, which nevertheless left the Venetians indifferent. The disastrous turn of the Crusade then against Constantinople was the result of dynastic conflicts within the Byzantine Empire. In 1195 Emperor Isaac II Angelus, together with his son Alexius, was deposed and imprisoned by his younger brother Alexius III; in 1202, however, Alexius was able to escape from prison and turned to his brother-in-law Philip of Swabia, promising the Crusaders that, if they regained his throne for him, he would reward them with the sum of two hundred thousand marks in silver, participate in and finance the Crusade and also subject the Byzantine Church to the pope of Rome. Now, Innocent III strictly forbade any attack on the Byzantine Empire, emphasizing the liberation of the Holy Land as the exclusive goal of the Crusades—but in vain. On July 17, 1203, Constantinople was captured, Isaac Angelus was set free from prison and reinstated, and his son Alexius IV was proclaimed coregent. The emperor was unable, however, to fulfill the promises that he had made to the Crusaders. He was deposed again and finally died in prison. Alexius IV was murdered, and Alexius V was crowned in late January 1204. His refusal to give the Crusaders satisfaction, together with the intrigues of Enrico Dandolos, the doge of Venice, thereupon led to the catastrophe of April 13, 1204: the fall of Constantinople and the establishment of the Latin Empire of Constantinople and the unauthorized installation of a Latin Patriarch by the Venetians. The attitude of Innocent III toward what had happened was not entirely unambiguous. On the one hand, he condemned in the severest terms the excesses of the Crusaders as soon as he heard about them; on the other hand, he believed that he could make use of the situation that had come about in that manner for the liberation of the Holy Land and for the reunion of the Churches—a hope that nonetheless was never realized.

War in God's Name?

More than anything else, this case shows that it was impossible to keep up the high religious standard that had been characteristic of the First Crusade. In the measure that the influence of the popes diminished, political and commercial interests prevailed in an undertaking that from the start had been planned quite idealistically.

An adequate historical judgment on the Crusades must above all take into account the extremely complex nature of this historical phenomenon. What provokes the most criticism is the idea of holy war, war in God's name! We must keep in mind, however, that this was not a purely Christian phenomenon but rather a universal idea of premodern cultures. It was an expression of a hierarchy of values in which the value of the sacred surpassed everything else and moved men to risk everything for it, even human life—the enemy's as well as one's own.

In the case of the Crusades also, instead of judging, one should seek to understand and reflect that our present age, too, will someday be judged by future generations.

VIII

MARTIN LUTHER'S REFORMATION
FROM A CATHOLIC PERSPECTIVE

Reformatio *in the Medieval Church*

Anyone who measures the life of individual Christians or of the Church as a whole against the moral standards of the Gospel is struck by the gaping discrepancy between demand and fulfillment—in himself and in the other members of the Church. Certainly, standing out from the great multitude in every century, more-or-less numerous and luminous, are the saints, in whose human weakness God's power took effect and was manifested and attained perfection. There are and always have been too few of them.

The recognition of this has led again and again from the very beginning of Church history to the call for conversion, for repentance; with regard to the Church as a whole, it expanded into a call for reform. The history of the medieval Church proves how open she was to this call at every stage.

At the beginning, after the debacles during the mass migrations and the Merovingian era, there was the Church reform during the time of the Carolingians, followed by the reform movements in monasticism proceeding from Cluny, Gorze and other centers, and then around 1050 the Gregorian reform, named after Pope Gregory VII. Less than a hundred years later, the Western Church was gripped by the mendicant movement, whose members tried to put into practice once again the lifestyle of the Apostles—the ideal of a life pledged to poverty and itinerant preaching. Francis of Assisi and Dominic were the names of the figures who soon loomed large and furthermore managed to lead back to the riverbed of ecclesiastical integration most of the religious forces that in many places had overflowed the banks of Church affiliation. Their influence spread throughout the Western Church, and by the year 1300 there must have been only a few European cities that did not have at least one friary or convent of mendicant religious. From the pulpits of these convent churches arose again and again the cry for penance, renewal and the imitation of Christ, occasionally in a very drastic, down-to-earth manner. For centuries, the pulpit became the domain of the mendicant orders. These preachers did not shrink from severe criticism of the clergy and even of bishops, when their lordly, even luxurious, way of life caused scandal. There are interesting studies of medieval critiques of the local Churches and of Rome, which show us how painful the distance between the ideal and the reality of Christian ecclesiastical life often was to pious observers.

Especially harsh tones could be heard at the time of the Great Western Schism, after Pope Urban VI was elected in 1378 and an antipope, Clement VII, was elected a few months later. This lack of unity in the supreme pastoral ministry, which metastasized into a tripartite division in 1409 after the Council of Pisa (since the council had unsuccessfully deposed the two competing pretenders to the papacy in Rome and in Avignon), threw Western Christendom into confusion and brought plenty of disorder into the life of the Church. The influences of secular rulers and financial interests gained the upper hand, and the Renaissance, with its this-worldly understanding of life centered on profit, enjoyment and importance, left lasting marks that were visible even in the Roman Curia and many a pope of the fifteenth century. Their brilliant deeds as statesmen and their cultural achievements cannot blind us to the fact that in some cases these popes did not truly correspond to their vocation to the supreme pastoral ministry in the Church. It is very uncertain whether they gave as much scandal to their contemporaries as to us: in their philosophies of life and in their lifestyles, they conformed all too much to the general mindset of the men of their time.

The fifteenth century, however, is also the century of the reform councils: Pisa in 1409, Constance in 1414–1418, Siena in 1423–1424 and Basel-Ferrara-Florence in 1431–1439. These were attempts, which met with more or less success, to reorganize ecclesiastical life so that the Church could respond to the demands of a transformed societal order. The great reform, admittedly, did not arrive: everyone talked about reform, but nobody wanted it to stay at his house, as a preacher at a council once said. "Reform" had been reduced to a slogan.

The ones who took the call for reform seriously, in contrast, were the orders. The Benedictines, the Franciscans, the Dominicans, the Augustinians, the Carmelites and their female branches experienced movements in their ranks that aimed at renouncing all the compromises that they had accepted over the course of time and at returning to the ideals of the orders' founders, although here and there too much emphasis was placed on externals and the observance of the rule. Martin Luther himself belonged to such a religious community.

This reforming impulse was not infrequently the driving force behind a critique of the Church that in its earnestness and fervor was reminiscent of the Old Testament prophets. Harsh words were uttered and prophetic warnings were issued. A classic example was the wool dyer's daughter, Caterina Benincasa [Catherine of Siena]: from her mystical union with the crucified Christ came her message to popes, cardinals, priests, the faithful, statesmen and generals. To Pope Gregory XI, who was at war with Florence, Siena and other cities, she wrote around 1377: "God's will is that you should make peace with Tuscany. You may punish rebellious sons, but not with war. . . . After all, you hold the keys of heaven in your hand. If you open for someone, it is open to him, and if you shut someone out, it is shut to him. Therefore, if you do not do this, the wrath of God will strike you." She relentlessly lashed out at luxury and moral failings in cardinals, bishops and priests, and when she appeared at the papal court in Avignon to summon Gregory XI to return to Rome, those who had been so harshly rebuked by her stepped aside respectfully. Pius II unhesitatingly declared her a saint in 1461.

The preachers at the Council of Constance struck a tone that was no less harsh. Now and then, they depicted the situation in such dismal colors that the historian hesitates, with good reason, to take their descriptions as a faithful reflection of the times.

What Is Reform?

The common element in all these reform movements, scattered about in such diverse times, regions and social strata, is that they pursued aims that were mainly practical, canonical and, even more important, religious and moral. They were concerned with the just management of ecclesiastical property; with the just and pastorally correct allocation of ecclesiastical offices; with fostering fear of the Lord and piety among the clergy and the laity; with the strict observance of the religious vows of poverty, chastity and obedience; with the conscientious celebration of the liturgy, administration of the sacraments and performance of the preaching ministry; and, over and over again, with maintaining the purity of the faith, given the individualistic and spiritualistic aberrations that were manifest in late medieval society.

To each of these reform movements, the Church as it existed concretely appeared to be in need of improvement but also capable of reform. On the eve of Luther's entrance upon the stage of history, the Fifth Lateran Council issued a series of positive reform decrees—the idea of reform was at the center of the conciliar activity. At the same time, reformers, such as the members of the humanist circle in the Upper Rhineland, headed by Jakob Wimpfeling, were at work. Particularly impressive, however, is the religious and ecclesiastical revival that took place in Italy and especially in Spain. One sign of the religious vitality of the Church in Spain was that the theological schools there posed the radical question of whether colonizing Latin America was morally acceptable; not only that, but they also managed, after thoroughgoing theological reflection on the human rights of the indigenous peoples, to limit the political will of the kings, even though there was only spotty success in putting these principles into practice.

No doubt the majority of Luther's contemporaries at first saw in Luther a reformer of the sort that had often appeared and accomplished good. Many might have imagined a new Savonarola when they heard about the Augustinian monk from Wittenberg.

It is therefore plausible when we are cautioned against believing that everything was clamoring for reform and Luther's appearance was just the spark that ignited the powder keg.

Rather, the German people as a whole were devoted to the Church and brought their own spiritual restlessness to the Church. "The ecclesiastical piety of the people, and in particular their devotion to the central elements of Catholic Church life, had reached maximum intensity in Germany in the latter part of the fifteenth century" (B. Moeller). That is doubtless correct. Even though there was at the same time a desire for reform, it still can be said that hardly anyone was thinking about reformation as Luther understood it. People wanted to renew the Church, not overturn it. There was as little doubt that the Church, as it existed concretely, was in need of reform as there was about the fact that she was nevertheless and would remain the Church of Jesus Christ. Once again, let us cite Catherine of Siena. Precisely because she profoundly grasped the salvific meaning of the Church, she could pray: "Eternal God, take the sacrifice of my life for the Mystical Body of Holy Church. I can give nothing else than what you have given me." She was thoroughly convinced: "We cannot obtain our salvation otherwise than in the Mystical Body of the Church, of which Christ is the head and we are the members. He who does not obey the Christ on earth who represents the Christ in heaven does not share in the Blood of the Son of God. For God has arranged it so that through his hands Christ's Blood and all the sacraments of the Church come to us. There is no other way and no other gate for us." Her disapproval of the pope and her warnings did not change this conviction in the least. It is the genuinely Catholic conviction and stance that she formulates here: although the actual conduct of the shepherd and the flock may be wrong—indeed, sinful—human failings can never prevent Christ from preserving his Word and his grace intact and effective in this, his one Church. Therefore, Catherine, without contradicting herself, could reproach Pope Urban VI because "he is sweeping out Holy Church in an excessive manner and by the fear that he inspires in his subordinates" but at the same time remain loyal to that very pope, in whom she discerned the legitimate shepherd. To the cardinals, whom she blamed for starting the division in the Church, she wrote:

> The poison of self-seeking . . . has turned you pillars [of the Church] into straws! You are not fragrant flowers but a stench that pollutes the whole world. Not lamps for spreading the faith. You have placed your light under the bushel basket of pride. You do not increase the faith, but as its disgraceful enemies you spread darkness in yourselves and in others. You ought to be angels on earth to save us from the infernal devil and to lead the stray sheep back to Holy Church. But you yourselves have become devils—and have deserved death a thousand times!

And nevertheless she was able to say: "It is God's explicit will: even if the shepherds and the earthly Christ" (by which she means the pope) "were incarnate devils instead of a benevolent father, we would have to subject ourselves to him . . . for God's sake."

Martin Luther—Reform or Revolution?

The answer to this question—did Martin Luther effect reform or cause a revolt?—presupposes a definition of the concept of reform. Initially, we can delimit the term negatively: reform can never result in something reformed that is no longer identical to the thing that previously was to be reformed. That means that reform in each instance pertains to the concrete form in which something appears, its concrete realization, but not to the essence of the thing needing reform. Otherwise, a change of essence would occur that would make the thing to be reformed into something other than what it was before. Applied to the Church, reform consequently means an increasingly full understanding of the faith that has been handed down, and purer, more vigorous life based on that faith, in an organic unfolding of the structure and content that at all times were given. Every development that would involve a contradiction, an opposition to the faith tradition that was foundational from the very beginning, to the traditional sacramental constitution and the basic hierarchical structure of the Church, should therefore be described not as reform but as revolution. Such a concept of reform also takes into account the full breadth of the Church's historicity, which is expressed in the tension between change in the concrete phenomenal form, on the one hand, and continuity in what is essential, on the other.

After this clarification of the concept of reform, we can discuss the question whether Luther's Reformation can be classified under this concept of reform. Even Martin Luther gave some sign of the fundamental and unshakable Yes to the Church of Jesus Christ that follows from such reflections when he emphasized, as late as 1519, that there could be no reason that would justify someone in separating himself from the Roman Church. In the commentary on Galatians that he wrote in that same year, he characterized the conduct of the Hussites as a falling away from Christ's Church, and he wrote:

> Consequently the falling away of the Bohemians from the Roman Church can in no way be excused and defended, either, as if it were not ungodly and contrary to all of Christ's laws; indeed, it offends against love, in which all laws culminate. For what the Bohemians allege—that they fell away for fear of the Lord and at the prompting of their conscience,

so that they would not have to live under wicked priests and popes—that is just what indicts them the most. For if the popes, priests or any other men are wicked and you ardently and truly loved, then you would not take flight; even if you were "in the uttermost parts of the sea" (Ps 139:9), you would instead hasten to come, complain, admonish, censure and do everything possible, and in following the plain teaching of the Apostle you would be aware that you are not supposed to take upon yourself the advantages but rather the burdens. And so it should be evident that it is vainglory when the Bohemians boast of this love and that the light in question is the one in which the angel Satan disguises himself [see 2 Cor 11:14].

Now, Luther's subsequent conduct was diametrically opposed to the principles just cited. Already in the Leipzig Debate (1519), it became evident that Luther had already traveled the path from reform to the Reformation. Whether and to what extent he was aware of this, whether or not he intended to make a break and, if so, since when, are controversial questions that are difficult to answer. Characteristic of Luther's standpoint, however, is his declaration in Leipzig: "Hence I wish to be free and not a prisoner of any authority: neither of the [Church] council nor of the supreme [governmental] power nor of the universities. The only thing that I will profess as trustworthy is what I recognize as true, whether it is maintained by a Catholic or a heretic, or whether it has been approved or rejected by a council." Luther made the above-cited remarks in his commentary on Galatians a few months later, and the contradiction is not easy to resolve. Nevertheless, in the Leipzig Debate, the real, genuine Luther may have spoken after being challenged roughly and relentlessly by Eck. Therefore, whatever he said and did after 1519 was the expression of his No to the Church, which he saw as being represented in the pope.

The following year, 1520, brought a significant intensification of his rhetoric, since in several of his statements Luther described the pope as the Antichrist, that is, the satanic opponent of Christ who was expected at the end of time. Especially in his written work *On the Babylonian Captivity of the Church* he championed this thesis. In another work, "Against the Bull of the Antichrist", Luther's battle against the papacy arrives at an initial climax when he declares that if the bull threatening him with excommunication is not retracted by the pope, no one should doubt that the pope is an enemy of God, a persecutor of Christ, a destroyer of Christendom and the Antichrist himself. A few months later, he wrote:

> If we punish thieves with the gallows, murderers with the sword and heretics with fire, then why do we not attack with every possible weapon these teachers of ruin, these cardinals, the popes and the whole gang of the Roman Sodom, who ceaselessly spoil God's Church, and wash our hands in their blood?

It was only consistent that on December 10, 1520, in a spectacular appearance at the Elster Gate in Wittenberg, Luther should throw the *Codex iuris canonici* (the book of canon law) and the bull threatening him with excommunication into the fire. "Arise, pious young students!" he had written, "and witness this holy and God-pleasing theatrical play. For perhaps now is the time when the Antichrist shall be revealed." On the next day, Luther wrote to Staupitz: "I have burned the pope's books and the bull, at first shivering and trembling, but now I am happier than after any other deed in my whole life."

"With that," says the Lutheran-Evangelical Luther scholar Franz Lau, "it was clear for all the world to see that Luther was not concerned with Church reform but rather with a fundamental ecclesiastical revolution." The historian Will Peukert, also a Lutheran, has arrived at this interpretation: "that Luther wants to bring about the new Reformation from without by a revolutionary act. . . . That is ecclesiastical revolution, . . . if one measures by the former standard."

The professor from Wittenberg remained on this trajectory until the end of his life. His repudiation of the papacy served from then on as the *continuo*, or figured bass line, for almost every other theme. Even Hadrian VI, a man filled with piety, erudition and zeal for reform, who at the Imperial Diet of 1523 in Nuremberg had his legate read aloud a moving confession of Rome's responsibility for the religious situation in Germany, was the object of Luther's invective. "The pope", he wrote with fawning mockery, "is a *magister noster* [schoolmaster] of lions; in this noble school such asses are crowned." Satan spoke through Hadrian, Luther wrote. Luther's polemic reached its climax in his work "Against the Roman Papacy Founded by the Devil". The title says it all. Even in his final illness, Luther, according to the report of one of his disciples, wrote in chalk on the wall the verse: *Pestis eram vivus, moriens ero mors tua, papa*—I was a pestilence to you in life, O Pope, and in death I shall be your death! This radical, total and—it must be said—hate-filled utterance, erupting from existential depths, was aimed at the papacy and, along with it, at the entire Church with her hierarchical-sacramental constitution.

This should come as no surprise, since already in his famous polemical writings from the year 1520 Luther had denied central tenets of the Church's faith. In particular, his No was aimed at the Catholic concept of Church.

With his famous saying that everyone hatched from the baptismal font was thereby already consecrated pope, bishop or priest as well, Luther proclaimed the universal priesthood of the faithful, the only priesthood that he acknowledged. That was simultaneously a repudiation of the Church's essential hierarchical organization, founded upon Holy Orders. Luther says:

> If we are all priests, then why shouldn't we also have the power to discern [*schmecken*] and judge what is right or wrong in the faith? We all have the same spirit of faith (2 Cor 4:13). . . . All this and many other sayings should make us bold and free, and we should not allow the spirit of freedom . . . to be intimidated by contrived words of the popes but rather courageously judge everything that they do or do without [*lassen*] according to our faith-filled understanding of Scripture, and force them to follow the better understanding and not their own.

With that, of course, the individual was proclaimed the highest authority in matters of faith. Now nothing was decisive for Luther anymore except one's own private judgment on the basis of personal insight and, as he occasionally indicated, on the basis of the divine revelation given to him. The self-assuredness with which Luther subsequently described and proclaimed his personal experience as the Word of God, ultimately making it the standard of orthodoxy even in controversies with the other Reformed theologians, is difficult to imitate.

Whereas in this treatise Luther had tried primarily to lift the Church's Magisterium off its hinges, he attacked her sacramental structure with similar intent in *De captivitate Babylonica ecclesiae praeludium* [Prelude on the Babylonian captivity of the Church]. This work appeared in Latin in late August of 1520 but was immediately translated into German. A superficial reading may lead to the conclusion that in it Luther was objecting only to the doctrine that there are seven sacraments, to marriage law, to celibacy and to the denial of the chalice to the laity [who receive Holy Communion]. In reality, however, he was objecting here to the traditional Catholic concept of sacrament in general. The climax of the work is his passionate repudiation of the Sacrifice of the Mass, with which Luther struck at the very heart of the religious life of the old Church. Luther's old friend and mentor Staupitz now withdrew his support. Erasmus opined that with this treatise the bridges had been burned. The University of Paris lodged a public protest against it, and Henry VIII responded by writing his *Assertio septem sacramentorum*. In denying the objective salvific efficacy of the sacramental action, "he formulated a Christianity that presents itself more and more as a product of a purely interior conviction. . . . Without even wasting a word on the subject, Luther declared in this work that the priesthood founded upon sacramental consecration was abolished; it had become completely irrelevant to him."

He made his statement as a man of letters and a publicist and then acted accordingly. In an enterprising collaboration with the princes and cities that followed Luther, established churches [*Landeskirchen*] were founded from 1524 on. Of all the territories, Prussia took the lead, and the Hohenzollern rulers in Franconia followed; Nuremberg had already reformed by 1524. Regulations for established churches were composed, and compliance was strictly enforced through visitation.

Thus, by the time the Augsburg Confession was formulated in 1530, new ecclesiastical communities had sprung up in protest against the old Church—alongside her ruins, so to speak—entities, furthermore, that contradicted one another on essential points yet were increasingly consolidated with the support of princes and magistrates. They had their own doctrine, their own liturgy, their own pastoral structures, indeed their own law—no doubt all the elements required to found a church. From 1532 on, the established churches everywhere appointed governing bodies, superintendencies or consistories—formal schism based on differences in faith had logically followed from division in the Church.

Reformation and Tradition

The question to be answered now is: Is such an ecclesiastical revolution theologically justifiable, that is, justifiable in God's sight? It should be emphasized in this regard that we are not judging the personal good faith of Luther and of his followers but rather the objective state of affairs.

The initial argument adduced for the necessity or inevitability of Luther's ecclesiastical revolution is the failure of late medieval Church reforms in view of the deplorable abuses of the Church of that time. This failure was in turn caused by a fundamental traditionalism of the Church, whereby "the numerous critics and reformers of the late medieval Church" were forced "to derive their principles again and again exclusively from one of the many traditions from the earlier centuries of the medieval period". Therefore, it is argued, they had merely gone around in circles and with few exceptions had remained within the narrow range of possibilities in the same Church that they felt called to cleanse. This traditionalism supposedly barred the way to an immediate, liberating return to the origin and the sources of the Christian religion and thus made a thoroughgoing

renewal of theology, piety and ecclesiastical life impossible
(G. A. Benrath).

This argument, meanwhile, raises the question of fundamental importance, namely the question as to the importance of Tradition, in Greek παράδοσις, for the Church.
Can the framework of "the possibilities of the Church" be
forced open at all; that is, may her doctrine of the faith and
her hierarchical-sacramental constitution ever be modified?
Wasn't this framework of the Church's possibilities established by Jesus Christ himself and thus withdrawn from human control? Paul, in any case, sees in unbroken Tradition
the genuine realization of the Church's nature. He expresses
this in the First Letter to the Corinthians (11:23) with classical poignancy: "For I received from the Lord what I also
delivered to you."

For this reason he can write also in the Letter to the Galatians (1:6–9):

> I am astonished that you are . . . turning to a different gospel
> —not that there is another gospel, but there are some who
> trouble you and want to pervert the gospel of Christ. But
> even if we, or an angel from heaven, should preach to you a
> gospel contrary to that which we preached to you, let him
> be accursed. As we have said before, so now I say again, If
> any one is preaching to you a gospel contrary to that which
> you received, let him be accursed.

Any change of the message that has been received and
handed down is therefore an attack on its integrity; to change
it would be to distort it, and that is ruled out. Anyone who
would do so would be accursed. The Apostle himself is
bound by the Gospel; it is beyond the reach of his control.
It is "an untouchable, hallowed matter" (F. Mussner).

Now, the Church herself is not merely the organ of proclamation but also the content of the Gospel. From her we learn

what Church is. That means that not only the fundamental elements of her doctrine and her mission but also the fundamental elements of her hierarchical-sacramental structure are contained in the New Testament. Hence these too are "an untouchable, hallowed matter". Inasmuch as the Church fulfills her duty of continuous proclamation, preserves unbroken her hierarchical structure and carries on her sacramental ministry, she makes it possible for each generation of mankind to have fresh, immediate access to the origins of salvation history and thus communicates salvation in Christ, until he comes again. This continuity has its hierarchical-sacramental expression and at the same time its efficacious instrument in apostolic succession; a break in it would mean a rupture of the [Church's] connection to her origins in Bethlehem and Golgotha. An ecclesiastical upheaval that attacks (1) the authentic, traditional doctrine of the faith, (2) the traditional Church structure founded on Holy Orders and mission, and (3) the sacraments that have been handed down by Tradition therefore affects the revelation of God in Jesus Christ, which has been received by the Church and is to be handed on faithfully.

One classic Reformation objection, which we must discuss now, went much deeper and was more fundamental: the papist Church was said to have fallen away from the Gospel in a centuries-long process and to have degenerated into the synagogue of Satan, the Whore of Babylon. Only Luther's achievement put the Gospel back on the lampstand. This so-called decadence theory has defined Lutheran-Evangelical church historiography since the *Magdeburger Zenturien* of Matthias Flacius Illyricus: the Church history of the Middle Ages was understood as a history of defection from the truth.

Now, of course, we should ask the critical question,

whether such a reading of Church history withstands comparison with the words of Sacred Scripture. The latter tells us, though, that the Church, built on Peter as the Rock, can never be overcome by any power, be it of this world or otherworldly. The passage from Matthew, "I tell you, you are Peter, and on this rock I will build my church, and the powers of death shall not prevail against it", must be read together with the parable of building a house that Matthew records in his chapter 7 and Luke in chapter 6. The wise man builds his house, not on sand, but on the rock, so that the torrential rains and the storms cannot cause it to collapse. Jesus, too, builds his Church on a rock, so that it can withstand the storms of human history and Satan's attacks, as long as this eon lasts. Certainly, this endurance is not due to men: it is the presence of Jesus through his Spirit that guarantees the continuance of the Church until the end of time. Jesus confers upon the Apostles his mission and his Spirit: "Go into all the world and preach the gospel to the whole creation" (Mk 16:15); "as the Father has sent me, even so I send you" (Jn 20:21); "[I will send you another Counselor, who] will guide you into all the truth" (Jn 16:13); "Lo, I am with you always, to the close of the age" (Mt 28:20).

Now, here and there some commentators try to divest these words of their full significance by saying that Jesus said these things only to Peter and the Twelve personally, in an altogether nontransferable way, and that they took those promises with them to the grave. Yet Jesus himself talked about remaining with his disciples until the end of the world. Furthermore, whether these are *ipsissima verba Jesu* [the very words spoken by Jesus] or whether they were formulated on the basis of the self-understanding of the original Christian community is immaterial: they are part of the canonical text of the New Testament and therefore the Word of God.

These passages do show that Jesus consigned his Church in her concrete historical form to more-or-less weak and sinful men but that by remaining in their midst through the Spirit who was sent to them on Pentecost he guaranteed that his Church would remain faithful to the mission that he himself entrusted to her—proclaiming the Gospel and continuing the work of salvation—in the measure that her identity remains the same from that Pentecost morning until the Parousia [Second Coming] of the Lord. Moreover, in the First Letter to Timothy (3:15), the Church of the living God is not called the "pillar and bulwark of the truth" in order to testify to her instability and frailty. Certainly this abiding in the truth occurs in the way that Paul describes in the Second Letter to the Corinthians, when he says about his own apostolic ministry:

> We have this treasure in earthen vessels, to show that the transcendent power belongs to God and not to us. We are afflicted in every way, but not crushed; perplexed, but not driven to despair; persecuted, but not forsaken; struck down, but not destroyed; always carrying in the body the death of Jesus, so that the life of Jesus may also be manifested in our bodies. For while we live we are always being given up to death for Jesus' sake, so that the life of Jesus may be manifested in our mortal flesh.

In this way the Church, too, has been "given up to death" throughout history, yet the life of Jesus is forever manifested "in her mortal flesh", that is, in her human frailty and wretchedness. But this happens in fulfillment of the promises that the Lord had given to his Church while traveling along with her on the path through history.

It is, on the other hand, astonishing, and yet consistent with his statement in the 1519 commentary on Galatians, that Luther himself in his answer to Prierias in August 1518 teaches no differently when he writes that the faith of all must agree with the faith that the Roman Church professes. He thanks Christ that this one Church on earth—namely, the Roman Church—has preserved the true faith in such a way that she has not swerved from it in any of her decrees and that, despite all the swamp of immorality, the devil has not been able to keep the authority of the canonical books of the Bible, of the Church Fathers and of their commentators from being preserved intact and being acknowledged in the Church of Rome.

In connection with the interpretation of Church history as a process of falling away from the Gospel, Luther's achievement is then further characterized as "an immediate, liberating return to the origin and the sources of the Christian religion", the only thing that was capable of reinstating the latter in its original purity (Benrath).

No doubt this is a fascinating thought. The notion of the dust and debris of the centuries, sifted over the original form of the Church, covering and thus distorting it, is understandable. Plausible also is the conclusion that this same debris must be removed in order to rediscover the original form of the Church. And that is just what Luther did, the Lutheran historians say.

But the Church that we are talking about here is not a first-century building to be studied by archaeologists and restored—the comparison does not hold, nor does the conclusion that follows from it. If any image should be used, then it is the image of healing a sick person, which does not merely consist of cutting the time of sickness out of a biographical "filmstrip" and splicing the two ends together again. Rather, the sickness must be overcome from within by new vital forces, and the patient is thus brought back to health.

After all, the Church is not something dead on display

in a museum but rather a community that is alive through history because it lives by God's Spirit. The fact that Jesus, according to John, compares it with a grapevine and Paul likens it to a living body permits or indeed demands that the Church be categorized as organic. But a living thing—and this is true even of the simplest organic life—can never be brought back to its initial stage. The tree in whose boughs and branches the birds of the air nest cannot be transformed back into the mustard seed from which it grew.

Similarly, it is not possible at any point in Church history to decide to jump back over all the stages of the development that the Church has gone through since and to begin again. History—whether regarded as the history of an individual person or as the history of a community—is absolutely irreversible. For the very same reason, an initially fascinating ecumenical idea, the idea of a *consensus quinque-saecularis*, was doomed to failure from the outset. Irenic religious leaders from the time around the Peace of Westphalia —for example, the Lutheran Georg Calixt or even earlier the denominationally borderline figure Georg Witzel, who died a Catholic—thought that it was sufficient to return to the situation in the Church's doctrine and discipline that existed at the end of the sixth century in order to find unity, for there was no controversy between Lutherans and Catholics concerning the development that had taken place until then.

But the architects of this plan for unity, too, as we have said, labored under a false concept of history. For history is open only toward the future, in the direction of the goal, and never backward toward the beginning. Therefore, the above-mentioned "liberating return to the origins" cannot take place any more than a return to some other development stage in the past. Such attempts are by definition reactionary and therefore destructive, not constructive.

But then another consideration comes to mind. If Paul already says with reference to the people of God in the Old Testament: "[T]he gifts and the call of God are irrevocable" (Rom 11:29), then this is preeminently true about the Israel of the New Covenant, the Church. Although the old Israel may have been overtaken and replaced in salvation history by the New Testament covenant people, this is unthinkable with regard to the Church. The history of God with mankind, rather, has entered into its irrevocably final stage with the coming of Jesus Christ in the fullness of time: we who live, as the Apostle Paul puts it, "in the last times" live also in the last Church, which consequently can never be replaced by another truer, better, holier Church but will be surpassed and simultaneously perfected only by the beginning of God's definitive rule. The true Church of Jesus Christ is therefore not only numerically one; she is one also in her historical dimension: she is and remains uninterruptedly, through the millennia, through all the inadequacies and failures of her members and her pastors and through all historical changes, one and the same foundation of Jesus Christ, regardless of the fact that at any moment in history her nature could and should be more authentically realized than will ever actually occur in this age.

Since Martin Luther disputed this and regarded this same Church as degenerate, as the Babylonian Whore, not just because of the sins of her members but as a result of a fundamental defection from the Gospel, we must say to him, with reference to the above-cited words of Sacred Scripture, what he himself had replied to Zwingli in Marburg in 1529: "The [Scriptural] word stands there too mightily [for that to be so]!" And just as he then took chalk and wrote on the table: "This is my body, this is my blood", so too in this case the Catholic must take his chalk and write on the table what Michelangelo wrote along the rim of the cupola of Saint Peter's in Rome: "The gates of hell shall not prevail against it!" This word, too, stands there too mightily for anyone to overlook it.

That is why there can in fact never be an objectively valid reason that would justify a division of the one, holy, catholic and apostolic Church. The Luther of the 1519 commentary on Galatians had been entirely correct. If someone really meant to say that the actual Church of 1517 was no longer the true Church founded by Christ because she had fallen away from the Gospel, then what else would the Lord's promises to his Church be but mere deceitful human words, pathetic prattle! This line of argument was taken already by the Catholic convert and former Lutheran preacher Laurentin Albert in his account of his conversion, "*Propositiones aliquot, in quibus . . . demonstratur, cur L. A. in gremium Catholicae Ecclesiae se receperit, Ingolstadii 1570*" [Some statements in which . . . it is demonstrated why L. A. was received into the bosom of the Catholic Church in Ingolstadt in 1570]. Identical arguments can be found even earlier in the writings of Thomas More and Georg Witzel as well.

These remarks are aimed, let it be said once again, at the objective historical and theological state of affairs. A judgment on the subjective, religious-moral side of the Reformation event is by no means intended thereby. Someone who does objective good can incur guilt on account of his morally inferior motives, while objective evil can be done for subjectively noble reasons. The fact that in the tangle of human motives both noble and base considerations, religious earnestness and guilt, are often inextricably intertwined is part of the human condition. No doubt, therefore, the motives of Luther and his followers, like those of his Catholic opponents in the hierarchy, academe and politics, were various and complex as well. Passing a moral judgment on them is not the task of the historian but belongs solely to the Lord of history.

Above all, however, it must be emphasized that the previous discussion had as its exclusive theme an objective, historical and theological evaluation of the events from 1520 on. In no way was the topic "The Currently Existing Churches of the Reformation from a Catholic Perspective". Something else would have had to be said about that. After all, the [Lutheran-]Evangelical Christians of today—aside from individual cases of a change in affiliation—have never separated themselves from the Church. They are, rather, born into their ecclesial community, where they have found their spiritual home and have also received truth and grace from Jesus Christ. Despite all divisions, the Church regards them as brothers and sisters in the Lord, as is sufficiently evident from the Decree on Ecumenism of the Second Vatican Council.

To arrive with them at a real and full communion in faith and ecclesiastical fellowship is the goal toward which all our efforts should be directed. Of course, that will also involve a sober and objective historical and theological reexamination of the history of the division.

IX

A PROFOUND SPIRITUAL REAWAKENING: THE "MIRACLE OF TRENT"

The historical profile of the Council of Trent (1545–1563) stands out clearly against the background of the experience that the Church had had with the previous councils of Basel (1431–1437), and Ferrara-Florence (1438–1439) and the Fifth Lateran Council (1511–1517), the last of which had taken place only thirty years before. At all of these councils, the episcopal and Petrine-primatial structure of the Church had been at issue, if not the actual theme.

The Council of Florence had finally succeeded in formulating the first rather detailed conciliar definition of the Roman primacy, and the Fifth Lateran Council had overcome the conciliaristic opposition to the primacy legislatively as well as politically. During the pontificates of Julius II (1503–1513) and Leo X (1513–1521), the papacy basked in its victory over conciliarism—only to become, through the protest of a monk in Wittenberg in the same year that the council concluded, a *petra scandali* [stumbling block], in a way and to a degree that was unprecedented, even at the height of the conciliarist crisis.

In those times and circumstances the Emperor, too, Charles V (1519–1558), saw a new council as the remedy with which to counteract the massive defections from the Church and also her destruction through doctrinal uncertainty, religious and moral disorder, and schism. Luther himself called for a council—one, of course, that he described as "general, free and Christian" that was to be held "in German territories [*Landen*]". By that he meant that this council was to be free of papal influence, that laypeople, in particular the princes, should be voting members and that the Bible alone would be the basis for its decisions.

This demand, which from Luther's perspective was certainly logical, went much further than the earlier idea of the supremacy of a council over a pope. Such a council was, of course, completely unacceptable according to the faith of the Church. The impending council would have to meet this challenge, and its physiognomy was also shaped by it. The question was posed, not theoretically but quite practically, as to the right cooperation between pope, council and emperor.

Again and again it is said that Rome's fear of a revival of conciliarism prevented Clement VII (1523–1534) and his successors from responding promptly to the demand of Charles V for a council, so that finally, after much hesitation, it was forced to do so. That may be true of Clement VII. Nonetheless, historical honesty requires us to admit that under Paul III (1534–1549) it was political circumstances, in particular the French-Habsburg conflict, that repeatedly frustrated attempts to convoke a council. Only the peace treaty signed by Charles V and François I of France (1515–1547) at Crépy in 1544 paved the way that finally led to Trent.

In the Mainstream of Tradition

The Council of Trent is aligned with the mainstream of conciliar Tradition. No other Council, not even Vatican II, was quite so formally and completely a new beginning, starting over both procedurally and with respect to the content of its decisions.

We have merely to examine the sources that are cited by the decrees. By doing so we discover not only the extent to which the earlier councils were influential but also how earnestly the fathers of Trent strove to base their own statements upon the authentic Tradition of the Church.

The general councils that are mentioned are Nicaea (I and II, 325 and 787) and Chalcedon (451), from antiquity; then the Lateran councils (with the exception of the first); Lyons II (1274); Vienne (1311–1312); and Florence. The Fourth Lateran Council of Innocent III (1215), nevertheless, surpasses all the others in the frequency with which its documents are cited. The fathers of the Council of Trent relied to an astonishing extent on the reform decrees of a council that antedated them by 350 years, and they initiated thereby a reform movement that is unparalleled in Church history! The concept of reform that is evident in such a procedure is significant also.

It is not surprising that the Council of Florence is cited in connection with the doctrine of Purgatory, and the Bull of Union for the Coptic Church in reference to the scriptural canon. It is astonishing, however, that even the controversial Council of Constance (1414–1418) has a say and thus receives the highest approval for its legitimacy from the Council of Trent. The decrees of Constance are referred to in condemning the necessity of Communion under both species—*sub utraque*—and in refuting the error of Wycliffe, who tried to make the efficacy of the sacraments dependent on the worthiness of the one administering them.

In this way the fathers of Trent silently made a statement that had great importance for the history of councils. Naturally, several particular councils were cited, too—

for instance, Toledo III (527) and XI (675), Orange (441), Carthage II (416) and IV (424), and Braga II (572). But Basel did not make its way into the documents of Trent. All these observations show how attentively the fathers surveyed the entire conciliar Tradition of the Church when they set out to counteract the dramatic process of ecclesiastical disintegration in their day.

On one very central point of its work, however, the council did not consider itself capable of citing one of the preceding councils. Only once—and only peripherally—is the Second Council of Orange (c. 528) mentioned in the centerpiece of Trent: the Decree on Justification. This was probably due to the novelty of the problem, which meant that no previous council had issued any decisions on the subject. Thus the fathers were obliged to refer to the primary source of any profession of faith, Sacred Scripture. Besides the New Testament, which is cited extensively, only the Church Fathers are quoted: Augustine copiously and Jerome and Tertullian once each.

Trent set foot here in new conciliar territory and produced a doctrinal decree that, as the renowned Protestant theologian from the turn of the twentieth century Adolf von Harnack said, would have made Luther's Reformation superfluous had it been issued by the Fifth Lateran Council.

The Theological Quality of the Documents

At this point we should evaluate also the theological quality of the doctrinal decrees of Trent in comparison with those of earlier councils. Whereas the Fourth Lateran Council (1215) and the Council of Vienne could still unabashedly make use of Scholastic terminology, the Council of Ferrara-Florence dealing with Church unity had to take into consideration the argumentation and vocabulary of its Byzantine dialogue partner. It was this consideration that had made it necessary to cite more extensively the Greek as well as the Latin Fathers of the Church. Now, at Trent it was important to keep in view the Reformation doctrines, which had gained so much ground that they had made the council necessary in the first place. So the council fathers relied to a great extent on Sacred Scripture, which the Protestants regarded as the sole source of the faith. This is especially true for the doctrinal decrees. It goes without saying that authentic Tradition —above all in the form of councils—was quoted also.

Besides this, however, the council succeeded in finding a language with both a high degree of conceptual precision and a tone that was capable also of moving the pious sentiments of the readers and indicating that the fathers were concerned about saving the souls of the faithful. Among other things, it was the flourishing humanistic scholarship of many fathers and theologians that made this manner of speaking possible by allowing increased access to the patristic literature.

The decrees themselves came about at Trent in a way that was unknown to either the early Church or the Middle Ages. Today we can say with great certainty that the great councils of Christian antiquity were by no means gatherings in which the final documents were produced by a common effort through speeches and responses. As a rule, the council's business was to confirm prepared texts by acclamation and to promulgate them. There was discussion—controversial discussion—when the council had to decide disputed matters as a tribunal.

The councils in the High and late Middle Ages were conducted in a similar way, until in Constance, Pavia-Siena (1423–1424) and Basel the subject matter, which was less theological than canonical, demanded a different procedure. Much the same is true of Ferrara-Florence, which was supposed to carry on the Greek-Latin dialogue.

A New Way of Proceeding

At Trent, in contrast, the decrees—aside from the one forced through by the cardinal legate Morone in the concluding phase of the council—were produced by the common effort of the fathers as they grappled to find the right expressions.

One particularly new feature in this process was the policy providing that the material in each case would be treated first in the gatherings of theologians. This was done through lectures given to the fathers by the council theologians, who had no vote; most of the talks dealt with the positions of Protestant theology. Afterward, the draft decrees presented by the legates were voted on in the general assembly, whereby the results of the fathers' votes were incorporated into the draft by ad hoc commissions. This process was repeated as often as was necessary in order to obtain a majority for the draft. Then in the "solemn session", the completed decrees were promulgated. No previous council had implemented such an intensive procedure for obtaining opinions. The role of the learned theologians in this process should not be underestimated; after all, the luminaries of contemporary theology were gathered at Trent. In this way, the decrees of Trent acquired the spiritual, intellectual and linguistic format that merits admiration even today.

In no way dependent on the quality of the contents of the council's doctrinal decrees is the question as to the nature and degree and scope of their binding force. The prerequisite for universal and irrevocable validity is the ecumenicity of the council that enacted them. In this regard one looks immediately to the presence of the *oecumene*, the universal Church, at the council. It was Gottfried Wilhelm Leibniz who not quite 250 years later in his famous correspondence with the great French bishop and preacher Jacques-Bénigne Bossuet radically called into question the ecumenicity of the Council of Trent. He claimed that, since the nations of northern Europe, the Greeks and the Eastern Christians were not present, a handful of papal fanatics took advantage of the situation to make their own strange ideas into articles of faith. Furthermore, the Spanish king is supposed to have been firmly in the hands of his monastic associates, and France controlled by an Italian woman, while the Italians dictated terms in Trent. Even France, the theory goes, was not able to resist them in the long run.

In order for a council to be ecumenical, the argument continues, the presence and collaboration of a large number of council fathers from various nations is required, which cannot be said of Trent. Therefore, Trent was not an ecumenical council, and for that reason, its decrees are not binding. Leibniz could have added that a whole hemisphere, namely North and South America, was absent from the council, although quite a few episcopal sees had existed there for half a century.

Now, naturally, it should be admitted that the physical representation of the universal Church at Trent was rather slight. The council was inaugurated in the presence of only twenty-nine cardinals and bishops, and the total number of participants of episcopal rank during the first period [1545–1547] did not even reach the one hundred mark. And even these few were not present from start to finish. Nevertheless, they came from all the European nations that had remained Catholic, except for Switzerland, Poland and Hungary. From Germany, only Auxiliary Bishop Helding from Mainz had showed up. It is indisputable that, for obvious reasons, the Italians outnumbered all the rest.

The situation was essentially unchanged during the second period (1551–1552). For the opening session, only fifteen participants had arrived, and without exception they belonged to the realm of Charles V. The arrival of envoys from Protestant diets—namely Saxony, Brandenburg, Württemberg and Strasbourg—did not change that. Only during the final phase of the council (1562–1563) were there more than two hundred fathers entitled to vote—236, to be exact. And most of those, too, were Italians.

The criterion that Leibniz took as the basis for the ecumenicity of the Council of Trent, however, was not appropriate. Leibniz was extrapolating from the circumstances in which the Council of Constance had taken place. During that *sede vacante* period—which continued until the election of Pope Martin V—the actual, physical representation of the universal Church was in fact the sole element that could establish the ecumenicity of the council in the situation prevailing at that time.

The Council of Trent, however, took place during the pontificates of legitimate popes, whose attendance and approval ensured the ecumenicity even of a sparsely attended council. The only member of the college of bishops that cannot be replaced by any other is its head, the pope. His collaboration makes up for any missing bishop. No council of the medieval or modern period demonstrates this so impressively as the Council of Trent.

Had any further corroboration been needed, the aftermath of this council would have supplied it. Whereas there have been councils that had little or no influence beyond their own day (for instance, the first three Lateran councils, the two councils of Lyons [1245 and 1274] and finally even the Fifth Lateran Council), the *Tridentinum* lent its name to an epoch that lasted three hundred years: we speak of a "post-Tridentine period" in Church history.

Reform Council

In sharp contrast to the so-called reform councils of the fifteenth century, the Council of Trent introduced a real reform, which Hubert Jedin has called the "miracle of Trent". At Trent there were no battles over the allocation of the Church's economic resources or exhausting debates about structural changes, as at Constance or Basel. Nor were the actual legislative measures the decisive factor that brought about the Tridentine reform. Rather, the council succeeded in setting before the majority of the bishops, and then of the priests as well, the authentic ideal of the apostolically minded shepherd in such a way that it could develop in all its attractiveness and thus become an effective force in pastoral care for the salvation of souls. This was not some new "Tridentine ideal of the bishop"; this image of the successor to the Apostles was, rather, a part of genuine Church Tradition that the council now disentangled from distortions and raised again as a standard. The real consequence of this council was not so much a new legislation as it was a new, profound spiritual and religious awakening. Furthermore,

Trent gave rise to a wave of regional synods and provincial councils, which transmitted its impulses to the individual dioceses. Indeed, even the councils in the Church of Latin America, which had been absent from Trent, were thoroughly committed to the Tridentine reform and to applying it to the local situation. Again, that cannot be said of any other council of the medieval or modern period.

So it is not surprising that, even though Vatican I cited Trent less frequently (due to the nature of the problems that it was dealing with), the Second Vatican Council referred extensively to the Tridentine doctrinal decrees, which it cited much more often than those of any other council. This fact alone makes it impossible to set up an opposition between Trent and Vatican II, although in some circles people like to talk about a "departure from Trent".

Departure from Trent?

Aside from the fact that everything that has been defined as a doctrine of the faith by a general council has entered once and for all into the *depositum fidei* [deposit of faith] and consequently is irrevocable, a "departure from Trent" would mean as well a departure from a period of our history and Tradition that has been extremely fruitful, intellectually as well as spiritually and culturally. What is called for is not a departure but rather a new and deeper assimilation.

And yet even today there are demands for a new departure from Trent for the sake of ecumenism, though of course in a rather disguised form. The Catholic-Lutheran dialogue produced in 1987 a work entitled: "Doctrinal Decisions— Ecclesiastically Divisive?" The gist was as follows: "If the two Churches [!] take the next steps recommended in the discussions, and informally declare that the repudiations of the sixteenth century can no longer be repeated, then they will find themselves on the path to a communion that binds them together ever more strongly."

In support of this thesis, it is alleged that the doctrinal conflicts that existed then have been rendered largely obsolete by modern developments and that they no longer apply to the dialogue partners today. On the contrary, the Lutheran-Evangelical theological faculty in Göttingen pointed out quite earnestly and emphatically that the anathemas of the Council of Trent are aimed at today's fundamental Lutheran convictions also. They go on to say that there is no getting around this ongoing opposition by means of discussion. And on that point, we should be in complete agreement. We might add that abandoning Trent for the sake of ecumenical rapprochement, as Leibniz once demanded, would mean the loss of Catholic identity. It would be throwing overboard not just a council but the entire Tradition of the Church. For even if the Council of Trent stands out in many respects from the series of the other councils, it is nevertheless so organically connected with them through the continuous stream of authentic Tradition that the removal of this council would cause the whole structure of Tradition to collapse. Just as the many characteristics of many ancestors are integrated into the genotype of a human being and form the basis of his identity, so too the *Tridentinum*—like any other council—has been integrated into the patrimony of the Church and is the basis for her identity.

It took twenty-five years for the council to come about, and then almost twenty more years passed before it could be concluded. That was, all told, almost half a century, during the course of which the laborious business of clarifying the faith and renewing the life of the Church had to be carried out in the midst of a struggle to overcome extreme resistance from without and crises within. On December 4, 1563, after the *Te Deum* and the *"Domini, ite in pace"*—"My Lords, go in peace"—pronounced by the legate Morone, as the fathers of Trent embraced one another with tears of joy and gratitude, the longest lasting council in Church history, and the one with the most salutary consequences, had come to a conclusion.

About no other council can the historian say what Hubert Jedin was able to say about the Council of Trent: that it initiated the "miracle of Trent". By that he meant the awakening of the Church, so sorely wounded by schism, from a deep swoon to a new flourishing of both religious and cultural life that has very few parallels in the history of the Church.

X

SENSUOUSNESS AND RATIONALITY

*Toward a Definition of the
Baroque Period in Intellectual History*

Writing an essay instead of a book with this subtitle may seem presumptuous. It is quite evident, after all, that the term "Baroque" summarizes a complex, many-layered cultural phenomenon. Not only does every department of life, each one of the arts and sciences present a specific aspect of the epoch; if we survey the geographical milieu in which the Baroque style developed—from Moscow to Mexico and from Sicily to Scandinavia—we find periodization that differs from one region to the next, as well as geographically and hence denominationally independent expressions of the Baroque. All this, naturally, would call for a differentiated and accordingly wide-ranging and in-depth presentation, which of course cannot be accomplished in an essay. There is no doubt that the opinion of Wilhelm Hausenstein is correct: "To say in a word what Baroque is, is as tempting as it is impossible." That is by no means the intention of this article; rather, it will examine one facet of the overall phenomenon "Baroque" in an effort to verify the thesis that the source of Baroque culture is to be found above all in the tension and harmony between sensuousness and rationality in the existential attitude [*Lebensgefühl*] of the Baroque period. The fact that this is done largely from the perspective of the Church historian is probably just as legitimate as the statement: "The whole colorful, infinitely varied world of the Baroque is . . . overarched [*übergriffen*] by a mindset that is oriented toward theology and trembles with a spirituality that takes its measure from the Last Things" (Benno Hubensteiner).

Roots in the Council of Trent

The roots of this are to be found in the two decrees of the Council of Trent that inaugurated a Christian rehabilitation of creation, of nature and thereby also of the senses and the sensory world: the Decree on Original Sin and the Decree on Justification, both of which were promulgated during the first period of the council, on June 17, 1546, and January 13, 1547, respectively. In both decrees the Church, now awakened from her paralyzing swoon in the first decades of the Reformation, responded to the pessimism of the Reformation, which had thrown into sharp relief the depravity of human nature resulting from original sin. Moreover, this was connected—through an exaggerated reading of a statement by Augustine—with a negative theological valuation of the human senses and of their function, which is amply demonstrated by the well-known phenomena of Calvinism and Puritanism. Furthermore, the exclusive emphasis on the saving Word of God fostered that iconoclastic intellectualism that turned against the abundance of liturgical forms and popular devotions and to which the graphic arts and the Church's works of art fell victim as well. This is precisely what the German playwright Schiller has the character Mortimer say in *Mary Stuart*:

> I never felt the power of the arts.
> The church that raised me hates the senses' charm.

It brooks no image, honoring alone
The disembodied Word.

In the above-mentioned decrees, the council now countered this pessimistic view of the Reformers with the genuine Catholic teaching. Already in the debates about original sin and the theological nature of *concupiscentia*, interpretations had come to light which, in contrast to Calvin even more than to Luther, were unwilling to characterize concupiscence as a sin or something sinful. The bishop of the Canary Islands, for instance, emphasized that *concupiscentia* is not a sin, since nothing belonging to human nature can be a sin. Here the statement itself is less interesting for us than the reason given for it, which clearly indicates that human nature is not sinful. This negative observation was ultimately included in the council's positive teaching that *"totum id, quod veram et propriam peccati rationem habet"*—"everything that is sin in the true and proper sense" is taken away and eradicated from man through justification and baptism.

Another theme that was stressed to offset the position taken by the Reformers was the necessity of human cooperation with the process of justification.

It was of far-reaching importance for the moral life of the individual that the clarification of the doctrine of justification declared that man's will is not completely deprived of freedom and that justification does not consist exclusively of grace. Thus grace maintained its value and dignity as prevenient and sanctifying grace, through which man is able to emerge from his passivity and perform good works. And the teaching on original sin had rejected the view that original sin is the proclivity to evil, thus avoiding a general condemnation of the inclinations and aspirations of the human heart, which according to Calvinism should be exterminated. Nature is not inherently sinful. Emotions can also be enlisted in the service of moral ideals. Herein lies the root of the great Catholic cultural accomplishment of the Baroque period. (H. Tüchle)

The Rehabilitation of the Senses

The teaching of the Council of Trent outlined here made it possible, not explicitly by its wording yet by the theological rehabilitation of the senses that followed logically from it, for the manifold forms of human, bodily activity to find expression, especially in worship and art. According to the Tridentine doctrine on justification, man, who had previously fallen calamitously, has become through baptism an entirely new creation—as Paul puts it (2 Cor 5:17 and Gal 6:15)—and is called to serve God in holiness and righteousness; this was perceived as an appeal to put all of man's intellectual, physical and sensitive faculties to good use in order to realize the one goal and purpose of creation, the *gloria Dei* [glory of God]. For the arts and for artists, this meant that they were able to proclaim God's work of creation and redemption in form, line, color, word and tone and to lend sensuous expression to man's faith, worship and devotion.

The very architecture of Baroque church buildings became a silent sermon through multifarious symbolism, based for example on the numbers three (the Divine Persons), four (the cardinal virtues), seven (the sacraments) and twelve (the Apostles). Furthermore, in the figures of the saints, the example of heroic Christian life was constantly placed before the eyes of the beholder. Painted altarpieces and the iconographic programs of frescos reminded churchgoers of scenes from both Testaments and of otherworldly things. Even

the macabre ornamentation of crypt chapels with countless skeletal parts and the portrayal of death and decay in
painting and literature were simply a *memento mori*—a re-
minder of death expressed in artistic language. "The art of
Bavaria", and no doubt one can generalize from this, "during that period develops from the close unity of the Church
and the world. Thus it can affirm creation and society and
place them at God's service. After all, the splendor serves,
even when justifiable pride in one's own accomplishment
and position is also expressed, to make visible the objects
of the faith. . . . Knowing, seeing and faith were one" (S.
Benker).

Then there was the shape of the liturgy, which was supposed to awaken in the devout participant an awareness of
the greatness of the mystery of redemption that is being
accomplished in the Eucharistic Sacrifice. The Council of
Trent had reaffirmed the belief in Christ present in the Eucharist *"vere realiter et substantialiter"*—truly, really and substantially—and this belief especially left its mark on liturgical forms. The most solemn worship of God, therefore, was
Mass celebrated in front of the Body of Christ, presented
to the view of the faithful in the form of a host placed in
a splendid sunburst of a monstrance. In his presence, the
clergy and the servers carried out a downright courtly ceremony, for which only the most beautiful and costly vest-
ments, furnishings and ornaments sufficed. This conveyed
to the eye—and so also the ever richer and more elaborate
music to the ear, and the incense and flowers to the sense
of smell—a vivid and profound impression of the nearness
of the Divine Majesty, which, by way of all of man's senses,
awakened and supported interior acts of faith, hope and
charity. In classical literary form, Friedrich von Schiller has
young Mortimer describe that impression of the Baroque

liturgy in *Mary Stuart*. It is remarkable and revealing how fully the nineteenth-century poet—in spite of the disdain for the Baroque that characterized his era—could sympathize with and express Mortimer's thoroughly Baroque experience.

Quite remarkable also in this connection are the dramatic developments of the official liturgy, especially on major feasts. The afternoon procession on Ascension Thursday, for example, is well known from the 1724 Bamberg *Rituale* of the renowned Bavarian liturgist Lothar Franz von Schönborn. A table was set up in the middle of the church, and on it was placed, between two lighted candles, a statue of Our Lord ascending into heaven. The clergy and servers knelt down before him, and then the statue was carried in procession through the church while the Ascension hymn *Aeterne Rex* was sung. Finally the procession returned to the table, where the statue was set down again, and after a psalm and a prayer, the congregation and the choir sang antiphonally the Gospel verse: "*Ascendo ad Patrem meum et ad Patrem vestrum, Deum meum et Deum vestrum, alleluia*"—"I am ascending to my Father and your Father, to my God and your God." Meanwhile, two boys had climbed to the loft of the church, representing the angels, and sang their question to the disciples: "*Viri Galilaei quid aspicitis in caelum?*"— "Men of Galilee, why do you stand looking into heaven?" The choir responded: "*Hic Jesus, qui assumptus est a vobis in caelum, sic veniet, alleluia!*"—"This Jesus, who was taken up from you into heaven, will come again in the same way." While this was being sung three times, the statue was drawn up slowly through an opening in the church roof. Once it was "taken out of their sight", the whole congregation sang *Christ fuhr gen Himmel* [a German hymn, "Christ ascended into heaven"]. And in order to exhaust the possibilities for theological symbolism, unconsecrated hosts were then thrown from above and water was poured down. The Lord had left his disciples, but only visibly: in the sacraments of baptism and Holy Eucharist, he remained with them.

There were similar practices on Pentecost, when amidst similar antiphons and prayers a dove was lowered from above after a threefold "*Veni sancte Spiritus*"—"Come, Holy Spirit". In many places, burning wads were tossed down to represent the Pentecostal tongues of fire. Representation, a sensible representation, of the mystery was the purpose also of the carved figures of the Christmas crèche, which likewise flourished artistically during the Baroque period, and of the *castrum doloris*, the Holy Sepulchre [on Holy Saturday]. The importance of all these things for the religious life of the faithful is evident from the fact that Catholics living in Protestant localities were forbidden to carry rosaries, or palm branches on Palm Sunday, to set up the crib or the tomb, to hold processions and much more, as we learn for instance from the principality of Ansbach-Bayreuth.

Very significant also were the processions, in which the faithful experienced what it means to be members of the Church Militant, the pilgrim Church that is accompanied on her way to heaven by Christ in the monstrance and by his saints, represented by their statues that were carried along in procession. The many pilgrimages were understood in a similar way.

Even the preaching and the astonishing number of religious and educational publications of this period, which ran to many editions, sought access to the hearts of the listeners and readers by way of their senses. Hence the wealth, colorfulness and graphic quality of the figurative language of the day. Francis de Sales, for example, in his *Introduction to the Devout Life*, said that everything in the world speaks a silent yet comprehensible language; there is no creature that does not proclaim God's praise and prompt pious thoughts. The mussels, plants and little oysters that are washed up on the shore are for him a symbol of the man who is driven to and fro [by the cares of this world]; a hare fleeing from the hounds represents the soul pursued by her enemies; a little lamb immediately recalls the Lamb of God; and the thorn-bearing rose symbolizes for him creation, wounded by original sin.

Finally, there are the unusually drastic and graphic comparisons with which someone like Abraham a Santa Clara seasoned his sermons—and many other preachers of the Baroque era after him, whose works are only now beginning to interest students of German literature.

In this connection we should also mention the religious-moral Baroque drama, which was brought to full literary flower by the Jesuits and the Benedictines. Quite in keeping with the allegorizing tendency of the Baroque style, virtues, vices, stirrings of the soul and other-worldly powers were personified onstage. Such playacting drew the spectators under its spell to such an extent that they often experienced an Aristotelian catharsis in a Christian sense. A performance in Munich of Jakob Bidermann's famous play *Cenodoxus, the Doctor of Paris* is described as follows in the preface to the 1666 edition of Bidermann's dramas:

> Although this play set the spectators to laughing so uproariously that the chairs were in peril, it still made such a salutary impression on the spectators that fourteen of them, high-ranking personages at the Bavarian court, were seen in the following days withdrawing into solitude in order to make a retreat and amend their lives; a hundred sermons would not have had such success. Indeed, during the final scenes, in which Cenodoxus appears before his eternal Judge, most

of the spectators trembled from head to toe as though they themselves were being judged. The actor who played the title role soon afterward entered our Society [of Jesus], in which he died after several years spent in innocence and holiness.

We know from his *Spiritual Exercises* that Ignatius of Loyola considered the so-called *applicatio sensuum*—the use of the imagination to picture, for instance, biblical events—as an important preparatory phase of religious meditation. In meditations on the life of Jesus, which normally were to be started in the second week of the Exercises, he instructs the person making the Spiritual Exercises to begin as follows:

> The Second Prelude is the "composition", seeing the place. Here it will be to see the great extent and circuit of the world, where so many and such various nations dwell; then likewise to see in particular the house and the chamber of Our Lady, in the city of Nazareth, in the province of Galilee. . . .
>
> The first point is to see the various persons: first, those on the face of the earth, so varied in dress and manners; some white and others black; some in peace and others at war; some weeping and others laughing; some in health, others sick; some being born, others dying; etc. Secondly, to see and consider the three Divine Persons as on their royal seat and throne of their Divine Majesty, how they behold the whole face and circuit of the earth, and all nations in such blindness, and how they are dying and going down into hell.

If we reflect now on the enormous circulation that the booklet of *Spiritual Exercises* had—by the suppression of the Jesuit order in 1773 more than six hundred commentaries on it had been written—then we can gauge the extent to which the spirit of an age spoke from it, and the extent to which the spirit of the Baroque period was in turn formed by it.

In all the instances mentioned here by way of illustration,

one thing is as plain as day: man's senses are understood here as the gateways to his inmost soul, through which the Gospel message should penetrate. This in turn is possible because the world, whose variety, splendor and beauty are perceived by the senses, was for the man of the Baroque period a reflection of heavenly glory.

Formerly, the human senses were often regarded with religious mistrust; but if they served as organs for apprehending and internally assimilating the Gospel, then they and the human body in general acquired also the function of giving expression to the interior life, the faith, hope and love of the Christian. In the process something analogous to electromagnetic feedback occurred: those events in the soul that found sensory expression in that way streamed back through the same gates from which they had flowed out, bringing fresh nourishment to the source.

Worship was expressed, accordingly, in the physical accomplishment of cultic forms—in bowing and genuflecting, in the gorgeous ornamentation surrounding the monstrance, which was understood as Christ's royal throne. The urgency of prayer spontaneously prompted the petitioner to throw himself down before the altar or before the image of the saint whose intercession with God was being requested. Repentance, sorrow for sin called for pain that could be sensed and felt: hair shirts, penitential belts, scourging, carrying heavy crosses or wearing shabby clothing served as means of expressing it. Interior devotion to Mary, the Mother of God, was supposed to be plainly visible through the wearing of rosaries, medals and scapulars.

This conscious or unconscious involvement of the human body and the senses in the process of salvation, which is evident in all the examples mentioned, constituted not only a vivid way of making faith concrete; it resulted at the same time in a sanctification of the sensory realm. What is manifest here is a tension-filled harmony of body and spirit in man, which in varying forms remains the task of human and Christian self-realization in every age.

From the depths of experience that are possible in this way, a scene like the following could also take place: Soon after obtaining a doctor's degree from the faculty of philosophy in Ingolstadt, the approximately twenty-year-old Jakob Balde from Alsace was walking one evening in 1624 through the streets of the university town. His destination was the house of Dolnhover the baker, whose daughter he admired. Under her window, he sang and played his serenade. But instead of a reply, midnight struck from the clock towers, and from the nearby monastery of Gnadental [Valley of grace] wafted on the wind the sound of Matins, which was just beginning. Then it struck the young man from Alsace, who was easily moved: *"Cantatum satis est: frangito barbiton!"*—"Enough singing, and may the devil take the lute!" He smashed the lute against the wall of the house and the next morning became a Jesuit. The spontaneous eruption of a Baroque man of action [*Kraftnatur*]! His volcanic character later led him to produce eight volumes of remarkable poetry by the time he died in 1668. In such figures as that great Jesuit poet, it becomes apparent how well spirituality and vitality had been joined in a creative harmony in that era. B. Hubensteiner describes Balde's work with a formula of T.S. Eliot: "an immediately sensual apprehension of thought or a transformation of thought into feeling".

Body and Soul

In olden times, Aristotle, in a critical reaction against Plato's doctrine of the existence of ideas in and of themselves, had understood the concrete world and the individual things in it as wholes composed of form and matter—we designate this understanding as hylomorphism. Now, in medieval Scholasticism, the immediate consequence was drawn from Aristotle's hylomorphism so as to define the relationship of spirit and body in man by the doctrine of *anima forma corporis*—the soul is the formative principle of the body. This understanding, then, recognizes spirit and body as mutually determining and interpenetrating "parts" of a whole. This same doctrine, further developed by the Spanish Jesuit Francisco Suarez, now swept once again Europe's institutions of higher learning. It is an astonishing phenomenon that shortly after their appearance in 1597, the Jesuit's *Disputationes metaphysicae* were introduced as a textbook at Protestant universities as well! It would be surprising if this did not have decisive influence on the entire Baroque culture. In Protestant circles as well, at any rate, it prevailed over Luther's theological approach, which, because of its failure to integrate man's imposing sensuality into religion, was suspicious of metaphysics and—to put it crudely—hostile toward nature. In the *anima forma corporis* doctrine of rediscovered Scholasticism, the holistic Baroque view of body and soul, of sensuousness and rationality and the experience of their unity, had their philosophical basis.

Now, if a philosophical understanding of the body-soul relationship in man that emphasizes their unity could produce a culture rooted in the harmony of spirit and body, then the obvious conclusion is that a philosophy which called into question the formerly advocated unity would have to result also in a change of spirituality and culture.

While Baroque culture was still in full flower, Descartes penned his epoch-making "*Cogito, ergo sum*" ["I think, therefore I am"], which incidentally subdivided reality into the *res cogitans* [the thinking thing] and *res extensae* [things having extension in space]. This affected the way in which the body-soul relationship was portrayed. "Accordingly, it is through this 'I', which is called the soul, that I am what I am, quite distinct from my body . . . and even if there were no body, it would still remain exactly what it is." The two things, spirit and body, *res cogitans* and *res extensa*, are separate from each other, and it is a paradox recognized by Descartes himself that they nevertheless have to do with each other. He thought that the pineal gland was the place where the soul has its effect on the body.

Subsequently, Johannes Clauberg (1622–1665), taking Descartes' approach a step further, opined that it is not clear from the concept of the *res cogitans* and the *res extensa* how they could affect each other. If there is nevertheless a relation between them like the relation between a helmsman and his ship, then it is only because God willed it so. That they could be essentially ordered to one another and interdependent is therefore out of the question.

The main proponent of so-called occasionalism, the Dutchman Arnold Geulincx (1624–1669), goes even further in this ontological separation of body and soul. Even sense perception, in his view, is no longer based on the ontological association between body and soul: "The world brings the image to my body and puts it down there, but the force that causes it to go further from there and to reach into my self, into my mind, is the Deity."

According to these philosophers, body and soul exist alongside one another, and only God himself, by his constant intervention, brings about an actual parallelism but not an essential connection between spiritual and corporeal phenomena. Leibniz thinks that this occurs on the basis of what he calls "preestablished harmony" (which therefore has no foundation at all in man's nature). A philosophical chasm had opened between body and soul, between sense and intellect.

Of course, it is a long way from the formulation of a philosophical opinion to the cultural and societal acceptance thereof. Nor should we overlook the fact that a seed of division was already present in the Baroque harmony. In a magnificent, breathtaking perspective, the Baroque world view had regarded heaven and earth, time and eternity, the divine and the human, the Church and the world, science, technology and faith as harmonious components of a mighty, all-encompassing cosmos of being that proceeded from God and tended toward God, and Baroque man had experienced this within himself in the unity of body and soul, of nature and grace.

But wasn't the range of opposites that were harmonized in this way too huge and comprehensive for man to be able to master it for more than one auspicious historical hour? Moreover, Baroque man had witnessed only temporary cease-fires in the conflict between intellect (truth) and the unconscious. Just one example: to this day, we often strive to understand the phenomenon of witch trials, but in vain. It was probably the calamitous experience of the Thirty Years' War that managed to trouble the depths of the people's soul in which the pre-Christian fear of demons still slumbered. Furthermore, the intellectual elite of the time had been all too ready and willing to assume that demonic influence on a human being, which the Bible and Church teaching had always recognized as a possibility, was a reality in the case at hand. Thus the witchcraft mania, which was by no means restricted to the Catholic milieu, gripped Baroque society like a fever. Only in the second half of the seventeenth century did it subside.

Despite the most intensive pastoral efforts, countless religious and theological publications, episcopal exhortations and even ordinances by the secular authorities, superstition was never completely eradicated from the wider populace. It could insinuate itself most easily at the very place where heavenly and earthly things, spirit and matter, rationality and sensuousness interpenetrated most intensively—in the sacraments and the sacramentals. Again and again, there are complaints about the sacrilegious use or superstitious understanding of holy water, palm branches, candles blessed on the Feast of the Presentation (Candlemas) and the blessing of stables. Exposure to sickness, pain, and inevitable poverty and dependence on the weather led not only to prayer for God's help and for the intercession of the saints but also to the attempt to coerce fate through magical practices. Through all these phenomena, which should probably be understood as a rebellion of what is dull and unspiritual and somehow sensual against the mind, the equilibrium of the universal harmony of the Baroque period was constantly being threatened.

Thus Baroque man may finally have grown weary of this constant existential tension, so that the time was ripe for the dualistic ideas of Cartesian rationalism, which, without reflection on the possible consequences, were put into practice and were able to shape culture and society. Whereas the ecclesiastical Rococo style reached its summit and perfection from 1740 to 1760, this was followed—according to Hubensteiner—by rigid formalization and decline. This final blaze of glory, however, was due to the still lively faith of the Baroque period, with its pathos, earnestness and gravity, which soon gave way to the light of reason. But that applies only to German-speaking regions: in France the end of the *Grand Siècle* [the 1600s] had already given rise to the enlightened Rococo period.

Whereas philosophical rationalism had made reason absolute, another almost parallel development can be seen in the Rococo style, which brought with it a sort of isolation of the sensual from the spirit. Egon Friedell is of the opinion that the Rococo style, as opposed to the Baroque, is a disintegrating style that in a merely painterly and decorative, playful and ornamental way dissolves the great forms of the earlier period into striking but tasteless effects. He describes Rococo as weary, muted, anemic and decidedly feminine—stylistic decadence par excellence. Symptoms of that hyper-refined, almost convulsive desire for pleasure are presented by that lady who ate a delicious sherbet and commented, "What a shame that it is not a sin!" Thus even the most frivolous and often willful subversion of marriage through the stipulation of paramours in the marriage contract itself —the Italian *cavaliere servente*, known in France as *le petit maître*—was considered a mark of so-called good breeding, and married men who kept no mistresses were ridiculed. The splendor "streaming from Rococo is the phosphorescence of decay". Of course, that is not all there was to the Rococo style.

We find a similar decadence also in expressions of piety, insofar as they proved susceptible to the fashionable influences of the day. There was altogether too much languishing, sighing and melting in the texts of hymns and prayers, so that devotees sang to young Saint Aloysius, for example, "Gonzaga, swiftly aim / at me the dart of love, / and pour into my blood / seraphic ardor." Equally tasteless are the hymns, which were common especially in Pietism, that tell about blood and wounds in macabre detail. On the other hand, things became playful again when, for instance, a song about the Way of the Cross began: "Sinner, come on, get up / and take a walk with me" (a folk song in the Upper Franconian dialect).

In short, isolated sensuousness, once it was detached from the larger contexts of natural and divine truth and the cosmic order, was deprived of its orientation to the whole and was abandoned to itself and thus to decadence.

Protest against Reason

Once the equilibrium was lost, it could not be regained. For the greater the protest, in the name of reason, against Rococo distortion, the more intellect and reason were isolated and made absolute, and the fact that man is also a sensory being, endowed with feelings and temperament, was forgotten.

From now on, in the name of Reason (which in the form of an actress would soon be raised upon the altar in Paris during the Revolution), a bitter, passionate battle was waged against the conventional forms of ecclesiastical, religious and artistic life. Princes and bishops forbade pilgrimages; processions, including those around the fields and vineyards [*Flurumritte*]; and other public displays of religion. A large number of feast days was abolished, and restrictions were placed even on the customs of tolling church bells as a storm warning and setting up Nativity scenes. All this, of course, could not be justified in terms of reason. The texts of hymns and prayers were treated harshly as well. Certainly, there was much in them that needed reform, as we have mentioned. But the new material was not much better than what was discarded. For example: "God, I believe with confidence / what Jesus Christ has taught. / He came and said: Let there be light! / And so it was enlightened." And still worse: "Wherefore let us wiser be and do today, / although it cause us hardship, / what we will wish that we had done / where wishing is of no avail."

What mattered, then, was "rational" religion, virtuousness, purposeful behavior. Even the liturgy and the administration of the sacraments had to serve this purpose. And in these circumstances instruction played the leading role: "Prayer, singing, the administration of the sacraments, church ceremonies, occasional devotional exercises, blessings and all other religious acts have the general and necessary purpose of enriching the understanding of the assembled Christians with new religious information or to impart more clarity and liveliness to the knowledge that they have already acquired" (L. Busch, *Liturgischer Versuch* [Liturgical essay], 1810). What a contrast to the courtly ceremonies of the Baroque liturgy, carried out in the presence of the Divine Majesty and enlisting the help of all the arts.

What experts praised now was the "noble simplicity and silent greatness" that Winckelmann found in the works of the ancient Greeks (1755). When the Catholics in the Protestant capital Ansbach were allowed to build an oratory, it was extolled in these terms: "[T]he dominant impression therein is not the excessive ornamentation usually preferred in Catholic churches but rather a noble simplicity and purity that inspires devotion."

The tendency to make man's reason the standard for the truths of the faith went hand in hand with this. Whatever did not seem "reasonable" was suppressed, opposed, ignored or reinterpreted. For instance, the death of Jesus was no longer regarded as the sacrifice that redeemed the world but rather as a virtuous example of enduring suffering that is inflicted unjustly. But by making reason the criterion for what is true, they had initiated the general attack on revealed religion per se. We recall here the famous fragments by Wolfenbüttler that portray Christ's Resurrection as a deceptive maneuver by the disciples.

Naturally, we cannot ignore the fact that the Enlightenment did not have the same measure of influence every-where. In Catholic Germany, especially in Franconia, the prevailing trend was considerably weakened and essentially deprived of its negative character, so that it could have ben-eficial effects on theology, spiritual life, pastoral ministry, education and care for the poor within the framework of an unbroken ecclesial faith. The realities in the everyday lives of the simple people, which could not be grasped in in-tellectual categories, were a remarkably salutary corrective. Still, that did not stop the enlightened bureaucracy of Count Montgelas in the Upper Palatinate in 1802–1803 from be-ing carried away by the rage for destruction and rampag-ing through churches and monasteries, leaving irreplaceable masterpieces of Baroque art in ruins, because they saw in them nothing more than loathsome relics of benighted su-perstition. The response of the people was unmistakable. They sang about Montgelas:

> He topples churches, plunders altars,
> Candles, bells and poorboxes—
> Be it only for a farthing—
> Vestments, albs and surplices.
>
> More than heretics, Turks and pagans,
> He brings ruin upon the priesthood,
> Dispenses with religious garb
> And then profanes the sanctuary.
>
> For the sake of a few gold braids,
> The relics [of a local saint] must be removed
> From the altar where they were revered
> To a common cemetery.
>
> Swede and Frenchman wreak less havoc
> Throughout all Franconia!
> Take up weapons, be not squeamish!
> Crush him with a righteous hand!

These expressions—and there are many others like them—demonstrate the protest of human nature, which has been deeply offended by the suppression of the senses.

We must conclude here this necessarily fragmentary overview of the changing fate of the relation between man's sensuousness and rationality as it can be observed in the manifestations of cultural and Church history during the Baroque period. The relation itself, which is so strained and variable, is not concluded. It confronts every epoch, including our own, as a task that must always be accomplished anew.

XI

NEW LIFE FROM THE RUINS

.

French Catholicism after 1789

Anyone who reflects on the present and future tasks of the Church and meditates on the new evangelization of Europe must ask himself an almost unavoidable question: Has there ever been anything like it? The answer is just as natural as the question: Obviously! Several times, in fact. Once, at the beginning of the Middle Ages, it was a matter of building anew on the remains of Roman Christianity in Gaul, Britain and Germany. Then the Reformation left in central Europe a heap of rubble that had to be built up again—and finally the de-Christianization of France brought about by the Enlightenment and the French Revolution confronted the Church with the task of a new evangelization.

We content ourselves here with a closer examination of the last-mentioned case. This is primarily because the intellectual-historical, societal and cultural conditions of to-day are still essentially marked by the events of 1789 and are in fact the fully ripened fruit thereof. Naturally, we should bear in mind that, although there is "nothing new under the sun", history does not repeat itself, either. Historical parallels cannot be constructed so easily. Nevertheless, it is always profitable to learn at the school of history, the *magistra vitae*.

Let us go about our task, therefore, in several steps. First we should ask what sort of picture the Church in France presented on the eve of the Revolution; then we must show how the Revolution acted toward Church and religion and what it hoped to gain thereby, and finally we will describe the re-Christianization of France and ask what factors were at work in it and what they were able to accomplish. Then in conclusion we will ask what insights or suggestions for today might result from this historical survey.

The Gallican Church on the Eve of July 14, 1789

Let us be content with the barest of statistical outlines: France had approximately 26 million inhabitants, of whom 500,000 were Protestants and 40,000 were Jews. The 25.5 million Catholics lived in 139 dioceses and in around 40,000 parishes. About 50,000 priests provided for their pastoral care, and in addition, there were approximately 15,000–18,000 canons regular, about 20,000 men in religious communities, and from 30,000 to 40,000 consecrated women religious. The Church owned around 10 percent of the land, which yielded an annual income of 150 million *livres*; the tithe brought in the same amount. Two percent of that was voluntarily paid over to the state. With this income, the Church covered the expenses of the entire educational establishment and of all social service programs as well. This meant that every part of French life was permeated by elements of Church-run institutions. So much for the institutional and societal statistics.

But how did the people regard faith and the Church? Jean de Viguerie distinguishes five types of religious attitudes during the *ancien régime*:

1. Enlightened opponents of religion from intellectual, artistic, commercial and official circles.

2. Enlightened Catholics: some tended toward Deism; others opposed only certain forms of piety that they considered suspect. Both groups could often be found in religious communities, especially among the Oratorians and the Benedictines of Saint-Vanne, also called the Maurists.

3. The Jansenists, who were still numerous: they bitterly criticized everyone who did not share their opinions.

4. Practicing Catholics with weaker convictions and lax morals. And finally:

5. Conscientious, pious Catholics—they were by far the largest group! They worked in all milieus, though less often in the world of business and finance. Innumerable good Catholics lived in the country as well as in the rectories and the cloisters. They met with as much opposition from advocates of the Enlightenment as from the Jansenists. Their attitude was called *fanatisme* by the "enlightened".

De Viguerie sums up: bishops and parish priests were as virtuous and dutiful as ever. But the situation was aggravated by the Enlightenment propaganda against religion and by the intellectual inability of Catholics to respond adequately. The writers of apologetical works argued from within their belief system: for example, unbelief is an insult to God, who is Truth and Love. But one can speak that way only to believers. Thus the defenders of the faith proved to be incapable of confronting unbelievers! The two sides were talking past each other on different levels. To that extent, the accusation of fanaticism leveled against believers by the Enlightenment thinkers was understandable. We are looking, then, at the phenomenon of a very lively, strong faith that was being put into practice but, because it no longer engaged in self-critical reflection, was not in a position to "give an account for the hope" that animated it. A reiteration of the theodicy of High Scholasticism would have been able to accomplish the task;

this proves the necessity of serious intellectual efforts to explain the foundations of faith and the danger of retreating into mere piety. The latter case can perhaps rightly be called "fundamentalism".

The Revolution and Its Consequences

Of course this is only a rough sketch, but such was the Church over which the Revolution swept. Aside from the aforementioned antireligious and in some cases hate-filled propaganda of the Enlightenment, there were several measures with which the Revolution proposed to stamp out the faith and the Church:

1. The nationalization and subsequent sale of all Church property. The buyers thus acquired a vested interest in opposing the Church. On the night before August 4, 1789 —the so-called Night of the Sacrifice—the clergy in the National Assembly renounced their privileges as a separate estate, and the confiscation of all Church lands followed on November 2. This destroyed the foundations for the Church's freedom and independence.

2. The Civil Constitution of the Clergy, dated July 12, 1790, which uprooted the faithful through a complete reorganization of diocesan structures and parishes, four thousand of which were entirely suppressed. Furthermore, the requirement of an oath of loyalty created in practice a new schismatic church and thus a devastating division in the clergy and among the faithful.

3. Next came the annihilation of the religious orders within the space of a year and a half (1791–1792), whereby the wide-ranging and influential pastoral works of the monas-

teries were destroyed also. There was a remnant of religious in Paris, but in the provinces their numbers dwindled to the vanishing point.

4. Banishment and persecution of the *refractaires*, those who refused to take the oath of loyalty. Only around 10 percent of those priests remained in the underground so as to administer the sacraments.

5. The closing and devastation of Church buildings. In 1793–1794 all churches were closed and all the material prerequisites for worship were destroyed.

6. The introduction of the revolutionary calendar, which abolished Sunday, now affected the time dimension of religious practice as well.

7. Marriage and the family were desacralized through civil marriage and divorce.

8. An anticelibacy campaign was then launched so as to sideline most of the clergy.

The decisive criterion was how one reacted to the oath of loyalty to the Civil Constitution of the Clergy and its result, the schismatic church. First we will discuss the clergy in this regard.

The real decision had to be made once Pius VI, after a long delay, had condemned the oath of loyalty to the Civil Constitution in early 1791. The result was that on average, around 52 or 53 percent refused to take the oath and thus gave expression to their loyalty to the pope and the Church in the midst of the most severe reprisals. Here it should not be overlooked that most of the priests who took the oath were by no means acting upon dishonorable motives. Fay sums up the situation as follows:

> Finally, despite the Jacobin clubs, the authorities that had been mobilized, and the newspapers, more than half of the

clergy, the bishops and the pious Catholics rose up en masse
from one end of the country to the other against the Civil
Constitution of the Clergy and against the brutal measures
that had been taken to impose it. Across the land an increasingly contested battle developed between the Jacobins and
the elite Catholics in most cities, marketplaces and villages.
The former did everything that they could to establish the
new schismatic church, even resorting to violence, while
the loyal Catholics vied with one another in enthusiasm,
discretion and ingenious heroism in order to maintain the
liturgy despite the persecutions that were now beginning.

Despite numerous compelling martyrdoms, a regular underground Church developed, which the priests and the
faithful kept alive by risking their own lives. Their mot-
toes were circulated on thousands of slips of paper that read:

> Obey men—but God first.
> Profess one faith—the faith of Rome alone.
> Submit to the pope and likewise to the bishop.
> In them alone acknowledge the Church and her pastors.
> Be unshakably devoted to the true shepherds.
> From them alone receive doctrine and the sacraments.
> Flee from the Masses and preaching of the schismatics.

Now, with the September Massacre of 1792, the great
persecution of Catholics was unleashed. In the course of it
about half of the priests, the ones who had taken the constitutional oath, fell away. Of the remaining priests, more
than a thousand paid for their loyalty with their lives. That
was also true of the laity, who likewise produced many martyrs. Among them was—to mention only one example—
a mother who was hauled off to the guillotine because she
had taken in her son, who was a priest. They died in the
most edifying circumstances in the full knowledge that they

were martyrs. "Fanatics", Voltaire used to say, "deserve no tolerance" (Viguerie).

Nevertheless, the de-Christianization brought about by the Revolution certainly must be called a success. After the persecutions ceased, we find the following picture: only two-thirds of the population, at best, still practiced their religion. There were regions where the rate sank considerably lower. The papal nuncio in Paris wrote in 1826: "More than half of the French are completely ignorant of their duties as Christians and live indifferently from day to day. It is doubtful whether ten thousand still practice their faith in all of Paris."

A New Beginning of Ecclesiastical Life

Now, however, we must describe and analyze the process that led to the new evangelization of France in the first half of the nineteenth century. Two important stages should be distinguished: the first during the reign of Napoleon and the second during the Bourbon Restoration.

It is testimony to Napoleon's genius as a statesman that after the fall of the Directory in early November of 1799, he plainly put an end to the official antireligious persecution and was intent on establishing new relations between the French Republic and the Church. It was the initiative of the First Consul that led to the 1800 concordat between France and the Holy See. The historical importance and momentousness of this agreement cannot be overestimated. What was at stake, basically, was nothing less than the initial attempt to incorporate the Church institutionally into a governmental system that no longer owed its foundations and legitimacy to Christianity. The basis for this attempt now was a purely statistical fact: namely, that the majority of

Frenchmen adhered to the Catholic faith. Another essential and consequential feature of this concordat was the fact that it was signed by the French Republic and the pope. Thus the old Gallican ideology, the concept of a "national Church" that for centuries had impeded relations between Rome and France, was basically overcome and an ultamontane orientation for French Catholicism was established. This concordat contained, no doubt, quite a few provisions that did not favor the Church, yet it was of inestimable benefit for her. The years of division between Constitutional Catholics and those loyal to Rome were over, a new ecclesiastical organization recognized by the state could be built again, and the persecutions were definitively ended. This fulfilled the prerequisite institutional conditions for a revival of the Catholic faith in France. The framework now needed to be filled in.

Decisive intellectual support along these lines was provided by several major authors who managed to have a lasting influence on the intellectual climate of French society and to counteract the effects of Voltaire and the Enlightenment. Here we will mention only one example, Chateaubriand, who in April 1802 published his famous work *La génie du Christianisme*, which was followed in 1809 by the novel *Les martyrs, ou le triomphe de la religion*. The edition of his complete works that appeared from 1826 to 1831 comprises thirty-two volumes.

Viscount François René de Chateaubriand, who was born in 1769 in Brittany and died in 1848 in Paris, is probably so representative of this process of intellectual change because his career followed the intellectual trends that defined his era. Having an enthusiastic temperament, he was initially an avid reader of Voltaire, the Encyclopedists and Rousseau; then he spent several restless and aimless years traveling in

America and England. In 1800, shaken by the deaths of his mother and sister, he returned to the faith. The product of this conversion was his aforementioned masterpiece of 1802.

> In marvelous, ingeniously evocative language he orchestrated themes that many eighteenth-century apologists had already broached, but he no longer channeled the religious yearning of his contemporaries toward a vague Christianity à la Rousseau but rather directly to the Catholic Church with her dogmas, sacraments and rituals. His book demolished the eighteenth-century prejudices that had accused Catholicism of barbarism and mediocrity and portrayed it as a salutary haven for all who are suffering in soul or body, and as a source of poetic inspiration that is just as fruitful as pagan antiquity. (Aubert)

The huge, long-lasting success that *La génie du Christianisme* met with shows what a deep longing for religion was present in all circles of French society in the postrevolutionary years and also that this longing reached a certain peak around the year in which the concordat was signed. Chateaubriand succeeded in satisfying the urgent existential longing for religion with Catholic content, and he thereby contributed, as quite a few other authors did, to the Catholic revival in France.

Religious Orders Founded

These institutional and intellectual developments, which affected all of French society, meanwhile led to individual religious initiatives that were nonetheless numerous. Of particular importance were the foundations of new religious communities. This was especially significant given the fact that in 1790 around half of all consecrated religious had doffed the habit and left the cloisters and monasteries. Now, after the fall of the *Directoire*, new life was stirring. The renowned seminary of Saint-Sulpice was reopened; the Sacred Heart Fathers, founded by émigré priests in Louvain, joined up with an Italian community that planned to replace the Society of Jesus, which had been disbanded. In the following year, 1800, Saint Madeleine-Sophie Barat founded the Society of the Sacred Heart of Jesus, which soon opened girls' boarding schools in Amiens, Grenoble, Chambéry, Lyons and Poitiers. The same Father Varin who had encouraged this foundation also inspired the foundation of the Sisters of Notre Dame de Namur, which likewise pursued an educational apostolate for girls. On Christmas Day of 1800, Father Coudrin, renowned for his heroic service in the underground Church, founded the Picpus Missionaries, which would soon find their field of action in Oceania. In the Cévennes, a mountainous region in southern France, Father Lapierre started the Basilian Fathers, who later worked in America, and in Bordeaux Father Chaminade brought the Society of Mary to life. The Sisters of Charity were formed in Besançon by Saint Jeanne Antide Thouret, while in Lothringen Madame de Méjanes founded the Daughters of the Holy Childhood of Jesus and Mary. The Holy Ghost Fathers, the Vincentians, the Paris Foreign Missions and the Brothers of the Christian Schools returned, and Father Clorivière founded an order of men and one of women modeled on the Society of Jesus, which had been dissolved. Other new women's communities were the Sisters of Saint Joseph of Cluny, the Sisters of Saint Mary Magdalene, of Saint Clothilde, and so forth.

In the years 1802–1814, at least 1,253 religious communities were approved, along with around 50 that had not re-

ceived authorization. In the year 1814, 12,400 women religious were living in 1,776 houses; there are no statistics for
the men's communities. Yet there was still more to the religious revival. The episcopate that governed the Church in
France under the concordat was generally distinguished for
its zeal and conscientiousness, especially in making the visitation of parishes. Catechetical instruction was reorganized,
and after the Holy Year of 1803 a wave of popular missions
began to spread through the land. A renewal of apologetical
preaching provided for the needs of the educated classes, especially in Paris and other cities. As an outstanding example
of this, we should mention the famous conferences held by
Monsignor Frayssinous in Paris, followed later by the even
more famous Lacordaire.

The Role of the Laity

Let us turn now, however, to the part that the laity played
in the religious reawakening in France. With this topic we
make a transition from Napoleon's consulate and imperial
reign to the Restoration of the Bourbon royalty after the
Battle of Waterloo. That event was of the utmost importance for French Catholicism. Convinced as ever of the
divine right of the hereditary dynasty, the broad-based legitimist circles saw a future for France only in a close association of crown and Church. Besides the fact that the immoral
conduct of several Bourbon kings was a slap in the face to
any religious claim of the monarchy, their legitimist adherents blocked the way to future democratic developments, to
the great detriment of the Church. Valuable intellectual and
political forces of French Catholicism were thereby bound
and crippled, and Catholics soon split into two opposing
wings.

At first, however, it was precisely the lay movements that stood up for the Church; they backed the king at the same time, however, which made it considerably more difficult, if not impossible, for them to dismantle the intellectual and social machinery of the Revolution, even though there was no disputing their apostolic activities and successes. The laypeople now came onto the scene, and there was good precedent for it. Back in the days of Louis XIV, the laity had formed at court a powerful elite in the *Compagnie du Saint Sacrément*, and wherever this association was influential, they promoted the interests of the Church to the best of their ability by personal sacrifices.

Now, in 1801 the so-called *Congrégation* had been founded by a former Jesuit in Paris. It originally comprised six students of medicine and law; three years later it already numbered 180 members, who belonged one and all to the highest and thus the most influential social circles. Soon they made headway in the provinces, too, where comparable associations were formed in around sixty cities, often after popular missions.

Close personal connections between the leading figures of the *Congrégation* and the monarchist secret society, the *Chevaliers de la foi* [Knights of the faith], made the *Congrégation* appear to historians to be a secret society also with the supposed purpose of dominating government and the civil service. More recent research, however, has brought to light the essentially religious character of the *Congrégation*. Nevertheless, its influence was great, since its members started quite a few highly effective charitable, social and apostolic lay organizations that cared for the poor and the sick, performed social work for members of the new industrial working class, provided catechetical instruction for children and distributed Catholic literature. An extremely impressive network of such initiatives soon extended throughout the land.

Incidentally, it should be noted that there was no centralized organization to speak of.

Besides Paris and Bordeaux, Lyons in particular was a center for religious initiatives by the laity; its far-reaching influence was felt even in Italy. Here, for example, a very young woman named Pauline Jaricot established the Propagation of the Faith for the financial and spiritual support of the missions, a work that is still flourishing today. When anticlerical tendencies resurfaced in the government and the civil service, the Association for the Defense of the Catholic Religion was formed in 1826; its publication became the famous newspaper *Le Correspondant*. We mention this as just one example of the Catholic press, which was thriving and expanding during those years and which soon found its outstanding exponent in the ingenious Breton convert and priest Félicité Robert de Lamennais, whose newspaper *L'Avenir* [The future] became in 1830 the mouthpiece of his ultramontane campaign.

Structures and Factors

Now we must analyze this process of Catholic revival, which could be presented here only in rough outline form.

In making this attempt, we first make two observations. Without exception, these undertakings harked back to the spiritual tradition of prerevolutionary times. There are hardly any substantially new accents in the spirituality; Catholics drew from the sources of Paray-le-Monial, Saint-Sulpice, Saint-Lazare and so forth. From them had flowed the strength that had empowered the resistance to the Enlightenment and the Revolution. One new and extremely fruitful element was the ultramontane orientation that characterized almost all the groups and initiatives of this new beginning, even those marked by the legitimist ideology. Napoleon had been the one who—contrary to all his intentions—by his brutal treatment of Pius VI and Pius VII, the plundering of the papal states and the abduction of the two popes to Valence and Fontainebleau, respectively, had suddenly directed the sights of the faithful of the self-assured, independently minded Gallican Church back to the pope as the visible center and foundation of the faith and the Church. The fact that both popes named Pius, despite their worldly helplessness, had opposed the reckless usurper and tyrant with unflinching courage earned them the admiration of all Europe. The journey of Pius VII to Napoleon's coronation, despite the latter's deliberate chicanery, became a triumphal procession of the pope, who was greeted along his way of the cross by waves of devout enthusiasm. The love and affection for the successor of Peter that were so typical of the nineteenth century, especially in France, had one of its deeper roots in that papal journey. Add to that the historical signing of the concordat: Napoleon had passed over the French episcopate, which no longer existed as a homogeneous corpus, and had selected instead the pope as the other party to it. In this turning of the "eldest daughter of the Church" toward Rome, after having been so emphatically Gallican, we see an essential factor in the re-Christianization of France.

An equally important factor was the *substance* of Napoleon's concordat with the Holy See, which has already been mentioned repeatedly. Only a spiritualistic dilution of the concept of Church could cause someone to disparage a concordat. Although a functioning diocesan or parochial administration is no substitute for faith, hope and charity, it is nonetheless an important prerequisite for an orderly proclamation of the faith and sacramental ministry. Often it takes the collapse of these structures to make their importance evident. Thus the religious reconstruction would have been unthinkable without the "Church of the concordat". And the religious awakening of the intellectual and literary circles in France must not be forgotten in this regard. Editions of religious and apologetic writings ran to the millions; their edifying influence could be compared favorably with the intellectual ruin that the Enlightenment and revolutionary propaganda had managed to accomplish before. Remarkable in the highest degree, however, is the absolutely explosive spread of revived or newly founded apostolic religious communities. That means that no less than thousands of young people committed themselves to a life ruled by strict ascetic principles, which was not possible without a corresponding religious motive. What is especially astonishing about this is that there was among them a succession of communities that, despite the religious situation in the French homeland, immediately turned their efforts to the foreign missions. If there is ever an unerring sign of the spiritual and religious vitality of the Church, then it is missionary zeal.

Now, though, an urgent question arises; to answer it requires the Church historian to walk a real methodological tightrope, on which the danger of falling to one side or the other is equally great and ever present: we mean the question about the causes of this Catholic reawakening in postrevolutionary France. The believing theologian could all too readily take up the handy axiom, venerable because it was formulated by Tertullian: *Sanguis martyrum semen christianorum* —"The blood of martyrs is the seed of Christians." But we must not make matters so simple for ourselves: God's grace and its pathways elude the glance of the critical historian, who knows that he must rely on verifiable information from sources and eyewitness testimonies if he wants to satisfy the strict requirements of the methodology. Nevertheless, one should not overlook the fact that the courageous witness to the faith, even unto death, that was given thousands of times by the victims of the Revolution, who came from all walks of life, must have made some impression on their contemporaries, to the extent that they were not completely brutalized and callous. Many who had been present at such a martyrdom must have remembered the events that they had witnessed for the rest of their lives. Moreover, memories often develop their own dynamic in the soul. It is true, furthermore, that the vigor [*élan*] that had driven so many of the French to put up religious resistance and had endured in the underground Church that was loyal to the pope and that was ultimately victorious could now unfold increasingly under the conditions of the concordat and during the Restoration. Here, too, the example of heroic fidelity given by so many priests and Catholics of every age, sex and social station produced its effects.

Similarly, the question arises as to the motives that prompted the First Consul to bring about the religious pacification of France. Some think that Napoleon was not so unreligious as it is generally assumed but rather allowed himself to be guided absolutely by rudimentary religious sentiments; others, however, speak about the cool, sober deliberations of statesmanship that provided the initiative. The latter, in any case, would be verifiable and could also be documented by appropriate statements by Napoleon. But how such reflections come about in the first place, how it happens that the good example—whether of martyrs or of confessors—really fires the popular imagination: these are the questions that methodological honesty forbids the historian to answer. One thing here is certain: sociological, psychological, formalist-cultural or political-economical categories

are inadequate to explain such historical developments. The
believer who knows that nothing good is possible without
the grace of God and who knows also that God's grace can
be obtained and indeed merited by prayer and sacrifice, cannot help recognizing in all these new religious beginnings
in postrevolutionary France the harvest of what was sown
in tears between 1789 and 1800 in the furrows that the Revolution had plowed up.

A Prospect

With that last sentence, we could and actually should conclude this essay. Yet the temptation that besets the historian,
to don the prophet's mantle after looking back in history,
entices us to venture a glance at future horizons. Naturally
there can be no question of prognoses for the third millennium of Christian history. The prophet speaks to the present
moment, speaks for today. What should and must happen
with our cooperation, therefore, if we want to accomplish
what we can in laying the foundations for a new flowering
of faith and the Church?

We observe in our days an awakening of the longing for
knowledge about the mystery of the world and of man,
which cannot be grasped by reason but can only be intu-
ited. This is expressed in such dubious phenomena as the
New Age movement, occultism or even satanic practices.
The goal of the Church's proclamation of the faith should
be to guide these longings, which are dimly felt rather than
fully conscious, to their true objects and to fill them with the
genuine contents of the Catholic faith. In much the same
way that a new approach to Catholic apologetics around

1800 managed to interest the educated public, which had been disillusioned with the Enlightenment and its rationalism, in the faith again and to win over a good number of them, so too today we should try to formulate clearly the deepest, to some extent unconscious but nevertheless troubling and urgent, questions of today's society and then to answer them out of the fullness of the Catholic faith. This would have to be done using a manner of argumentation and a language that reaches the ears of contemporary man, just as Chateaubriand and de Maistre were able to do under different circumstances almost two hundred years ago.

XII

GERMAN CATHOLICISM AND ITS OCCASIONAL BOUTS OF FEVER

The 1995 *Kirchenvolksbegehren* [Church-people's petition drive], which to many observers may have seemed like a menacing monster, assumes its proper dimensions (which are quite modest) when examined from the perspective of the historian. "Nothing new in Germany!" It is enough to recall similar disturbances in the last few centuries.

In nineteenth-century Baden and Württemberg, there was a late-blooming Enlightenment flower that heralded the Revolution of 1848: the "Attack on Celibacy" ["*Zölibatssturm*"] and anticelibacy societies. Twenty-three laymen from Freiburg, headed by the privy councilor Duttlinger, filed a petition in 1828 with the Chamber of Deputies of the Diet in Baden (of all places) formally requesting that the government abolish celibacy. The chamber had enough sense to reject the demand. An attempt to mobilize the masses by means of the press failed. The renowned theologian from Tübingen Johann Adam Möhler, in contrast, had success with his persuasive defense of celibacy.

Now protest was stirred up in Mainz. The chief agitator against celibacy was the Protestant professor Wilhelm Hoffmann, who now claimed to have proved that celibacy was patently detrimental to the state and society. His fiasco did not prevent him from presenting his proposal again in 1832–1833. This time, in fact, 156 priests of the Archdiocese of

Freiburg and fifty candidates for the priesthood joined in his demands, and there were big waves in the Diocese of Rottenburg, too. An anticelibacy society was soon founded, which within a short time numbered almost two hundred clerical members.

The response of the Catholic populace, however, was severe: they boycotted the anticelibates, who soon found themselves alone in their churches. More than forty localities declared to the king of Württemberg that they would rather have no pastor than a wedded one. Under pressure from the mordant satire with which this topic was soon bandied about in the press, the government prohibited the anticelibacy society. The annals of history record no response whatsoever on the part of the bishops.

Campaigns for Democratization

The reaction was more energetic in Limburg, where such attempts were nipped in the bud by the bishop. Yet it wasn't just a question of celibacy there—it was also a matter of democracy in the Church! There were loud demands for "synods": mixed synods to be attended by both clergy and laity, as a sort of provincial diet.

Archbishop Boll of Freiburg im Breisgau, who saw through the hidden agenda and suspected what was meant by the demand that Catholics "march forward with the spirit of the age", said No, and ultimately this attempt at democratization ran aground against his refusal. It was only to be expected that the maneuver would be imitated in Rottenburg. There the matter led to an interesting alignment of forces, whereby the cathedral rector Jaumann spouted polemics against those Catholics who "were more papal than the pope, more

Catholic than the Catholic world" and defended the democratizers, while the politician Baron Hornstein decisively opposed them.

A new initiative followed in Freiburg, where in 1845 Dean Kuenzer set in motion a signature campaign calling for a "mixed" diocesan synod; he eventually took over the presidency of an association for "the promotion of ecclesiastical life", which had been founded in 1838 by Professor Fischer —a priest from Luzerne who lived with a concubine—for the purpose of "forcibly warding off the excessive interference of the papacy". They tried especially to recruit teachers. The somewhat feeble archbishop turned to the state for help in counteracting this association—in vain.

Ethnic-German Catholicism

All this was only the prelude to a substantially more far-reaching movement that was supposed to produce an "enlarged and expanded edition" of the anticelibacy propaganda, the "democratization" of the Church and the repudiation of the "foreign influence of Rome": this was the *Deutschkatholizismus* [Ethnic-German Catholicism] of Father Johannes Ronge, an assistant pastor from Breslau.

Theologically ignorant and without a real vocation, he had been ordained a priest after squandering his years as a student and immediately made a shipwreck of his faith and celibacy. Relieved of his ministry after a conflict with the diocesan chancery in Breslau, he realized—provoked by the approaching pilgrimage to Heilig-Rock in Trier—that his opportunity to attack Rome had come. He rose to the occasion with an aggressively bombastic and equally stupid open letter to Bishop Arnoldi of Trier in which he made fun of the pilgrimage to the shrine, defamed the bishop and announced his slogan: Christianity without Rome, without dogma, without sacrament and without priests (and of course without celibacy)!

He turned to "his fellow German citizens" and exhorted them "with all their might and decisively to counter at last and put a stop to the tyrannical power of the Roman hierarchy"—thus spoke the former assistant pastor from Breslau. And he became the hero of the day! He was called a new Luther. He found an ally in Father Johannes Czersky, another parochial vicar who likewise had been suspended for breach of celibacy and had then founded a "Christian Catholic Church" in Schneidermühl. And now Ronge began a triumphal procession through northern, western and southwestern Germany, which had to come to a halt, though, at the border of Bavaria. His audience consisted of Catholics who were personally at odds with their Church, Protestants (mainly the petty bourgeoisie and upper middle class of the cities), and discontented Protestant pastors and Catholic priests fleeing from celibacy. From among them were recruited the preachers of the "German Catholic Church".

There was even a council in Leipzig in late March of 1845. Its president: the stenography teacher Wigard. The leading role was played by the theater cashier Robert Blum, later the leader of the extreme left-wing movement at Saint Paul's Church in Frankfurt, who after the collapse of the Vienna Revolution in 1848 was executed there by firing squad.

There was nothing left of genuine Christianity; the dogma of the new "church" was stale rationalism, and its morality was restricted to social and educational initiatives. The Leipzig "council" also left the interpretation of the Bible up to each individual, along with the decision as to whether one wanted to believe in the divinity of Jesus Christ or not.

The papacy, confession and specifically Catholic spirituality were discarded. They devised for themselves a German-language liturgy and for the "Lord's Supper" passed around bread and wine. It went without saying that preachers were freely chosen by the congregations.

Elated at having accomplished a great deed, Ronge exclaimed: "Ah, I shudder to think that we nearly perished! But now it is over. The great gamble was successful, the progress of this century has been salvaged. Germany's genius is already reaching for the laurel wreath—and Rome must fall!"

The enthusiastic applause that Ronge received from the rationalist camp of Protestants was significant. Even the court in Berlin paid him notice, and the Prussian regime supported him also at first. Yet Rome did not fall, and around 1860 the uproar was over. The remnants drifted off into the godless movement of the *Lichtfreunde* [Friends of light] and elsewhere.

National Church?

Meanwhile, the ultramontane movement, a distinguishing mark of the pontificate of Pius IX that was made up of Catholics who were consciously Rome-oriented and loyal to the pope, developed strength in Germany as well, and of course it precipitated "antiultramontane" reactions. The "Syllabus" of Pius IX with its condemnation of rationalism, liberalism, communism, the all-powerful state and so forth, had elicited the shrillest protests from the liberal bourgeoisie. In their view, modern culture and civilization as a whole were being threatened by a sinister Roman-Jesuitical, medieval conspiracy. Its goal: world domination by the pope!

Now, during the preparations for the First Vatican Council, an alliance was formed [in German-speaking lands], based on their common protest against Rome and its "ultramontane machinations", between antiultramontane-nationalist Catholics and liberal Protestantism, represented by the Protestant Union [*Protestantenverein*], the leaders of which had long since broken with the authentic faith in Christ.

"Catholic unions" sprang up everywhere, especially in southwestern Germany; their goal was nothing more and nothing less than a common Protestant-Catholic German national church that would be Rome-free, and of course dogma-free as well. The *Allgemeine Zeitung*, the German newspaper with the largest readership, became the mouthpiece of this movement, which then led to the *Kulturkampf* after the council in 1869–1870 promulgated its dogmas concerning the papacy. The fruit of this anticonciliar agitation was Old Catholicism. It was essentially a movement of university professors and middle-class citizens that initially gained a following but soon dwindled away. Although the anti-Roman protest was openly supported by the government bureaucracy also, the Catholic people never joined in with it anywhere.

On the contrary: in the wake of the council, German Catholicism, which proved to be increasingly loyal to the pope, exhibited an amazing resurgence. Popular piety, social and charitable projects, associations, religious communities, commitment to the worldwide missions—all of this flourished mightily, and resistance to the arrogance of the state-based *Kulturkampf* united Catholics, clergy and the episcopate into an impressive phalanx, against which even the efforts of a Bismarck failed.

The later movement to "separate from Rome", which was the talk of the initial years of the twentieth century, had hardly any success in Germany, either. It was a different story in Austria. Through the 1882 Linz program of the German nationalists in Austria and the Pan-German Union founded in 1893, which was both anti-Catholic and anti-Semitic, the leaders of the latter sought to bring about the incorporation of German-speaking Austria into the German Reich and also the separation of Austrian Catholics from Rome as preparation for the establishment of an "ethnic-German" ["*deutschrassigen*"] united national religion. In Austria, however, this movement had considerable success well into the years after the First World War. Therein lie the historical roots of the present-day crisis of Austrian Catholicism.

At the end of this rapid review of the "bouts of fever" that German Catholicism has suffered, an insight comes to mind: besides the temptations of rationalism and liberalism, that is, of untrammeled Enlightenment thinking and attitudes about life, there was always a nationalist current at work as well, which valued German culture [*Deutschtum*] more than being Catholic. In this German national sentiment, some liberal Catholics were in agreement with the Protestants—and both groups were suspicious of "foreign Roman influence". Liberalism sought a German Christianity as a national united religion, as the basis for national unity, long before Hitler invented his "German Christians".

And Today?

Nevertheless, all these bouts of fever passed. Ultimately, the healthy sense of the faith remained resistant to the tones of the Pied Piper's flute. That being said, however, we have still not answered the question as to whether we can rely on that proven resistance in the present crisis as well. And it is to be doubted. Conditions today are different. The power of the mass media, to which the great majority of Catholics are exposed; the lack of spiritual leadership from a theologically disoriented and diffident clergy—all this makes Catholics susceptible to the spirit of the age. And its prophets have it very easy in dealing with a television society that to a great extent has lost its critical faculties. Then, too, there is the cultural collapse that has affected almost all departments of social life, which is expressed also in an acute crisis of faith in German Catholicism. What made the latter so capable of resistance in the upheavals of bygone history were the close ties of the bishops with the pope; the intellectual uniformity and consistency of the clergy; and the unity of the lay faithful with the pope, the bishops and the priests.

If German Catholicism is to emerge from its present crisis reinvigorated, as it has done from past storms, then a high degree of commitment is required. That, however, will be possible only if bishops and the pope, priests and their bishop, the laity and their priests once again stand shoulder to shoulder, as has proved to be effective in the past, and if people awaken from the delusion that the cure for the Church is the German way of doing things.

XIII

THE COUNCIL
AND THE COUNCILS

Vatican II in the Context of Conciliar History

"From now on, general councils are superfluous!" This remark, hawked for popular consumption [in the late nineteenth century] by the famous Protestant historian of canon law Paul Hinschius of Berlin, probably reflected just as accurately the general opinion after the First Vatican Council had promulgated the dogmas concerning the supreme pastoral authority and the magisterial infallibility of the pope on July 18, 1870. That this view was groundless, however, is demonstrated by the fact that the [project of drafting a comprehensive] code of canon law that was taken up after the conclusion of the council and incorporated much of the preliminary work done for the council—which had to be interrupted on account of the Franco-Prussian War—that this *Codex iuris canonici*, I say, which was enacted in 1918, contained eight canons defining the canonical status of the general council in the life of the Church and regulating the manner in which it is to be carried out. That is not surprising, for throughout the existence of the Church of Jesus Christ, there have always been councils in one form or another. That this would remain so even after the definition of papal authority at Vatican I was as clear to the participants then as it is to us today. This quite effortlessly leads us to the topic of this essay, which attempts to portray Vatican II (1962–1966) both in comparison and in connection with the previous general councils.

What Is a Council?

But first let us clarify our terminology and ask what a general or an ecumenical council is. That can be stated in a few dry words which, however, do not make the matter at all comprehensible. A council, then, is an assembly of those invested with ecclesiastical teaching and pastoral authority for the purpose of exercising this teaching and pastoral authority collectively. If participants are invited to this gathering from all regions of the Universal Church, and if they conduct their business under the presidency of the pope or of his representatives, then this assembly is called a general or an ecumenical council, whereby "ecumenical" here, in contradistinction to our modern use of the term, refers to the origin of the council participants from the *oikuméne*, that is, the entire inhabited world.

"*Concilium episcoporum est*"—a council is the bishops' business. Thus the wording of a principle that the Council of Chalcedon had already formulated in the year 451 as something uncontested and self-evident.

The exercise of teaching and pastoral authority within the Church is, of course, connected inseparably, albeit in a differentiated way, with Holy Orders. That means that only a man who has become a member of the college of bishops through the reception of episcopal consecration and the canonical conferral of pastoral authority can participate *iure proprio*, by his own canonical right, in such a collegial decision-making process. Since the High Middle Ages, higher-ranking religious superiors have been invited also; although they are not bishops, they do have quasi-episcopal jurisdiction over their orders, which is conferred upon them by the pope.

This episcopal consecration, which imparts to the recipient the fullness of the sacrament of Holy Orders, at the same time leaves on the soul of the ordained man an indelible mark that conforms him personally [*in seinem Personsein*] to Christ as the real Pastor, Teacher and Priest. In this supernatural, ontological *configuratio cum Christo* is also rooted his participation in the teaching and pastoral ministry of Jesus Christ. This same sacramentally grounded participation is therefore also the real basis for his fully authorized participation and collaboration in a council. Now, because a council is made up of participants who stand in such a sacramentally constituted relationship with the glorified Christ, one can apply to a council also the Lord's promise to his Apostles: "He who hears you hears me, and he who rejects you rejects me, and he who rejects me rejects him who sent me."

From this follows logically and immediately the authority and legally binding character of conciliar decrees that claim to define the doctrinal and moral teaching of the Church. Very early on, at the latest around the year 400, Church leaders cited in this regard chapter 15 of the Acts of the Apostles, which tells about the assembly of the Apostles in Jerusalem, the so-called Council of Jerusalem. Its decisions, however, are introduced by the formula: "It has seemed good—ἔδοξεν—to the Holy Spirit and to us", that is, "the Holy Spirit and we have decided." Therefore, it is in keeping with the most ancient belief of the Church that a collegial act of those responsible for the teaching and pastoral ministry owes its binding character and authority to the cooperation of the Holy Spirit. Definitive doctrinal decrees of a council are therefore the expression of magisterial infallibility, that is, of the Church's inerrancy in matters of doctrine, which is why they bind the faithful in conscience.

We see, therefore, that a council by its very structure is light-years away from a church parliament, understood democratically, even though certain external similarities in their manner of proceeding could suggest otherwise. For instance, there is voting at a council, but doctrine is by no means created by the decision of the majority. It is contained, rather, in the Church's deposit of faith, which has been revealed and handed down; the bishops testify to it as authentic witnesses to Sacred Tradition and if need be act as judges to distinguish it from error. That is the meaning of a conciliar vote, which, as we have said, is essentially different from a democratic majority decision. It goes without saying that this is precisely the reason also for the fundamental difference between a council or a synod of the Catholic Church and what is referred to within the context of the Protestant Reformation as a synod. A Lutheran or a Reformed synod is in fact an instrument for democratic consensus building and decision making. That is out of the question within the Catholic Church or even the Orthodox Church.

A general council, also called a general synod, is accordingly the organ for the communal exercise of the teaching and pastoral ministry of the Church by the members of the college of bishops assembled under the leadership of the pope. We speak about a regional or a provincial synod when the bishops of a region or an ecclesiastical province gather for the same purpose. Such a synod (i.e., such a particular or local council) then exercises ecclesiastical teaching and pastoral authority over that particular region or province whose bishops have assembled.

"*Concilium episcoporum est!*" This means also that a diocesan synod can be called a synod only in the broader sense, since only one bishop who is vested with his own ordinary authority as pastor is present and active at it. Auxiliary bishops have no autonomous pastoral authority and therefore cannot form a real council or synod together with the local ordinary—not even if there are five active auxiliary bishops, as for example in the Diocese of Münster. The only one who exercises teaching and pastoral authority at a diocesan synod is the chief shepherd of the diocese. He alone, then, is responsible for the decrees that he enacts after consultation with the synod participants—it is not their decision at all. So much, then, for clarification of terminology.

Now, of course, someone could say that this is a holy icon bathed in a mystical glow by the light of many little oil lamps rather than a realistic historical depiction of the institution known as a council. One might ask, doesn't conciliar history provide instead an abundance of data about all-too-human events at councils, about power struggles, intrigues, vanities, even expressions of aggressiveness, and so forth? Wasn't the man right who once said in reference to Vatican I that that council had gone through three phases: first the phase of men, second that of the devil and finally that of the Holy Spirit?

No doubt there is much truth to that. Nor is it surprising, provided that one does not overlook the fact that divine truth and grace in the Church are never "chemically pure" but rather always appear in the earthly garb of a pilgrim, which not infrequently is covered with dust and in need of mending here and there. This experience, however, is not prejudicial to the fact—which can be grasped only by faith, of course—that a general council, whenever it deserves the name and makes this claim, indeed governs the Church and teaches in Christ's name and by his authority.

A List of Councils?

Now, if we ask which councils this applies to and how many there are in all, we must take another step in treating our topic (which is to describe Vatican II in connection with and against the backdrop of the previous ecumenical councils); not only that, but we have also brought up a central problem in historical research into the councils in general. When John XXIII convoked the Second Vatican Council and numbered it the twenty-first general council, he acted with his characteristic nonchalance, without first consulting at length the Church historian that he himself was. The historian surely would have told him that so far there is no historically certified list of the general councils, much less an official ecclesiastical count.

The list to which Pope John simply added Vatican II as the twenty-first ecumenical council was drawn up by a commission of experts headed by Cardinal and later Saint Robert Bellarmine in the year 1595. That means no more and no less than this: the number of general councils, now as then, is the object of scholarly research. It also implies that the number and names of the councils with which we intend to compare Vatican II in this essay are by no means settled. But we need not go into those details now, nor should they be an obstacle. Material for comparison is available in such abundance that it cannot all be marshaled. We just won't describe Vatican II simply as the "twenty-first" council.

What sort of a figure, then, does the ecclesiastical assembly of the years 1962–1966 cut in comparison with its predecessors? Well, at Vatican II, we don't encounter, as we do for instance at Trent, two bishops who tore each other's beards out in the heat of the debate. Nor do we hear that a group of Frenchmen threw their fellow synod fathers from

England off the seating platform, as happened at Basel. Nor was what occurred at Constantinople in 786 repeated in 1962 in Rome, namely, that the imperial troops prevented the first attempt of the seventh ecumenical council to convene by attacking and dispersing the council fathers, so that the council finally had to be held in Nicaea.

The Council of Superlatives

Joking aside: the first impression that Vatican II makes on the conciliar historian is that in many respects it was the council of superlatives. Let's start with the fact that never before in the history of the Church was a council prepared so thoroughly as Vatican II. Certainly, the previous council was also very well prepared when it began on December 8, 1869. The theological quality of the prepared schemas was probably even better than that of the following council. Nevertheless, there is no overlooking the fact that the number of the initial ideas and suggestions sent in from all over the world and the method of processing them surpassed anything that had gone before.

Vatican II conspicuously proved to be the council of superlatives on October 11, 1962, when 2,440 bishops—a huge number—processed into Saint Peter's Basilica. Whereas Vatican I still had found room for its approximately 642 council fathers in the right transept of Saint Peter's, now the entire nave had been turned into the council hall. It was strikingly evident here that in the hundred years between the two councils, the Church no longer merely claimed to be a worldwide Church but had de facto become one, a fact that was now reflected in the number of bishops—2,440 of them—and in their countries of origin. Furthermore, for the first time in the history of the Church, a council voted by means of electronic technology, and acoustical problems, which had still been a nuisance to the participants in Vatican I, now did not even need to be mentioned.

While we're on the subject of modern communications media, never before 1962 had some one thousand journalists from all over the world been accredited at a council. Thus Vatican II became also the best-known council of all time, a worldwide media event of the first order. It is the council of superlatives in a very particular way, however, with respect to its results. Of the 1,135 pages in one edition of the decrees of all the councils that are usually regarded as being ecumenical (there are about twenty), Vatican II alone produced 315 pages, which is considerably more than one-quarter. Thus our council without any doubt takes up a special position in the series of ecumenical councils, already by material, external criteria.

A Unique Profile

Yet above and beyond these, there are other special features of this council that make it stand out from its predecessors, for instance with relation to the functions of a general council. Councils are supreme teachers, supreme legislators and supreme judges under and together with the pope, to whom, naturally, all these prerogatives belong even without a council. Not every council has exercised each of these functions. Whereas the First Council of Lyons in 1245, for instance, acted as a tribunal by banishing and deposing Emperor Frederick II and furthermore enacted laws, Vatican I neither sat in judgment nor enacted laws but rather decided doctrinal questions exclusively. The Council of

Vienne (1311–1312), in contrast, both sat in judgment and also enacted laws and decided questions about the faith. The same is true about the councils of Florence (1414–1418) and Basel-Ferrara-Florence (1431–1439).

Vatican II, in contrast, neither sat in judgment nor legislated, strictly speaking, nor definitively decided questions of faith. Rather, it exemplified a new type of council, inasmuch as it understood itself to be a pastoral council, concerned with the care of souls, which wanted to present the teaching and instruction of the Gospel in a winning way as a guide to today's world. In particular, it issued no doctrinal decisions whatsoever. John XXIII spoke explicitly about this in his inaugural homily: "The Church has always taken steps against heresies. Many times she has condemned them most severely." Nowadays, however, "the Church prefers to make use of the medicine of grace. . . . She believes that she is responding to the needs of the present time by demonstrating the validity of her teachings rather than by issuing condemnations." Now, as we know many years after its conclusion, it would have been for the council an honorable page in the annals of history if it had followed in the footsteps of Pius XII and found the courage to condemn communism repeatedly and explicitly.

Meanwhile, this aversion to issuing either doctrinal condemnations or dogmatic definitions also led ultimately to conciliar statements having different degrees of authenticity and consequently greater or lesser binding force. Thus, for example, the constitutions *Lumen gentium* on the Church and *Dei Verbum* on divine revelation quite certainly have the character and binding force of authentic doctrinal pronouncements—although even here nothing was taught definitively, in the strict sense—whereas on the other hand the Declaration on Religious Freedom, *Dignitatis humanae*, according to Klaus Mörsdorf, "takes a position on contemporary issues without any apparent normative content". Therefore, the council documents have binding force in widely varying degrees. This was likewise something quite new in conciliar history.

But let us compare, in conclusion, Vatican II with the First Council of Nicaea and with the two councils that preceded it, the Council of Trent (1545–1564) and Vatican I, with regard to their consequences. It is evident that schisms occurred after both Vatican councils. In 1871 the Old Catholics split from the Church in protest against the definitions of the primacy and the infallibility of the pope, and after Vatican II Archbishop Lefèbvre, with a following that to this day [2007] continues to grow, especially in France and America, set out on a path that, unless it takes a turn, will necessarily lead to schism. As contradictory as these two movements may appear, they coincide in their "No" to legitimate developments in the teaching and practice of the Church, a refusal rooted in a disturbed relation to history. Whereas the Old Catholic movement dried up for lack of religious content and was doomed to insignificance because ecclesiastical developments since 1871 pulled the rug out from under their protest, Lefèbvre's movement challenges the Church of today to prove that their protest, too, is unjustified. We can still hope that she might succeed in doing this.

Historical experience might also offer hope in this regard. Councils are not for the short of breath; their work is accomplished over long stretches of history. After the First Council of Nicaea, which defended and defined the true divinity of Jesus Christ against Arius, new battles over the faith then began, which during the postconciliar years increased in bitterness and vehemence until the Nicene dogma finally prevailed, thanks above all to the authority of the popes. The process took more than a generation.

This is quite comparable also to the postconciliar phase of the Council of Trent, which, after the debacles of the Reformation, led to a new flourishing of religious practice, missionary efforts and culture in those parts of Europe that remained Catholic. To describe it, Hubert Jedin coined the expression "the miracle of Trent". We would be mistaken, however, if we thought that this flowering occurred overnight, as it were! After the conclusion of the council in 1564, it took almost a hundred years until its dogmatic and reformatory decrees took effect across the board! This process began, though, wherever and whenever the bishops required that their priests, teachers and officials swear to uphold the Tridentine profession of faith, which Pius IV formulated and prescribed in 1564, about a year before the council ended.

In view of this experience, it seems high time that an analogous profession of faith and loyalty should be made and lived out by all those who serve the Church. The point in time at which that happens could mark the beginning of a genuine implementation of Vatican II, as it did in those days after Trent. Certainly, we could expect from it great things for the Church and the world of today.

In the Mainstream of Tradition

Now, of course, there are many other perspectives, especially of a substantial, theological sort, from which a comparison could be made between our council and other councils in the past. But there would be no end to the investigation. And the only final result of such a study would be that practically every one of the councils known to history, and naturally Vatican II as well, has its own unmistakable character with respect to its structure, progress and substance yet has this in common with all the others: that every council, considered formally, was a collegial exercise of the supreme teaching and pastoral authority of the Church—but with regard to its substance was concerned with presenting, interpreting and applying Sacred Tradition to the contemporary situation. Now, each council makes its specific contribution to this Tradition. It goes without saying that this cannot consist in substantially new additions to the Church's deposit of faith, and certainly not in a departure from the doctrines of the faith previously handed down. It is, rather, a process of unfolding, clarifying and making distinctions that goes on here, indeed, with the help of the Holy Spirit, so that each council with its definitive doctrinal pronouncements enters as an integral part into the Church's Tradition as a whole. To that extent, councils are open and always look forward, toward a more comprehensive, clearer and more relevant proclamation of Church teaching, but never backward. A council can never contradict its predecessors; it can supplement, further define and continue their work.

It is, of course, a different matter with the council as a legislative organ. Legislation can and indeed must always respond to the concrete demands of a particular historical situation—again, naturally, within the framework provided by the faith—and thus is fundamentally subject to change.

One thing may have become clear from these remarks: all this is true of Vatican II as well. It, too, is nothing more —but nothing less, either—than one council among, alongside and after others. It stands neither above nor outside but rather within the series of the Church's ecumenical councils. That this is the case follows, not least importantly, from the way in which almost all the councils understood themselves. It suffices to quote their statements on the subject as well as those of the early Church Fathers concerning this question. They regard Tradition as being the very essence of the councils.

Vincent of Lerins (d. before A.D. 450) already reflects on this expressly in his *Commonitorium*:

> What else has ever been attempted by the decrees of councils except this, that what before was believed in simplicity, this same truth should afterward be believed more earnestly; that what before was preached more indifferently, this same truth should afterward be preached more fervently; that what before was reverenced more carelessly, this same truth should be honored more carefully. This, I say, nor anything beyond, has the Catholic Church (roused by the innovations of heretics) always accomplished by the decrees of her councils; namely, that what at first she had received from the Fathers by Tradition alone, this she should thenceforward also attest to posterity through the autograph of writing; by summing up a great mass of matter in few words, and mainly for the sake of the light of understanding, not for the sake of a new meaning of the faith, by distinguishing them with the property of a new name.

This genuinely Catholic conviction is reflected in the definition of the Second Council of Nicaea (787), formulated as follows:

> We, continuing in the regal path, and following the divinely inspired teaching of our Holy Fathers, and the Tradition of the Catholic Church, for we know that this is of the Holy Spirit, who certainly dwells in it, define in all certitude and diligence . . .

and then follow the crucial sentences of the conciliar decree. Especially important also is the last of the four condemnations: "If anyone rejects all ecclesiastical Tradition either written or not written . . . let him be anathema."

Finally, Vatican II also clearly acknowledges the extent to which it stands in the mainstream of Tradition. The abundance of references to Tradition in the documents of Vatican II is very impressive. The council incorporates a great breadth of Tradition when it cites councils (especially Florence, Trent and Vatican I); the encyclicals and other writings of numerous popes; an abundance of patristic literature; and the great theologians, above all Thomas Aquinas, as the sources from which it draws its teaching. In holding a council, the Church actualizes what is most essentially her own [*ihr eigenstes Wesen*]. The Church—and thus the Council—hands on the faith by living, and she lives by handing on the faith. Tradition is the actual accomplishment of her nature [*ihr eigentlicher Wesensvollzug*].

Break with Tradition?

These observations have already included essential statements concerning the interpretation of any council, of Vatican II as well. Some years ago [1988], Cardinal Ratzinger made the following remarks on this issue, which are internally consistent with what has been said above, while speaking to the bishops of Chile:

> Certainly there is a narrow-minded view that isolates Vatican II. . . . There are many accounts of it which give the impression that, from Vatican II onward, everything has been changed, and that what preceded it has no value or, at best, has value only in the light of Vatican II. The Second Vatican Council has been treated, not as part of the entire living Tradition of the Church, but as an end of Tradition, a new start from zero. Although the Council itself defined no dogma and rather modestly intended that it be understood as a pastoral council, many treat it as though it were a sort of superdogma which makes everything else unimportant.

This impression is heightened especially by what is going on in practice. That which previously was considered most holy—the form in which the liturgy was handed down—suddenly appears as the most forbidden of all things, the one thing that can safely be prohibited. It is intolerable to criticize decisions which have been taken since the Council, but when the great, ancient truths of the Faith are at stake —for instance, the corporal virginity of Mary, the bodily resurrection of Jesus, the immortality of the soul, etc.— there are no complaints or only muted ones. I myself, when I was a professor, observed how the very same bishop who, before the Council, had fired an irreproachable professor on account of his somewhat crude way of speaking, was not prepared, after the Council, to dismiss a professor who openly denied certain fundamental truths of the Faith.

All this leads a great number of people to ask themselves whether the Church of today is really the same Church as the Church of yesterday, or whether something else has been foisted [*untergeschoben*] on them without anyone asking them. The one way in which we can make Vatican II plausible is to present it quite clearly as it is: one part of the one, unbroken [*ganzen*] Tradition of the Church and of her faith.

Thus far Ratzinger's remarks. The only way to comply with them is to interpret the decrees of Vatican II, not in isolation, but rather in light of the whole Tradition. Many times this was not as obvious as it ought to have been. Indeed, in the postconciliar years it was fashionable to compare the Church with a construction site, on which demolition and new construction or rebuilding was going on. Very often in sermons, God's command to Abraham in Genesis 12— "Go from your country and your kindred and your father's house to the land that I will show you"—was interpreted as a challenge to the Church to leave her past and her Tradition behind. People used to say enthusiastically that the bark of Peter was putting out to sea and sailing to new shores. A departure for the unknown, for what is far-off and new was preached—and Tradition became a derogatory term. On the contrary, it should be stated quite emphatically that an interpretation of Vatican II that contradicted Tradition would contradict the nature of the Catholic faith, the Church and the council. Tradition, not the spirit of the age, is the essential element in framing the interpretation.

Certainly a view of today is absolutely indispensable. Today's questions are the ones that have to be answered. But the components of this answer can come from nowhere else but from divine revelation, which was given once and for all and which the Church has handed down to us in unadulterated form through the centuries. This Tradition then represents the criterion for what is true and valid, and each new answer must stand the test.

Against this background, the popular distinction between "preconciliar" and "postconciliar" proves to be extremely dubious, both theologically and historically. A council is never an endpoint or a point of departure, marking off eras into which Church history or even salvation history can be divided. A council is a link in a chain, the end of which no one knows except the Lord of the Church and of history. It can never cause a break; it must remain in the continuity effected by the Spirit.

Neither Beginning nor Conclusion

Now, continuity has something to do with continuation, too. Will there be a Vatican III, then? It is no surprise that many even make such a demand—and this demand is coming from the most contradictory quarters. Some think that a new council should come right now and finally tear down the barriers to today's world, thoroughly democratize the Church, grant access to the sacraments to those who after a failed marriage have entered into a new union, open the way for women to become priests and for priests to become husbands, and bring about reunion with the separated Christians; others think that the confusion and crises of the tumultuous postconciliar period urgently require the regulatory and guiding hand of a Vatican III.

One thing is certain: that Vatican III, Nairobi I, or even Moscow I would stand in turn in the mainstream of Tradition; it would just be another item of this venerable series. Did Vatican II itself, perhaps, by understanding itself as a pastoral council and by refraining from definitions and dogmatic judgments, show the way to a future council that will see its precise task as the clarification of essential questions of doctrine that touch on the foundations of the faith? Doesn't the collapse of the socialist ideologies and utopias, which had shackled minds and peoples for almost a hundred years, raise questions that beset mankind in the depths of its being, the solution to which will determine also the earthly fate of a world that is constantly growing closer together? And who can answer these questions, if not the Church, through whose voice the glorified Christ speaks to mankind?

Vatican II was, in any case, neither the beginning nor the conclusion of conciliar history, and we still are faced with the task of implementing it before we talk about the future.

XIV

"STATE THEOLOGIANS"
THEN AND NOW

Within the context of the extensive range of problems created by the rise of the modern liberal state after 1848, theological faculties [at European universities] were from the
very beginning at an intersection of state and Church interests, and this became the starting point for the endeavors
of German Catholicism to emancipate itself from the all-
powerful state. During the years before Vatican I, stoked by
the debate over the Syllabus of Pius IX and by Bishop von
Ketteler's decision to withdraw his seminarians from the
short-lived theological faculty at the University of Giessen
(he subsequently turned the major seminary in Mainz into
an outstanding school of theology for their training), the
controversy over "state-run faculties" flared up again and
again. Under these circumstances it was precisely the ultramontane party, with its intention of freeing ecclesiastical life from the shackles of the authoritarian State, which
demanded the "disestablishment" or "denationalization" of
priestly formation as well as a separation of church and state
in general. Their real adversary was the ideologically liberal
state, which was all the more authoritarian, however, in its
political behavior.

Yet that was not the only ultramontane position. Such
leading exponents of a resolutely ecclesiastical, Rome-ori-

ented course of action as Franz Xaver Hettinger and Joseph
Hergenröther—both of them professors at the University
of Würzburg and renowned scholars; the latter was created
a cardinal by Leo XIII—were downright enthusiastic sup-
porters of "state-run faculties". Probably their personal, very
positive experiences with the faculty at Würzburg, which
was predominantly Neoscholastic in its approach, prompted
them to make that judgment. Hergenröther was correct
when he wrote:

> The complete demise of Catholic theological faculties at our
> institutions of higher education, which to a very great extent
> have contributed to the strengthening of the ecclesiastical
> sense . . . would lead also to disdain for and disparagement of
> the clergy in the eyes of the other educated and profession-
> ally trained classes and make it grievously more difficult for
> them to exert influence on those classes. . . . The Church
> could scarcely do a greater favor for her mortal enemies.

Hettinger, too, is right when he notes that in Italy the enemies of the Church had succeeded in doing just that. Indeed,
the Italian clergy suffered for these reasons as well from an
unmistakable inferiority and isolation in society.

Hettinger is likewise correct when he declares that "our
German clergy could not have accomplished what it did accomplish precisely in the difficult days of the *Kulturkampf*",
even though he, like the large majority of the French clergy,
had not had a university education. Bismarck unintention-
ally confirmed this judgment by explaining the resistance
of the Catholic clergy in terms of their university training.
Even the crisis in the theological faculties in Munich, Bonn,
Braunsberg and Breslau resulting from the debate over infallibility (1869–1871) was resolved according to the mind
of the Church; the renowned Church historian Sebastian

Merkle from Würzburg attributed this to the decisive action of the bishops, who made sure that the lectures of those professors who had ventured to contradict Vatican I would no longer be heard by their seminarians.

After that, the turn of the twentieth century brought on a new crisis in the theological faculties. Now the intellectual opponents of the Church were demanding their abolition in the name of the ideology of a "science without presuppositions". Theology, much less Catholic theology, could not be recognized as a "science", since it has been forced into the cage of Church dogma and lacks the academic freedom to conduct research and teach [new findings]. Professor Merkle, mentioned earlier, was the one who brilliantly defended the existence of theological faculties at state universities in a major lecture presented to scholars in Berlin in 1905. In doing so, he had to fight a battle along two fronts: on the one hand, against the aforementioned liberal-agnostic prejudices, but then also against demands within the Church for a strict seminary formation of the clergy. Despite a certain patriotic tone aimed at his listeners, many of his arguments for the continuation and the importance of the faculties were convincing—and still are today. They would be even more so if Merkle the historian had viewed concrete historical experiences with the "state-trained theologians" a little more realistically.

What he presented in Berlin was a speech for the defense, whereby he started from an ideal construct both of the discipline of theology and also of the state (or the university). Things had gone differently, however, in the rugged reality of history. Whereas the Bavarian government had reorganized the once-Catholic theological faculty in Würzburg into an interdenominational faculty in the first quarter of the nineteenth century and had forced the candidates for priesthood to listen to lectures given by declared atheists, in Freiburg likewise scholars with anticlerical leanings occupied professorial chairs—one of them, Reichlin von Meldegg, even denied the divinity of Christ and ultimately left the Church for Protestantism—while Heinrich Schreiber and the layman Amann fomented the anticelibacy campaign in Baden. The situation was no better in Giessen, a faculty that soon ceased to exist. Breslau likewise was not very distinguished for being of one mind with the Church; in 1817 the faculty declared that some courses, on the Bible, for example, could just as well be taken with Protestant professors. That men like Ronge and Czersky—the fathers of German-national Catholicism—could be trained in such a milieu is not surprising.

No wonder, then, that the state theological faculties met with complete skepticism within the parameters of the nineteenth-century Catholic movement. Again, the status of the faculties during the Modernist crisis at the turn of the twentieth century was by no means unproblematic. It is simply not true, although it is the generally accepted opinion today, that Modernism—which in practice tended toward the denial of revealed truth in general—did not exist in Germany, at least, and that the Church's condemnations did not really affect any German theologian (with the possible exception of Joseph Schnitzer in Munich).

The fact that the anti-Modernist oath could not even be required of German theology professors, however, speaks volumes. And here it was not just a matter of protecting them from the odious accusation of a lack of academic freedom. Typically enough, in this context, the professors in Dillingen were not deprived of their authorization to teach but rather, with remarkable inconsistency, of their permission to preach.

In short: the existence of Catholic theological faculties at state universities, with the result that those holding professorships conduct their research and teach on behalf of both the church and the state, is per se an ideal construct—under ideal or at least normal circumstances. That would, indeed, guarantee that future priests could receive a broad intellectual and cultural education in an atmosphere of academic and methodological rigor. The societal integration and the intellectual influence of the clergy into and upon the rest of the academic community would be ensured. Above all, however, theology could make her voice heard in the chorus of sciences and make her indispensable contribution in an age of intellectual disorientation and ethical crises.

Therefore: Yes to the state-run theological faculties and to their mission for the Church and scholarship. But: Yes under all circumstances? By no means! This Yes is valid only on the condition that these faculties follow the law under which they started out, that they fulfill the conditions under which they were certified by a concordat between church and state. But that means that they have to represent authentic Catholic theology at the academic level in their research and teaching. When it is no longer guaranteed that the students and also the learned discussion partners from other faculties can find theological teaching that completely agrees in substance with the teaching of the Catholic Church, then these faculties have lost not only their ecclesiastical and their civil legitimacy but also their significance for the world of scholarship.

Now, one might object that the academic freedom of the individual theologian is constitutionally guaranteed. It is, and that is very fortunate, but that by no means gives a professor the right to advocate within a Catholic theology faculty a doctrine that contradicts the Catholic faith. Therefore, if a theologian comes into conflict with the Church's faith, he must either resolve that conflict—or else resign. That is an elementary demand of intellectual honesty that is easy to fulfill, inasmuch as no loss of status whatsoever is connected with it. Anyone who nevertheless does not fulfill it thereby betrays an intention to undermine the faith of the Church from within. That this applies not just to one particular case or another but rather describes a phenomenon that by now has become widespread has been obvious for a long time, just like the utter bafflement of many Catholics when they notice that such professors can continue to train religion teachers and candidates for the priesthood, as though their teaching were unobjectionable, that is to say, Catholic—which the impartial student assumes.

Under these circumstances, in fact, the question arises as to what interest the Church could possibly have in continuing this state of affairs. Is the real solution to abolish these faculties? If Church-run institutions took over theological training, would that end the present and indisputable crisis in these faculties? Would theology in Germany thereby regain its former scholarly level, which was recognized throughout the world, and regain its ecclesial character? Merely institutional changes improve nothing, absolutely nothing! Change depends almost exclusively on the individual persons who are involved. Not one of the theologians who are justly criticized today obtained his professorship without ecclesiastical approval [*Placet*], and not one of them can remain in his position against the will of the competent bishop. Responsibility for the ecclesiastical correctness of academic theological teaching clearly lies with the bishops. The confidence that they occasionally express in the self-cleaning capacity of academic theology has thus far been disappointed. The ideological power structures created since the sixties (that golden age!), which control the academic theological enterprise and especially academic personnel policies, are too strong. Maybe for that very reason, though, given the extreme situations today, extreme solutions ought to be considered.

What remains, then? At least the hope that what is decayed and withered will someday fall by itself, or perhaps will be swept aside by political storm winds, and that new life will spring up and make its way through the debris. That, too, is a lesson taught by history.

XV

FORGIVENESS:
THE WAY TO PEACE

The Penitential Act of John Paul II on March 12, 2000

In his apostolic letter, *Tertio millennio adveniente*, in which John Paul II had exhorted the faithful to prepare for the celebration of the two thousandth anniversary of the Incarnation of God in Jesus Christ, he had already announced the theme of "Sin and Guilt in the Church's Past" also and thus initiated a wide-ranging and controversial discussion. With considerable satisfaction among circles that have a negative view of the Church, a series of cases was rehearsed in which the Church of the past allegedly must be accused of failures, indeed, of crimes. The approval of slavery, forced conversions to Christianity, the Crusades, the Inquisition, witch hunts, discrimination against and oppression of women, but also the suppression of freedom of thought and of inquiry—people still mention Galileo Galilei and Giordano Bruno in this regard—as well as compliant cooperation with National Socialism [Nazism]: all this, in addition to many other charges, was subsequently referred to as the sin of the Church. With something of a self-righteous attitude, many now believed that they should express satisfaction with the Church's awareness of her limitations and praise the long-overdue confession of sins by the leader of the Church before the whole world.

Possibly such misunderstandings of the pope's intention

explain why in the bull *Incarnationis mysterium* [*IM*], with which John Paul II proclaimed the Great Jubilee, formulas suited to preventing that sort of misinterpretation were chosen when it deals with, among other things, the relation of today's Church to the sin and guilt in her past.

In particular, the pope directed the International Theological Commission to study this problem, and consequently it drew up a document entitled "Memory [Remembrance] and Reconciliation", which was released to the press on March 7, 2000. [See *L'Osservatore Romano*, weekly English ed., vol. 33, no. 11 (1634), 15 March 2000, special insert, pp. I–VIII.] On this occasion, the chairman of the commission, Joseph Cardinal Ratzinger, presented a remarkable discourse [See *Pilgrim Fellowship of Faith* (San Francisco: Ignatius Press, 2005), pp. 274–83.] that served to clarify the correct interpretation of the eagerly awaited penitential act, which was the subject of lively discussion even before the pope performed it on the First Sunday of Lent during the Jubilee Year in a solemn (not to mention dramatic) ceremony in Saint Peter's Basilica in the presence of the famous Romanesque crucifix from the Church of San Marcello al Corso.

Understanding the Penitential Act

After that, John Paul II himself repeatedly indicated how he wanted this penitential rite to be understood in speeches that he gave during his pilgrimage to the Holy Land. Thus he admitted during his visit to the chief rabbis in Jerusalem: "I have always wanted to be counted among those who work, on both sides (!), to overcome old prejudices" (*L'Osservatore Romano*, weekly English ed., 29 March 2000, p. 6). Even clearer was his statement on the occasion of the interreligious meeting on March 23: "We are all aware of past mis-understandings and conflicts, and these still weigh heavily today upon relationships between Jews, Christians and Mus-lims (ibid., p. 8). The pope went on to say that this know-ledge should be for us an incentive to "do all we can to turn awareness of past offenses and sins into a firm resolve to build a new future" (ibid.). [Two days later, during an Ecumenical Meeting with representatives of the Churches and ecclesial communities of the Holy Land,] the pope ex-pressed the desire "to overcome the mistrust and rivalry in-herited from the past" so as to make possible a new and fuller communion (ibid., p. 11, par. 1). This, however, can-not be achieved simply by human effort. Rather, the Holy Year 2000 is "a providential time for us to turn to the Lord in order to *ask forgiveness* for the wounds which the members of our Churches have inflicted upon one another down the years" (ibid., par. 5).

The pope's statements on this subject reached their climax during his visit to the Yad Vashem Monument on March 23. There he spoke remarkable things about the meaning of remembrance and thus of the historical consciousness in general:

> We remember, but not with any desire for vengeance or as an incentive to hatred. For us, to remember is to pray for peace and justice, and to commit ourselves to their cause. Only a world at peace, with justice for all, can avoid repeating the mistakes and terrible crimes of the past. (*L'Osservatore Romano*, 29 March 2000, p. 7, par. 3)

This is followed by a declaration that can only be described as solemn:

> As Bishop of Rome and Successor of the Apostle Peter, I as-sure the Jewish people that the Catholic Church, motivated

by the Gospel law of truth and love and by no political considerations, is deeply saddened by the hatred, acts of persecution and displays of anti-Semitism directed against the
Jews by Christians at any time and in any place. (Ibid.,
par. 3)

John Paul II had just emphasized that all this must not be
blamed on the Church, on Christianity, when he posed the
question: "How could man have such utter contempt for
man?" And the answer: "Because he had reached the point
of contempt for God. Only a godless ideology could plan
and carry out the extermination of a whole people" (ibid.,
par. 2).

With these statements, the pope further elaborated and
thus interpreted himself what he had said in his homily on
the Day of Pardon, the First Sunday of Lent, March 12. Re-
calling his demand for the "purification of memory", the
pope had then made an appeal, "that in this year of mercy the
Church, strong in the holiness which she receives from her
Lord, should kneel before God and implore forgiveness for
the past and present sins of her sons and daughters" ("Let us
forgive and ask forgiveness!", *L'Osservatore Romano*, weekly
English ed., vol. 33, no. 11 [1634], 15 March 2000, p. 2, par.
3, citing *IM* 11). This request for pardon, expressed here and
now, is "based on the *objective responsibility* which Christians
share as members of the Mystical Body, and which spurs
today's faithful to recognize, along with their own sins, the
sins of yesterday's Christians, in light of careful historical
and theological discernment" (from the text of the homily,
12 March 2000, ibid.).

In the interest of theological precision, the pope then mentions membership in the Mystical Body of Christ, which
unites the redeemed of all generations with one another, as
the reason why the living have to bear "the burden of the

errors and faults of those who have gone before us" (ibid., citing *IM* 11). Behind this idea are probably the Pauline passages from the Letter to the Galatians (6:2), "Bear one another's burdens", and the First Letter to the Corinthians (12:26), "If one member suffers, all suffer together." A qualification follows that is well worth noting: with this request for pardon—which by its nature presupposes the existence of guilt—one must not encroach on "the judgement of God who alone knows every heart" (ibid., citing *IM*, 11).

This is the necessary preamble to the statement that "we cannot fail to recognize the infidelities to the Gospel committed by some of our brethren, especially during the second millennium" (homily, 12 March 2000, ibid., par. 4). After that, he expresses a request for pardon "for the divisions which have occurred among Christians, for the violence some have used in the service of the truth and for the distrustful and hostile attitudes sometimes taken towards the followers of other religions" (ibid.). It should not be overlooked that the pope not only asks pardon for the sins of Christians but in the name of the Church also grants forgiveness for "*the sins committed by others against us*". "Countless times in the course of history Christians have suffered hardship, oppression and persecution because of their faith. Just as the victims of such abuse forgave them, so let us forgive as well" (ibid.). It should be noted that this formulation clearly expresses the fact that both the request for pardon and the granting of it is meaningfully possible only among the living and that anything beyond that would be mere rhetoric dictated by political correctness. The hermeneutical framework [*Horizont*] within which the pope's admission of guilt and request for pardon should be interpreted points out another factor, however. We mean the impressive remembrance of the twentieth-century martyrs that took place in an ecumenical ceremony in the Colosseum on May 7, 2000. We mean also the unprecedented number of beatifications and canonizations performed during the pontificate of John Paul II. Already during the preparations for the Jubilee Year, the pope had directed all the conferences of bishops to ascertain and keep in mind [*festhalten*] the names of all those who in their respective land gave witness to their faith in Christ by sacrificing their lives; during the Jubilee Year itself, he planned numerous beatification and canonization ceremonies. In doing so, he impressively highlighted the sanctity that was heroically lived out by members of the Church in all centuries, but especially in the century just completed.

Therefore, the professions of guilt and requests for pardon that were expressed during the solemn penitential rite on the First Sunday of Advent are to be interpreted against this background and in the light of the previous and subsequent papal speeches mentioned already so as to avoid painting a distorted picture of the Church.

Forgiveness for What?

There were, in all, seven requests for pardon, which were introduced by representatives of the Roman Curia and pronounced by the pope in a prayer to God. [See *L'Osservatore Romano*, weekly English ed., no. 12 (1635), 22 March 2000, p. 4.] In each instance, a confession of guilt was also formulated. There were references to "men of the Church [who], in the name of faith and morals, have sometimes used methods not in keeping with the Gospel in the solemn duty of defending the truth" [II]. "[S]ins which have rent the unity of the Body of Christ and wounded fraternal charity" were acknowledged [III], by which obviously not just the sins of Catholics were meant. Against the Jews—according to the fourth petition—"not a few" have committed sins, and injustices have "often" been committed by Christians against members of other religions, and migrants and itinerants as well, through pride, hatred, the desire to dominate others or enmity, whereby the Christians have "often denied the Gospel, yielding to a mentality of power" [V]. There are similar prayers asking pardon for acts of humiliating women and discriminating against them, as well as for a lack of respect for the personal dignity of the poor, the marginalized and the abandoned [VI]. Next—and here the ceremony abandons the pattern of prayers for forgiveness —there is intercessory prayer for children who are "killed in their mother's womb or even exploited for experimental purposes" [VII].

In the formulation of these petitions, equal attention is given to the sins of the present and those of the past.

Sinful Church or Church of Sinners?

A systematic analysis of all these statements by the pope reveals the position that he takes with regard to guilt and sin in the Church's past and that he intends the Church to take as well.

First it is unambiguously clear: the Church has not sinned, but rather "some of our brethren", and attitudes of distrust and hostility toward those members of other religions have been adopted "from time to time" by members of the Church. This clearly distinguishes between the Church as the spotless Bride of Christ and her members, who certainly are sinful again and again. We can hardly agree with the introduction to the German edition of "Memory and Reconciliation" (*Erinnerung und Versöhnen: Die Kirche und ihre Verfehlungen in ihrer Vergangenheit* [third ed: Einsiedeln, 2000]), which reads: "In this (in what?!) sense we can also speak not only about the sins of individual members of the Church, but also about the sins of the Church, especially when they were committed by those who were authorized to act in her name" (*Erinnerung und Versöhnen*, "Einleitung", p. 13). Just as definite conditions must be fulfilled in order to say that "the Church teaches", so too this is required if, conversely, one is to say that "the Church" has sinned! But when and where is that supposed to have happened? Nevertheless, in an interview with the KNA [Katholische Nachrichten-Agentur, Catholic News Agency] published on February 24–25, 2000, there is talk about "offences of members of the Church and of the Church herself".

A distinction between the Church and the members of the Church is necessary, however, since membership of an individual in the Church in no way sets aside his personhood or the individual's responsibility for his morally relevant behavior. A collectivist concept of the Church, which would affirm a responsibility of the whole for the action of the individual members of the Church and/or a merging of the individual into the whole, contradicts both the nature of the human person and also that of the Church. Consequently, we can apply analogously to the Church what the Second Vatican Council declares in *Nostra aetate* about the responsibility of the people of Israel for the death of Jesus:

> True, the Jewish authorities and those who followed their lead pressed for the death of Christ (cf. John 19:6); still, what happened in His passion cannot be charged against all the Jews, without distinction, then alive, nor against the Jews of today. (*Nostra aetate* 4)

This document speaks, therefore, about the impossibility of a collective responsibility of those living at the time for what took place on Golgotha, but likewise about the impossibility of charging later generations with it. According to the same principle, the entire Church cannot be saddled with a collective responsibility for the deeds or omissions of individual Christians, nor, a fortiori, for the actions of generations that are long gone. Yet we, the members of the Church living today—united by the bond of grace to the Mystical Body of Christ and thus with its members in all generations—carry together with them the burden of the errors and guilt of those who went before us.

A comparison might illustrate this: The heir of a debt-ridden farm inherits, that is, assumes together with it, the mortgages that encumber it, even though he himself could in no way have helped to incur the debt. It is his task to pay off the mortgages. Accordingly, A. Baumgartner remarks: "The moral achievement that is required of this generation is not the acknowledgment of some responsibility for the past but rather the willingness to take on the inherited burdens, the debts from the past, for which they share the liability, although they themselves are not responsible for them." This is an expression of solidarity reaching across generations—solidarity that in this case is based on kinship. At the same time, one acknowledges that in one's own family, too, there have been "black sheep". Now, with regard to the Church, this state of affairs is expressed in a striking image by the Gospel passages that say that good fish and bad are to be found in Peter's net and that the good wheat in the field of the Church continues to grow amid the weeds until the harvest.

The preceding considerations add up to a weighty proviso in connection with any attempt to pass a historical, much less a theological-moral, judgment on events in the Church's past. As the International Theological Commission emphasizes, a "precise historical and theological evaluation" and clarification is necessary for every judgment of this sort ("Memory and Reconciliation", 4.2).

Certainly, that points in a few words to a big and complicated problem, the problem of historical judgment, which of course can be dealt with here only by way of suggestion. No doubt it is possible to demonstrate the causes, connections and consequences of historical actions. To that extent, with due caution, the question as to the responsibility for them can be answered also. Now, whether a particular historical event should be judged negatively or positively does depend largely on the vantage point of the observer. It depends no less upon the criteria selected for such a judgment. Furthermore, we should point out the relativity of such criteria, which are conditioned by the historical era and culture. By what standards should one judge the human sacrifices of the Aztecs, which were still the practice in the fifteenth century, and accordingly the measures taken against them by the Spanish colonists? This example alone makes it clear how problematic historical judgments are in general.

The careful historical evaluation demanded by the International Theological Commission, however, runs into considerable difficulties even before any attempt to pronounce a judgment. In a whole series of cases in which so-called public opinion supposes that it has identified unmistakable failure on the Church's part, the very prerequisites for a serious historical judgment are lacking. Research into the Crusades, the Inquisition, the witch trials—to mention only the best-known issues—once again finds itself at a stage where new inquiries, new methods and new sources lead occasionally to surprising results that debunk the stereotypical, popularized notions that were previously taken for granted.

No Judgment on Conscience!

Given this state of affairs, an attempt to pronounce a judgment nevertheless in these cases or others of the sort could not be justified [*zu verantworten*] scientifically. Especially important, however, is a second proviso mentioned by the pope: No historian, no theologian, and not even the Church can sit in judgment on the conscience and thus on the guilt or innocence of another human being. The Second Vatican Council clearly states this: "God alone is the judge and searcher of hearts, for that reason He forbids us to make judgments about the internal guilt of anyone" (*Gaudium et spes* 28). With that, the council expresses an elementary moral demand of the New Testament. Obviously, there were considerations of this sort that prompted the pope to point out "problem areas" where such things might have happened but not to mention any concrete cases at all in which one would have to impute sin. It testified to great prudence and a realistic view of history when, for instance, the bishops' conference in Spain on the one hand asked God's forgiveness for the atrocities committed during the Spanish Civil War yet avoided asking pardon for the conduct of the Spanish episcopate during the Franco regime, since the historical facts are still too murky and complicated to allow for a judgment at present.

Such caution certainly does not mean to deny the existence of sin in the Church's past. The Church has always been conscious of the fact that in every age she numbers saints as well as sinners among her members. This awareness is expressed in the religious practice of the Church, which through her liturgy is familiar with the confession of sins and requests for pardon, with seasons in the liturgical year devoted to penance, but especially with the sacrament of reconciliation, in which sins are forgiven (to paraphrase Cardinal Ratzinger at the Presentation of "Memory and Reconciliation" on March 7, 2000; see *Pilgrim Fellowship of Faith*).

That is why, in spite of repeated claims to the contrary, there was nothing extraordinary or spectacular about the pope's admission of guilt, which was especially emphasized in view of the Great Jubilee Year 2000. It is worth noting, moreover, that contrary to many expectations, the pope, in pronouncing the admission of guilt and request for pardon for the sins of Church members in the past, did not address individuals or human communities of our time but rather presented both in the form of prayers to God. God alone is the judge of men's consciences, which is why forgiveness, too, is reserved to him—at least when the people to whom injustice has been done can no longer themselves be asked for pardon. Therefore, God was asked to forgive the guilt of those who have sinned over the course of Church history. But even that is only a special case of the intercession for the departed members of the Church that is offered daily in the liturgy.

No Rehabilitation

This very thought, that everything that has crossed the threshold of the present is consigned once and for all to the judgment and the mercy of God, also makes it impossible officially to rehabilitate anyone posthumously. In recent decades, there have been repeated demands that the excommunication of Martin Luther be lifted, but these could not and cannot be met any more than the demands for the rehabilitation of Girolamo Savonarola or even Giordano Bruno. All other considerations aside, the very concept of rehabilitation—insofar as it refers to personages in history—is highly problematical in itself and furthermore is encumbered with well-known Marxist-Leninist connotations.

Meanwhile, John Paul II has not hesitated to express sorrow and regret, for instance, about the fact that Jan Hus, who had been condemned as a heretic by the Council of Constance, was handed over to the secular authorities and then burned at the stake (address to the international symposium on Jan Hus in Rome in December 1999; *L'Osservatore Romano*, 22 December 1999, p. 3). In similar fashion, the pope has regretted that Galileo Galilei had to suffer as a result of measures taken by ecclesiastical agencies (address to the Pontifical Academy of Sciences in October 1992).

The pope, however, has deliberately avoided going any further than that. Such a step, which nonetheless had been demanded repeatedly in the interests of political correctness, would have meant that proceedings and judgments that in their context and according to the criteria of their time had nothing unjust about them would have been evaluated after the fact, in the wake of such "rehabilitation" efforts—hundreds of years later—by current standards and criminalized. In such a process, entire periods of Church history would have to stand trial, with the present as the prosecuting attorney. To mention only one example, the Apostle Paul would be charged with approving of slavery. The absurdity of such an anachronism is plain to see! And so it was impossible for the pope to follow the rather superficial public opinion on this matter. In his thoroughly critical review of two thousand years of Church history, moreover, the pope has looked for guilt and sin not only among members of the Church. Mentioned also are sins [*Verfehlungen*] of which the Church herself has become the victim.

Looking Ahead

The penitential rite celebrated by the pope on March 12, 2000, like the more in-depth statements of John Paul II that preceded or followed it, display, as we have noted, an unmistakable orientation toward the future. The pope was concerned about the purification of the past, which only God's mercy can bring about, as an indispensable prerequisite for shaping a future that is freed from the burdens of history.

With the key concept *purificatio memoriae*, the "purification of memory", John Paul II designated what can and must be done on the part of mankind for the sake of this goal. This is indeed a very felicitous expression. It captures what is meant much more accurately than the formula that had been decided on, *faute de mieux*, during preparations for the historic meeting between Paul VI and Patriarch Athenagoras in 1971, in order to answer the question of what position the two parties should take toward the momentous mutual excommunications of the year 1054. At that time, the phrase was that they should "be erased [*getilgt*] from the Church's memory" (*Tomos agapis* [Rome/Istanbul, 1971], nos. 127–30, pp. 278–97). Such a manner of speaking could, however, create the appearance that everyone is supposed to shut their eyes to the historical reality—a behavior that could be reminiscent of the pathological phenomenon of "repression", which itself then causes psychological dysfunction. In contrast, the concept of "purification of memory" has the advantage of referring to an active confrontation with the historical reality, to the work of coping with it intellectually and existentially by the power of faith and in light of it.

This is precisely what the pope demanded, not only from members of the Church but from all "people of good will". In doing so, the pope showed an indispensable way to reconciliation and peace in general. This should be explained now in greater detail.

Purification of Memory

Anyone who investigates the root causes of today's conflicts must in fact dig deep. Events that date back centuries still unfold their dire consequences in the present and become grounds for war and violence. Examples of this are too plentiful to be listed here. Rare is the ethnic group [*Volk*] or religious community that does not have some such dragon-seed sown in its past. For instance, the French and the Germans were described for a long time as hereditary foes. The bloody assassination attempts and street battles in Ulster today are unthinkable without the firmly entrenched memory of the political and religious oppression of Ireland since the seventeenth century. Even in our day the fate of Jan Hus has burdened relations between Germans (and/or Austrians) and Czechs. Similarly, the memory of the conquest and sack of Constantinople by the army of the Fourth Crusade in 1204 is still a more serious obstacle to agreement between Greek Orthodoxy and Rome than their dogmatic differences, for instance, concerning the *Filioque*. Romans, in turn, cannot forget the date May 6, 1527, when the "*Lanzichenechi*", the *Landesknechte* or mercenaries of Charles V, king of Germany, overthrew Renaissance Rome in an orgy of devastation.

Too numerous and too multifarious are the burdens originating in the past for them to be named even in general terms. Mentioned most often in our days is the destruction of the Jews by the Nazis, the far-reaching consequences of which cast a shadow to this day over Israel's relations with Germany, and even with the Catholic Church. Generally speaking, one can scarcely find a conflict that has no historical roots, that isn't constantly fueled by memories that are deliberately kept alive. This constitutes the backdrop before which John Paul II, from the beginning of his pontificate, urged peace, showed the way to peace and called for the "purification of memory".

The need for this purification [*Reinigung*], however, is based, as we have indicated, on the preceding contamination [*Verunreinigung*] of the collective memory, of the remembrance and thus of the traditions of social structures, both political and religious. Not infrequently—and this aggravates the problem—such "poisoned" memories have become the very points around which their national and/or religious identity crystallizes. The papal call for a *purificatio memoriae* is therefore relevant in the highest degree. Naturally, it is directed first and foremost to the guild of historians. Down to the present day, they have been the ones who all too often have seen their task as serving the political, economic or even religious interests of their own society— through a selective, deliberately slanted presentation of history or even by means of a version that colors the facts, if it doesn't manipulate them outright. Furthermore, this nationalistic, confessional sort of historiography has been carried over into wide sectors of the various populations through literature, theater, the graphic arts and folklore. In this way, historians have managed to convey a predominantly black-and-white picture of history, which on the one hand was able to justify identifying with one's own community and its traditions yet on the other hand could lead to a more-or-less emotional refusal to acknowledge the other "blackened" group.

The Tasks for Historians

Although certainly it is an essential task of historiography to create social identity by illuminating and raising consciousness about the origins of a society, it is both possible and imperative that this be done sensibly and responsibly, on the basis of unadulterated historical truth. To that extent, the call for the purification of memory is addressed primarily to historical scholarship. Both secular and Church historians must take as their program what Leo XIII wrote in his letter *Saepe numero considerantes*, dated August 18, 1883, on the occasion of the opening of the secret Vatican archive; in this letter, which is addressed to historians, the pope points to a lesson learned from Cicero: "*Primum esse historiae legem ne quid falsi dicere audeat deinde ne quid veri non audeat, ne qua suspicio gratiae sit in scribendo ne qua simultatis*" (Acta Leonis XIII [Romae, 1884], 3:268): "This is the first law of historiography: do not dare to say anything false, nor to leave anything true unsaid. Let there be no hint of favoritism or rivalry in your writing." Another comment that was made on the opening of the archive: "*Non abbiamo paura della pubblicità dei documenti*": "We have no fear of making our documents public."

Thus the investigation of historical truth—insofar as this can be comprehended at all through the methods of historical scholarship—is selected as the supreme guideline. This categorically demands, however, the resolute avoidance of any sort of manipulation [*Instrumentalisierung*] of historical truth. Instead, that truth should be brought to light, objectively interpreted and elaborated into a realistic historical picture, in which both the light and the dark colors are not muddied by sympathy or antipathy or by any interests but are applied according to the truth that has been discovered. The historian's love for his people, for his religious community must never compete with his love for the scholarly elaboration of the truth. This is where the *purificatio memoriae* begins. It takes place when errors or crimes on one's "own" side are noted and recognized as having in fact occurred just like the successes, accomplishments and greatness on the "other" side—and vice versa. The fact that such a perspective on history demands not only intellectual effort but also a conscious overcoming of inherited resentments doesn't make the purification of memory any easier. Nevertheless, respect for historical truth and a responsible attitude toward it can enable the historian to make the effort, even if the hallowed monuments of many heroes are toppled in the process.

To require that due honor be paid to known historical truth is not to demand, however, that the historian have no standpoint at all or that he give up his identity. What is expected of him, though, is a willingness to understand and to refrain from hasty or partial judgments. The job of the historian—and that includes the historical writer and the teacher of history—is not that of a prosecutor or a defense attorney or a judge. Aware of the relativity and thus of the provisional nature of his assessments and judgments, the historian who is firmly committed to the purification of memory will concentrate his efforts on conveying as complete an account of the facts as possible and on investigating their causes, multiple interconnections and consequences, before he very carefully attempts evaluations.

The recognition of historical truth is then followed, in a second step, by opinion and commentary on it. That is not possible, however, without the previous attempt to understand the reasons for what happened and the attendant circumstances, as well as the consequences. It should not be surprising that the historical method itself, for all its scholarly apparatus, frequently runs up against limits in this endeavor, since the historical actions of an individual, and even more so those of communities, are in the final analysis impenetrable tangles of human freedom, external and interior prerequisites and conditions, not to mention the latent conflicts within man between grace and sin. Without an acknowledgment of the reality of sin, and also of grace, the course of history can hardly be understood at all, or only superficially.

The purification of memory comes about by making due allowance for all the factors mentioned above, and especially for the [admission] *"non liquet"* ["it is not clear"], which is sometimes unavoidable in sketching an accurate historical picture. Nevertheless, experience teaches that errors in this process can be made not only by defect but also by excess. The more serious the resolve to purify memory, the more easily it can happen that the negative elements in the past of one's own community—nation or church—become the focus of the investigation rather than the positive elements. In these circumstances, the result can be a historical picture that may make identification with one's own history (which is essential for the life of the community in question) burdensome, if it doesn't actually lead to aloofness from it, or even to self-contempt. The sociopsychological consequences of such an attitude are comparable to those that appear in the analogous case of the individual who refuses to accept his own heritage or past.

Such reflections clearly lead to the conclusion that it is necessary to be reconciled with one's own history before one can come to be reconciled with other persons or communities. In each case, the journey must proceed by way of a recognition—which often demands courage and self-denial—of the reality of evil in one's own past, which leads to the request for pardon by God—to which must be joined a request for the forgiveness of those to whom injustice was done, if they are still alive. When one's own past and that of the other party have been commended in this way to God's mercy, it then becomes possible to face up to that past without prejudice and to accept it with inner composure. Then the moment will have arrived also in which *Historia* can exert her influence as the *vitae magistra* [schoolteacher of life]. This could happen, for instance, with regard to the divisions among Christians that were particularly addressed by John Paul II. As it becomes better and more widely known what a decisive role political, cultural and even economic factors—in other words, absolutely irrelevant secular matters—have played in almost all schisms, it might become possible to examine, once the aforementioned reasons have fallen away, whether we could set out on the path to reunion. Thus the way of the purification of memory that the pope pointed out could in fact lead to peace among the Christian denominations, but also among peoples and religions.

"DEFYING THE ULTRAMONTANE GANG
WITH BRAZEN ASSURANCE"

*Nineteenth-Century German Catholicism:
National Church or Universal Church?*

The political upheaval of the French Revolution, which also marked a radical change in intellectual and cultural history, ended an era in which church and state, religion and culture (sometimes politics, too), had formed a unity that was full of tension yet withstood all vicissitudes. Now both spheres —secular society and the Church—were faced with the task of redefining their mutual relations.

On the Catholic side, essentially two points of view developed, each of them being further differentiated. The two viewpoints were based respectively on their own theological schools and led to different positions and approaches with regard to society, culture and politics. In particular, a decisive role was played by the attitude that one took toward the state (and thus toward the nation), which increasingly understood itself in the Hegelian sense and acted accordingly. The two currents of thought differ also when examined from sociological and, obviously, political perspectives as well, as we will demonstrate.

These contrary and highly charged developments, which finally went off quite violently in the debate over the First Vatican Council, can be presented here only in bold strokes and schematically while of course dispensing with distinctions that are necessary per se. Basically the question was:

What position should a Catholic and should the Church take
with regard to society, which in the wake of Enlightenment
philosophy and revolutions—1789, 1820, 1830, 1848—had
become secularized?

A rather optimistic view of so-called modern society pre-
dominated in those circles that were still under the influence
of the Enlightenment but were also open to the national
sentiments revived by Romanticism, which became increasingly pronounced in the years leading up to the Revolution
of 1848. The year 1840, for example, saw the composition
of the songs "*Die Wacht am Rhein*" and "*Sie sollen ihn nicht
haben, den freien deutschen Rhein*" ["The watch on the Rhine",
"They must not take it, the free German Rhine"]. The universal German songfest in Lübeck and conferences on German literature in Lübeck and Frankfurt proclaimed and
promoted a growing national-German enthusiasm that eventually led to the 1848 Parliament at Saint Paul's Church,
which had a typical sociological profile: it was made up of
academics and members of the middle class. This ethnic-na-
tional consciousness, which initially was still along "greater
German" lines and thus included German-speaking Austria,
was replaced in the wake of later developments by the "lesser
German" concept, which excluded Austria and amounted
to a Prussian-Protestant hegemony that was to culminate in
the establishment of the *Reich* in 1871 and play itself out in
the *Kulturkampf*.

"Liberal" Catholicism

Specifically, [the aforementioned groups] were circles of
academically trained Catholics, the "educated bourgeoisie",
who in the decades before Vatican I were eager to annex
the Catholic populace to the general trend of modern cultural and national development. Based on the diligently peda-

gogical tradition of Catholic Enlightenment thinkers such as Ignaz Heinrich von Wessenberg, they perceived it as an urgent imperative to overcome the "Catholic" lack of education and the associated cultural and societal inferiority of the Catholic sector of the population, the root causes of which lay in the destruction of the Catholic educational system, which had comprised seventeen universities and hundreds of *Gymnasien* [classical secondary schools], over the course of the [late eighteenth-century] "secularization". It will come as no surprise that compromises with the rationalistic and later with the liberal spirit of the age were not always and everywhere avoided, as well as compromises with the increasingly virulent ideas about the nation that ultimately developed into nationalism.

But what was it like in the field of theology? Specifically, in the theological faculties in Tübingen and Bonn, distinguished minds were at work—here we mention only Johann Adam Möhler and Georg Hermes. One might think, not of Möhler, but of his colleagues in Tübingen and of Hermes, who taught in Bonn, when Leo Scheffczyk speaks about the "do-it-yourself thinking of these schools, which often drifts into brilliant subjectivity", which resulted from a reliance on the philosophical idealism of Kant, Fichte and Hegel. In this intellectual circle, one can also note a certain national fervor and a rather close reliance on the state.

The "Ultramontanes"

The other current—let us call it for now the "ultramontane" current—had two principal sources. On the one hand, there was the older Mainz school, led by thinkers such as Liebermann, Räss, von Weis and Klee, who out of their experience of the French Revolution and the subsequent upheavals, among other things, developed a biblical-speculative theology in conjunction with Scholasticism and laid the groundwork for a new kind of theological formation that was ecclesiastically minded and pastorally oriented.

In the 1820s, after the Napoleonic disturbances were over, a similar process played out in Rome, which consisted of a new revival of the Scholasticism of the High Middle Ages and was promoted by the Jesuits at the Gregoriana. Around midcentury, Giovanni Perrone, Carlo Passaglia, Clemens Schrader and Johann Baptist Franzelin taught on the faculty there, and Joseph Kleutgen was especially influential. Perrone studied German idealist philosophy intensively and critically, while Passaglia was an outstanding specialist in patristic literature. All of them taught several generations of "*Germaniker*"—seminarians who resided at the *Collegium Germanicum* in Rome—who, upon returning home, transplanted to Germany that style of theological inquiry. Here we should mention above all Matthias Joseph Scheeben, who taught at the major seminary in Cologne, and also Heinrich Denzinger, Franz Hettinger and Joseph Hergenröther, all three former *Germaniker* who dominated the faculty in Würzburg; Hettinger in particular was a highly educated and inspiring teacher, whose five-volume manual on apologetics went through numerous editions. Hettinger also shows in his two rather journalistic volumes entitled *Aus Welt und Kirche* [From the world and the Church], in which he describes his travels, how the seven years of study in Rome could broaden one's horizons. Proximity and also emotional ties to the center of the Universal Church and meeting dozens of fellow students and teachers from all over the world left no room for nationalism to take root, however much one might love one's homeland. Ecclesiastically and also culturally, though by no means exclusively, these former students were Rome-oriented, and thus the ex-*Germaniker*, together with such renowned non-Roman Neoscholastics as Johann Baptist Heinrich and others, assumed leading posts in the ultramontane popular movement that first took shape at the 1848 Catholic Congress [*Katholikentag*] in Mainz and involved the socially active forces of the Catholic populace.

Lay Initiatives

It is noteworthy in this connection that the real political leadership of this movement, which was organized along union lines into pious associations and Catholic *casinos*, was in the hands of the laity. Viewed sociologically, those who joined these groups were from the lower middle classes, and later even the working classes, from the old-established Catholic nobility and the rural population. It should be added: civil servants, entrepreneurs and academics were more often to be found in the so-called liberal, nationally minded camp. In the ultramontane circles, the endeavor to free the Church and religious life from the very restrictive fetters of the liberal-authoritarian state set the tone for their common activities, which led to the organization of German Catholic life around such associations [*deutschen Vereins-katholizismus*], which were extraordinarily effective until Vatican II. In 1868 the First Central Committee of Catholic Associations was founded in Bamberg.

With regard to politics, their thinking was greater-German, anti-Prussian (which is to say antinationalistic), antimilitaristic and socially minded, as is strikingly evident from even a cursory reading of their most important publications, the *Mainzer Journal*, *Der Katholik*, *Historisch-politische Blätter*, and the *Augsburger Tagespost*. This movement was also the theological and political home of the younger clergy, whereas certain groups among the older priests toed the so-called liberal line. A phenomenon that can be noted again and again is the strong social commitment of this ultramontane clergy and their close acquaintance with the people. An attitude that was critical of the state and oriented toward Rome—the sociopolitical element was less important here —was characteristic also of an influential group of theology professors in Tübingen around midcentury; Carl Joseph von Hefele, the renowned historian of the council [Vatican I] and later bishop of Rottenburg, should be considered the leading thinker of the group. Moreover, the theological faculty in Munich, too, while not critical of the state, was nonetheless thoroughly ultramontane in its thinking, although that did not mean either there or in Tübingen that they adopted Neoscholasticism also. However, in both cases, we can note a certain departure from this viewpoint toward the end of the 1850s.

An Initial Collision

The Mainz-Würzburg school first clashed with the Tübingen-Munich school in connection with the so-called Munich Convention of Scholars in the year 1863, which naturally had been preceded by several controversies, concerning both personalities and Church polity. The course and content of the discussion cannot be detailed here, since we are dealing with a narrower issue: whether nineteenth-century German Catholicism was conscious of being a national Church or part of the universal Church. Of great significance in this connection, however, was the speech given on that occasion by Ignaz von Döllinger, who had been elected president of the convention. The speech was extremely well informed, composed on a grand scale and at a high intellectual level. The only part of its contents that should interest us is what pertains to our topic: the speech had an unmistakably German-national, if not nationalistic, tendency. Some evidence of this: after an appreciation of the earlier achievements of theologians from the cultural area of Romance languages, he continued:

> Thus in our days the lamp of theological science has been removed from its former places and at last it is the German nation's turn to become the foremost representative and custodian of the discipline of theology. . . . The charism of scientific acuity and thoroughness, of unceasing, in-depth research and of assiduous intellectual work has now been given to us Germans. . . .
>
> In Germany, therefore, we should look in the future for the homeland of Catholic theology. After all, no other people has cultivated the two eyes of theology— history and philosophy—with such care, love and thoroughness as the German people; in both fields, indeed, the Germans have become the teachers of all nations.

Döllinger, who was engaged like no other German theologian of his time in international scholarly exchange, considered the outstanding achievements of the Roman school and the works of a John Henry Newman—to name only two—as not worth mentioning! This could not have been the result of rational reflections; it was a painful display of German-national arrogance. That Döllinger was aware of the nationalistic slant of his speech is indicated by the fact that he himself prevented it from being translated into English, remarking that his speech was intended only for German ears!

Indeed, Germany assumed a leading role in the technological-industrial and thus the economic progress of Europe, and a national enthusiasm for progress defined the general mood in Germany during those decades.

One Nation—One Church

The momentousness of this national thinking is illustrated also by the fact that liberal circles, especially those affiliated with the liberal Protestant Union, whose leaders were influenced by David Friedrich Strauss and had long since taken leave of Jesus Christ as the Son of God, seriously propagated the idea that a reunion of Protestantism and the Catholic Church at the lowest common liberal denominator was a prerequisite for the rise of the German nation to the summit of power and importance. It is telling in this connection that Cotta's newspaper, the *Allgemeine Zeitung*, wrote: "German unity is the union of the confessions in Germany."

A message dated April 20, 1870, sent from Wartburg and addressed to the German people protested against any sort of dogmatic or priestly control (even Protestant!) and expressed the hope that "our Catholic brothers will summon the courage to cast off at last the shackles of foreign Roman rule" so that "the confessional rift which has divided the life of our German people like nothing else, can finally be healed. . . . Only then can the German people go forth on a straight path to meet its noble destiny, for the salvation of mankind. . . . This German people's Church is the indispensable inauguration of German unity and German freedom. If the Roman poison remains in the German ecclesiastical body, then political unity is only a patchwork stitched together."

After the council of 1869–1870 had ended and the Old Catholic split had occurred, this gave new hope to those affiliated with the Protestant Union, and they immediately wrote a prescription for Old Catholic church polity, since they were sure "that the Protestant and the Catholic reform movements . . . would in time have to meet in the common goal of a national church". Therefore, the following strategy was recommended to the Catholic reformers (i.e., Old Catholics):

> No withdrawal from the previous [ecclesiastical] communion, no renunciation of rights or shares in material goods, no separation! Rather, a firm alliance with like-minded members within both confessions and a courageous, tireless battle against the coercion of consciences within one's own confession. Thereby the cornerstone will be laid for the unification of Germany on the hallowed ground of religion and the work of political unification will be crowned most splendidly.

The Prussian general superintendent, who also served as the court preacher of Wilhelm I, had already indicated another way to accomplish this in 1868: the German [Catholic] Church, liberated from the "southern European" ["*romanischen*"] element, should assemble her bishops at a national council and unite under a primate. A "historical honorary preeminence" could then be conceded to the pope, and then they could enter, not a union, but a confederation with the likewise unified Lutheran-Evangelical church. Wilhelm Hoffmann opined "that this would not be a protestantization of the Catholic Church but rather a rejuvenation proceeding from her best and inmost life". For him the ultimate goal was a Lutheran Evangelical-Catholic national council, which perhaps would need to be held only every twenty-five years. The persuasive effect of such slogans on certain Catholic circles should not be underestimated.

Another factor, of course, was that all this played itself out against the backdrop of Bismarck's "Germany Policy" —since 1862 he had been the minister president—which increasingly steered toward war, which was supposed to create the conditions necessary for Prussian hegemony and to prepare for the foundation of the empire. It is no secret that the left-liberal Progress Party [*Fortschrittspartei*], which in 1863 took up residence in the Bavarian Chamber of Representatives, saw itself as the "spearhead of national, political and ideological liberalism" and found adherents particularly in educated, middle-class circles.

There was criticism from the so-called ultramontane camp, the meeting place of those German Catholic forces that resolutely looked to the pope, engaged in social action and were critical of the state. A leadership role in this movement was played by the increasingly numerous young priests who had received their theological training at the Gregorian University in Rome while residing at the *Collegium Germanicum*, had founded many Catholic associations, especially socially oriented ones, and had found therein their field of pastoral ministry. On the other hand, the nobility was heavily represented also, since many noble families regarded themselves as honor-bound to support the Church and to champion the cause of her freedom from the shackles of the all-powerful state. Precisely in ultramontane circles, the awareness of being united with the pope, who was enthusiastically revered, and with the worldwide Church was an important religious motive. As a result, streams of young farmers and noblemen enlisted in the papal army, which tried to defend the papal state against the forces of the *Risorgimento*; not only that, but the ultramontane circles were typically involved in charitable works and especially promoted the foreign missions—along with devotion to the Sacred Heart of Jesus and the Blessed Virgin Mary. The appearances of the Mother of

God at Lourdes gave strong impetus to Marian devotion. Nor should we forget that during the pontificate of Pius IX alone, 150 new religious communities were founded, which devoted themselves with great zeal to Catholic education, works of charity and the missions.

Concerning Vatican I

These two "camps", which, as we have said, differed sociologically, politically and also theologically, stood in opposition to each other also in the debate about the so-called Syllabus of Errors together with the encyclical *Quanta cura* of 1864. In the latter and in the appended list of errors of the time, Pius IX had characterized as errors and condemned philosophical rationalism, ideological liberalism, and communism, along with the enthusiasm for progress that is inspired by atheism and the conclusions about the relationship between church and state that are drawn from the Hegelian concept of the state. The so-called liberal Catholic circles, which were intent on bridging the opposition between the Church and the liberal-authoritarian state, the ideologically liberal culture, and modern science, which is to a great extent atheistic, passionately rejected this action by the pope.

Now, when the First Vatican Council was convoked, these opposing fronts came to light once again, whereby the close ties of the nationally minded, so-called German theology to the state became clearly evident. Ignaz von Döllinger, imperial councillor/senator of the Bavarian Crown, who was closely connected with the minister president Prince Chlodwig von Hohenlohe-Schillingfürst and the anticlerically minded minister of public worship and education, Johann von Lutz, now began to devise his strategy against the impending council. This strategy was two-pronged: on the

one hand, politics, and on the other—public opinion. The
early Döllinger had already used public opinion as an instrument by which theologians might exercise power within the
Church, and of course he had also dabbled in politics.

Now, in March of 1869, in response to the impending
council and to an article of the Roman Jesuit publication
Civiltà cattolica, he began to make use of this instrument with
a virtuosity that for a scholar was astonishing. As his mouthpiece for publicity, he chose the *Allgemeine Zeitung* that appeared in Augsburg and belonged to the publisher Baron
Cotta; its influence then could be compared with that of
today's *Frankfurter Allgemeine Zeitung* [FAZ]; under the editor in chief Dr. Otto Braun, it had set for itself the goal
of "defying the papist deceit of the ultramontane gang with
brazen assurance".

In these sensational articles, which Döllinger had the
newspaper publish anonymously and for which he received
considerably more than the usual honorarium, he tried to
stir up the sentiments of the German educated middle class
against Rome, partly through the deliberate distortion of
facts but also with unmistakably false statements. Expanded
to several times their original length, the articles appeared in
book form under the pseudonym "Janus" in the summer of
1869. At the same time, however—and from the perspective of our topic, this is even more interesting—Döllinger
had the Bavarian minister president Prince Hohenlohe issue
a so-called circular dispatch that he himself had drafted and
that was sent on April 9 to all the Bavarian embassies. These
were supposed to prompt the European governments to take
concerted action against the impending council, since the
council clearly was pursuing aims that were extremely dangerous to the state, namely—to summarize—the abolition
of more-or-less democratic constitutions and the reestablish-
ment of the universal papal rule of the Middle Ages, a specter

that Döllinger had already successfully conjured up in his series of articles in March.

With that, however, both Döllinger and Hohenlohe had overdrawn their accounts. Not even Bismarck joined their cause. But why is this of any interest at all for our topic? Well, it was an attempt to play the national element against the universalism of the Catholic Church. The *Kulturkampf* that broke out soon after the council and the support given to the "Old Catholic Church" that immediately split off in protest against the council were along the very same lines of a national consciousness that was loyal and obedient to the state. Still in the background behind all these endeavors was the dream, propagated by the Protestant Union and the *Allgemeine Zeitung*, of German national unity based on a religious unification of all Germans. All this was opposed by the so-called ultramontanes decisively and intelligently but also with indignation. Döllinger's attacks were perceived not only as attacks on the pope and the Church but also as a disavowal of all attempts by Catholics to fight for freedom from the shackles of an anachronistic state-church system. In this regard, as far as Bavaria was concerned, the Patriots' Party [*Patriotenpartei*] presented itself as the political spearhead of Catholicism. The actual mood among the Catholic people—and again we are speaking about Bavaria—is demonstrated by the fact that the ultramontane Patriots' Party, which was established in 1868, achieved a parliamentary majority as early as 1869.

From Kulturkampf to Imperial Allegiance

An analogous development took place in Germany under Prussian rule, where the Center Party [*Zentrumspartei*] immediately brought the ultramontane forces together politically. Organized politically in this way, above all through the network of Catholic associations with an ultramontane orientation, German Catholicism managed to withstand quite impressively in 1871 the extraordinary challenge of Bismarck's opportunistic *Kulturkampf*. Even though in Prussia more than a thousand parishes and ten dioceses were then orphaned, because their pastors and bishops were in prison or in exile, not one of the bishops and only twenty-four out of the four thousand priests had yielded to the coercive governmental measures.

As the *Kulturkampf* calmed down after the change in pontificate from Pius IX to Leo XIII and was eventually set aside, this orientation was modified in a certain sense. Weary of the constant accusation of hostility toward the empire, the leading circles of centrist, politically organized Catholicism no longer wished to be content with an outsider role in the new empire, which was in every respect successful. Thus a process of *rapprochement* began, which after the parting of Bismarck and the liberals allotted an increasing significance to the political center. Interesting, too, is the fact that the center, Cardinal Kopp of Breslau, the leading Protestant circles and the Berlin court understood that they were in agreement in rejecting plans for a nunciature in Berlin.

The political motto of the Catholics now was "national cooperation", and this call for "the fulfillment of national duty" found spectacular expression (for reasons of parliamentary tactics, of course) in the approval of the center for Bismarck's naval policy, which was controversial among centrists as well and ultimately was a major factor contributing to the conflict with England. This national tendency became rather hardened in some circles of reform-minded Catholics [*Reformkatholizismus*], which in their repudiation of so-called papal centralism became very much, too much, involved with nationalism. With the end of the empire, a new chapter was then opened.

APPENDIX TWO

ON THE ARROGANCE
OF THEOLOGY

The fact that Catholic theology in German-speaking lands finds itself in an academic identity—crisis, indeed, that this crisis is hurrying at a swift pace to its climax—is clear to everyone who surveys the theological scene.

The so-called Cologne Declaration of January 25, 1989, the foundation in that same year of the European Society for Catholic Theology [ESCT] and finally the reactions to the declaration by the Congregation for the Doctrine of the Faith [CDF] concerning the relation of theology to the Church's Magisterium have removed all doubt as to the critical state that theology is in at present. That all of these statements and initiatives are part of a carefully planned campaign is evident from the fact that the instigators of the Cologne Declaration are identical to those of the European Society for Catholic Theology. And the German-speaking members of the executive committee of this society, who were elected in Mainz on December 1–2, 1989, are signers of the Cologne Declaration also. Given these circumstances, we may safely assume that the real raison d'être for this society is the propagation of the purposes and content of the Cologne Declaration. The question arises also whether such initiatives would have succeeded without encouragement on the part of the authorities.

Therefore, it is appropriate to read the "Suggestions for

273

the Society's Work in the Coming Years" initially in light of the aforementioned facts and circumstances.

Theology in Europe is faced with specific tasks in the service of the Church and society. They are based on the following challenges, among others:

1. The Christian faith is practiced by a minority. In many cities, not even 10 percent of the children are baptized now as Christians. To many, the faith no longer seems capable of making a decisive mark on the world of tomorrow.

2. There is a demand for religion, but less so in the major churches [*Grosskirchen*, e.g., Catholic and Lutheran-Evangelical; cf. North American "mainline denominations"].

3. Consensus about fundamental moral criteria is increasingly difficult to reach in European societies.

4. The ecumenical movement among Christians is stagnating in many respects.

5. The relationship between husband and wife [*or:* between man and woman] is currently being fundamentally redefined. The women's movement is important and influential.

6. Responsibility for future generations is inescapable.

7. Economically and politically, developed Europe bears increasing responsibility in relation to the [Third] World of poor nations.

8. European integration demands reconciliation, new structures and circumspection based on historical experience.

9. Nations and cultures are growing closer together, which demands a new understanding of history.

10. In Europe, too, Christians encounter other religions; they must respect them and reflect on their relation to them.

On the basis of this analysis, the following questions arise:

1. What signs of the times help or hinder the task of communicating the Gospel in word and deed?

2. Are there new movements within European Christianity, and what are their chances?

3. What new ethical questions and answers (norms, virtues, institutions) present themselves?

4. What sorts of renewal does theology need as an ecclesial service?

5. Can the renewal of the Catholic Church be continued on the basis of the council and national synods?

This question is aimed especially at the possibilities of *actuosa participatio* [active participation] in the ecclesial *communio*. Church and society [i.e., the ESCT] are perceived and developed as spaces for free speech and constructive criticism proceeding from theological expertise [*aus theologischem Sachverstand*]. Open discussion, methodological standards [*wissenschaftlicher Anspruch*], and service to the whole Church and to human dignity are prerequisites for this work.

The Society sees in the ecclesial ministry of theologians, both men and women, an independent [*eigenständigen*] service to the People of God. It commits itself, on the basis of the Second Vatican Council, to the concerns of the Lima Document and to the conciliar movement for peace, justice and the conservation of creation. These suggestions were discussed on December 2, 1989, by the founding assembly. Proposed revisions were accepted.

Certainly, in this document, just a few correct observations are listed initially, no doubt, and then from them questions are derived for today's theology, some of them justified. Answers are not given; substantial positions are not taken. Still, quite a lot can be learned from it about the positions and aims of the writers. The attentive reader immediately notes that questions about fundamental theological research are not posed here, nor are corresponding research projects formulated. Yet there are so many desiderata for academic theology and also remarkable modern facilities —such as electronic data processing—to help fulfill them! Just think of the great need for adequate modern editions of theological sources and literature. Yet those who drew up this program apparently don't perceive research into Church Tradition as a significant task at all. That goes even for Sacred Scripture. It is just as momentous, if not downright alarming, however, that this catalogue of topics does not mention God, the One and Triune, the Creator; nor Jesus Christ, sin and redemption, grace and the sacraments; nor Mary, the Virgin Mother of God. The urgent themes of eschatology are entirely absent also. In this whole program, not a single article of faith—indeed, not even one of the problems of substantiating the faith—appears as something worth reflecting upon. Then, too: if one feels obliged to be relevant, why not bring up for the moral theologians the questions about abortion and euthanasia, which immediately affect everyone?

The items of interest, instead, are mainly political, sociological and academic-religious questions—and naturally those from the field of ecumenism. The Lima Document is mentioned and the "conciliar movement for peace, justice and the conservation of creation". Here it is obvious that the positions taken in the Lima Paper are affirmed, although that is out of the question as far as the non-Catholic dialogue partners and even the Catholic Church are concerned.

Through such proceedings, of course, Catholic theology, and indeed theology in general is robbed of its original and most characteristic object and is de facto watered down to a special case of sociology, psychology and political science.

There is little, if anything, in the program of this society to indicate that theology stands and falls with divine revelation, its proper object. However, if the connection with revelation, which defines theology in its inmost being, remains so much in the dark, then one cannot establish a connection between theology and the Church or the Church's Magisterium, either. After all, these two things, Church and Magisterium, amount to more than sociological entities only if divine revelation is entrusted to them by virtue of divine institution so as to be preserved and proclaimed, and only if the authenticity and purity of that which the Church preserves and proclaims is guaranteed by the divine founder of the Church. That is why theology, rightly understood, accepts its object, God's revelation, from the Church's hands, so as to question it scientifically, then, with the reverence due to the matter, with the help of all methods suited to its object, thus to understand and present it in greater depth.

This society, then, is speaking a completely different language when it claims that "the Church and society are . . . spaces for free speech and constructive criticism proceeding from theological expertise". There is talk also about "the ecclesial ministry of theologians, both men and women" and about their "independent (!) service to the People of God". Tradition and the Magisterium of the Church, in contrast, are not even mentioned. It is difficult to see what rationale there could be for the expressly emphasized "methodological standards" of that sort of theology.

"Crises of Modernism"

Additional light is now shed on the motives and aims of this society by two articles, one from the pen of the actual initiator, Norbert Greinacher, the other signed by the president

of the society, Peter Hünermann. Common to both statements is recourse to history, resulting in the discovery of
two Modernist crises in recent Church history, followed by
the comment that a third crisis of Modernism has been brew-
ing for several years. This procedure per se is not only legitimate but necessary. Only by analyzing lived experience can
one get help in understanding and solving present-day problems. The decisive things are one's approach and method,
and naturally a comprehensive knowledge and appreciation
of the historical facts.

Hünermann cuts corners, however, when he deals with
the subject of the first major Modernist crisis during the
pontificate of Pius IX simply by citing a controversial essay by Roger Aubert in Jedin's *Handbuch der Kirchengeschichte*
[Manual of Church history]; he mentions only the editor,
Jedin, thus allowing the reader to assume that the passage
quoted was actually the work of the leading German Church
historian of the twentieth century.

Aubert and Hünermann, as well as Greinacher, in their
negative judgment on Pius IX, ignore the fact that precisely during his pontificate (1846–1878), which was distinguished for its resistance to all the "-isms" that were modern then, the Church's internal life in the areas of missionary
and charitable work, popular piety and the care of souls, as
well as in religious-social lay initiatives, experienced an astonishing revival and in fact flourished marvelously. It may
suffice to point to the more than 150 newly founded religious communities that that pope approved. The Catholic
lay movement—which made its first public appearance in
1848 at the Catholic Congress in Mainz, proved its mettle
impressively in the *Kulturkampf* and furthermore opposed
nationalism and militarism energetically—is the product of
that spirituality which characterizes the pontificate of Pius
IX and which some Catholics today like to think they can

disparage by calling it the "ghetto mentality". Moreover, in view of the events of 1989–1990 [e.g., the fall of the Berlin Wall], one should not overlook either the fact that Pius IX was the first pope to condemn Communism, at the very beginning of his pontificate.

Roman narrow-mindedness and intransigence was not primarily to blame for the fact that during the course of these philosophical-theological controversies some theologians were finally disciplined by the Church. When Ignaz von Döllinger, for example—he is usually mentioned in this context as a representative for other, less important figures—demanded that the extraordinary authority of public opinion, to which "in the end all bow down, even those who head the Church and hold authority", should be set up alongside the ordinary authority of the Church hierarchy, and opined that through public opinion "theological science exercises the power rightly belonging to it, which in the long run nothing withstands", then the professorial chair was being set up in place of the episcopal *cathedra*, and an ecclesiastical response was necessary. It is obvious that such an understanding of the function of theology in the Church contradicts the genuine, Catholic concept of Church, revelation and Tradition. Of course, that was true not only in the days of Pius IX and Döllinger. This must be noted in response to Greinacher's comments on the subject. Theology's claim to arrive at the scene as the "magisterium of the Magisterium" is and remains theologically illegitimate.

Hünermann sees the second major crisis in the Church's repudiation of Modernism in the 1907 encyclical *Pascendi* by Pius X. Greinacher in his article states that this crisis occurred because in reaction to the "triumph of ultramontanism" under Pius IX a movement among German Catholics had formed, a coalition of "liberal elements, opponents of centralist Roman Church governance, heirs of the liturgical reform movement, opponents of obligatory celibacy, and opponents of political Catholicism". Their representatives are said to have been Franz Xaver Kraus, Hermann Schell and Albert Erhard. Greinacher's statement is completely undifferentiated, and will hardly meet with the approval of historians! In his version of the story, the Curia responded with the terrible decree *Lamentabili*, the encyclical *Pascendi* and the authoritarian order to take the anti-Modernist oath (1910).

In contrast, Hünermann admits that in this connection "it goes without saying [that there were] publications and initiatives that overreached". Yet he, too, thinks that Rome at that time, "on the basis of a chimerical image of the 'enemy', so-called Modernism, . . . also condemned things that belong to a sound modern theology". Here, of course, concrete examples would be very interesting. Only then would a substantial debate be possible. Now, it would be difficult to find among the sixty-five theses that were condemned by *Lamentabili* any "that belong to a sound modern theology". It all depends on how one defines "a sound modern theology". And was Modernism really just a bugaboo, a "chimerical image of the 'enemy' "? That is by no means the case. To prove that the foundations of the Christian faith were actually being threatened, it suffices to reprint verbatim the following passage from the *Frankfurter Zeitung*; the unsigned newspaper article appeared on July 22, 1907, three weeks after the publication of *Lamentabili* (July 3, 1907):

> The current of Catholic intellectual life that has been called "Modernism" for short pursues two goals. Catholics want to benefit from advances in science and scholarship [*Wissenschaft*]; they want to bridge the chasm that has opened between faith, religion and Church, on the one hand, and science and scholarship on the other; they want the Church

to become more scientific with her whole being, so that she can adapt to the demands of more-mature academic findings [*Erkenntnis*]. This is true for scholarship in general, that is, for the natural sciences and the humanities, as well as for ecclesiastical science in particular, namely for the exegesis of the Sacred Scriptures, from which the whole system of Christianity, Catholicism and the papacy derives its existence and its justification with the claim that in those Scriptures is contained a supernatural, divine revelation. Now, there is no field in which science has been revised so thoroughly and expanded so fundamentally as this one. We know now that the Old Testament contains no divine revelation but rather drew its religious ideas from merely human sources, from Egypt and especially from Babylon. We know that the Gospels do not intend to give historical facts but only edification and that they therefore contain many things that do not stand up to critical examination, and in particular much that was added later, and thus give no reliable information about the origins of Christianity but only about the opinions and dispositions, the conditions and circumstances of the Christian community that had already developed. One need not go so far as Kalthoff, who has maintained that Jesus never lived; yet biblical scholarship in general regards it as a proven fact that the sayings of a certain Jesus, along with the legend about that figure, provided only the core around which the new religion crystallized and formed in Rome under the influence of messianic, Greek philosophical, Roman proletarian and Roman universalist ideas.

Even today, any theology that identified with such trends or criticized the repudiation thereof by the Church's Magisterium could no longer call itself "Catholic". When Hünermann goes on to say that he is convinced that individual sentences in the anti-Modernist oath are "untenable", again he ought to say precisely which sentences he means. Now, of course, if his statement really does apply, then Hünermann is confronting his readers with questions that can scarcely be answered. Let us listen to him: "I still feel shame today that I took this oath eight times as a young cleric at the urging of my spiritual director. This practice, which lasted a half a century, was not a *formatio* but rather a *deformatio conscientiae* by the ecclesiastical authorities." Certainly, it is scarcely comprehensible that anyone should be required to take the oath so often. That was far from the general practice.

Nevertheless, these sentences are of inestimable importance for the intellectual attitude of several generations of theologians. They provoke serious questions: Can someone take an oath eight times (!) against his conscience—and over long intervals of time? What sort of spiritual director is it who can advise someone to do that? What must happen, necessarily, as a consequence of this "deformation of conscience"? Can such trauma ever be healed? What Hünermann writes here is evidently true, as we have said, for many clerics and theologians. Quite a few of them who went through the same training, or even had the same spiritual director, held and hold tenured positions teaching theology. How many of them swore the anti-Modernism oath against their convictions? How many refused to take it for reasons of conscience? How many took it with conviction?

Basically, the question for someone who believed that he had to reject the content of the anti-Modernism oath was this: If the Church demands that I abandon my conviction, can I enter the service of such an institution in the first place?

Be that as it may: this way of treating the anti-Modernism oath, which obviously was taken by quite a few men contrary to their convictions, is a relatively plausible explanation for the divided and even now double-dealing and hence insincere relation of certain theologians vis-à-vis the Church and her Magisterium and their intention, manifest in their abundant literary output and their behaviors, to create "another Church". A Church in which "Modernist" convictions could take up permanent residence [*Heimatrecht haben*, have right of domicile]. Of course, then that would no longer be the Catholic Church that was built by Jesus Christ upon Peter and is animated by the Holy Spirit.

The Stumbling Block of the Papacy

Then it is a question of the primacy and teaching authority of the pope. An occasion for a direct attack by Hünermann on Rome is now provided by the 1988 apostolic constitution *Ecclesia Dei* of John Paul II, along with the papal commission by the same name, headed [then] by Cardinal Mayer, the function of which is to reintegrate former disciples of Lefèbvre and other "Traditionalists" into the Church. Hünermann assumes that they reject the Vatican II documents on "freedom of religion and of conscience, the collegiality of the bishops, and so forth", which in fact could hardly be proved! At any rate, the [German] Catholics in question have acknowledged the pope's authority and shown him such obedience as is not often encountered in other quarters. In this same connection, Hünermann accuses the pope of "suspending the decisions of a legitimate council", that is, of Vatican II, through the document *Ecclesia Dei*. That is absurd—although it goes without saying that conciliar decrees which contain no definitions of faith and those that are of a disciplinary or a practical, pastoral nature can be modified or revoked. Nonetheless, not one single decree, not even the mere Declaration on freedom of religion, is "invalidated" or disavowed by *Ecclesia Dei*.

While we are still on the subject of Vatican II, it must also be said emphatically that it is Hünermann's and Greinacher's understanding of the ministry of the pope and in particular of his teaching ministry that is in blatant contradiction to *Lumen gentium, Christus Dominus* and *Dei Verbum* and thus to the oft-invoked Second Vatican Council. And, to return to an earlier point: Which thesis condemned by *Lamentabili* and *Pascendi* and rejected in the anti-Modernism oath could be reconciled with Vatican II, in particular with the above-mentioned decrees?

What Is "Church"?

What is striking, moreover—and here, once again, Greinacher and Hünermann agree—is the application of political terminology to the Church and ecclesiastical life. Hünermann notes the typical efforts of modern societies to protect against the abuse of power and argues that the forms of this protection that have developed, namely the separation of powers, the limitation of authority, checks and balances among the branches of government, monitoring authorities and transparency, should be introduced in the Church in an analogous fashion through public agencies. Then, when he goes on to say that this should not involve any sort of democratization, it certainly sounds strange. Furthermore, when Hünermann sees the "emphasis on collegiality, the independence (!) and particular character of the local and regional churches, of the bishops' conferences" and so forth as the initial fulfillment of his demands, since Vatican II produced "prospects for a differentiation and subdivision of the use of power", hasn't he then misunderstood the concepts of collegiality and particular Church?

Basically, though, it gives the appearance of striving for a Church whose structures correspond to the ideas, experiences and outlook on life of a pluralistic, democratic society. Remarkably, the reference to Tradition and the "inner, mysterious life" of the Church pales in contrast and seems to be just a rote theological exercise. Greinacher is clearer when he asks, "Will the Catholic Church in Europe remain the sole refuge for feudal and authoritarian structures of governance?" His "hope that *perestroika* and *glasnost* will someday be adopted in the Catholic Church as well by the power of the Holy Spirit" goes to show what a thoroughly sociological—one might almost say *political*—concept of Church is presupposed here.

Hünermann and Greinacher are right: we are in the midst of a crisis of Modernism that, because it expresses itself in the widest possible public forum, is much more dangerous than formerly was the case. To speak about a "new" crisis would not be accurate, since we are dealing with one and the same crisis that has confronted faith in supernatural revelation and in the Church since the Enlightenment. The question here is whether faith and Church should be adapted to modern man's horizon of understanding and experience, or whether modern man must be required and helped—if at all possible—to have the ability and willingness to deal with the complete Otherness of God and of his Church. There is no removing the scandal that is involved for the person who thinks in a worldly, naturalistic way: "Blessed is he that shall not be scandalized in me" [Mt 11:6, Douay-Rheims]. Then when the Rock of Peter becomes a stumbling block as well, the pope will manage to endure it. A Church that no longer causes scandal for the world would no longer be the Church of him who is destined "for the fall and rising of many in Israel, and for a sign that is spoken against".

What is needed in this crisis, which is then naturally also a crisis of the missionary proclamation to the world of today, is a concentration of forces, not intraecclesial confrontation and controversy [*Kontestation*]. In this perspective, the *professio fidei* and *juramentum fidelitatis* [profession of faith and oath of loyalty], as newly formulated by the Congregation for the Doctrine of the Faith, is nonnegotiable. The vantage point of a theologian is not the Olympian heights but rather the communion of the Church. She and the public at large have a right to be certain that preachers, religion teachers and theologians do not present their private opinion but rather the authentic faith of the Church. This leads to the demand for a reconsideration of the self-understanding of the theologians. The relevance of the most recent Roman instruction concerning Magisterium and theologians is demonstrated by precisely those who oppose it.